Help! I'm a Pastor!

Encouraging pastors to **be more effective,
preach better sermons,**
and **get through difficult situations**.

Joe McKeever

Parson's Porch Books

Help! I'm a Pastor!
ISBN: Softcover 978-1-960326-85-0
Copyright © 2024 by Joe McKeever

Parson's Porch Books is an imprint of Parson's Porch *&* Company (PP*&*C) in Cleveland, Tennessee. PP*&*C is a self-funded charity which earns money by publishing books of noted authors, representing all genres. Its face and voice is **David Russell Tullock** who you can contact at: dtullock@parsonsporch.com.

Parson's Porch *&* Company *turns books into bread & milk* by sharing its profits with the poor.

www.parsonsporch.com

Help! I'm a Pastor!

Contents

Dedication 9

Foreword..11

Introduction 15

Chapter One.. 16

   Be a pastor, change the world.

Chapter Two..20

   A special word for those who would help people worship.

Chapter Three..25

   Blind-sided by opposition

Chapter Four..31

   10 foundational truths to remind your people of again and again

Chapter Five...39

   What's a pastor to do when his biggest competition in town is another preacher?

Chapter Six 45

   Preachers are different. You've noticed? Here's why.

Chapter Seven..49

   The pastor will sometimes feel like a failure. Sometimes he is.

Chapter Eight...52

   Should the pastor confess his doubt?

Chapter Nine..55

   An effective minister must learn to say 'no' sometimes. Want to hear my tales of woe?

Chapter Ten 59

   I urge pastors to read constantly

Chapter Eleven...62

   High standards are great but lose perfectionism

Chapter Twelve 65

   The worst kind of Christian faith

Chapter Thirteen..69

   The most striking thing about leaders

Chapter Fourteen 72

   Things the pastor cannot do

Chapter Fifteen..75

   The promise Jesus has made to the obedient

Chapter Sixteen..78

   What you need to know about those celebrity pastors

Chapter Seventeen 81

   Everyone fails from time to time. Learn to fall forward

Chapter Eighteen 85

   Some preaching is a waste of time

Chapter Nineteen..88
  Humor is good, when done right
Chapter Twenty..92
  Lazy, uninspired preaching is an insult to the Lord of Heaven and earth!
Chapter Twenty-One 95
  Pastor, make your people think!
Chapter Twenty-Two... 102
  Help someone find their calling in life. Scripture calls that 'discipleship.'
Chapter Twenty-Three 106
  Mediocrity is so easy, comfortable even. But we can do better than that.
Chapter Twenty-Four 109
  Preaching is easy. Unless you want to do it well
Chapter Twenty-Five 112
  One question we in ministry are not allowed to ask
Chapter Twenty-Six.. 116
  For the young Timothys entering the ministry
Chapter Twenty-Seven 122
  Perhaps the hardest thing a pastor will ever have to do
Chapter Twenty-Eight.. 125
  Think God can't use you? Think again
Chapter Twenty-Nine 128
  Bogged down in minutia: the occupational hazard of ministers
Chapter Thirty 132
  Pastor, leave sports partisanship out of the pulpit. Here's why
Chapter Thirty-One.. 135
  The arrogant pastor: peacock in a mudhen parade
Chapter Thirty-Two... 139
  You're a pastor; you're not like us
Chapter Thirty-Three... 142
  The burden and fear of handling the Word of God
Chapter Thirty-Four... 145
  10 lessons on leading God's church, all learned the hard way
Chapter Thirty-Five.. 149
  Scripture has some strange heroes; we can learn from them all
Chapter Thirty-Six 152
  Ten of the scariest times in a pastor's life
Chapter Thirty-Seven 159
  True Humility in the Pulpit. What a Rarity!
Chapter Thirty-Eight 162
  Pastor, ask something great from us

Chapter Thirty-Nine.. 167
    Let the pastor decide he's going to preach the Bible
Chapter Forty.. 171
    How to take criticism and make the most of it
Chapter Forty-One... 175
    Preaching the Word in a climate of fear
Chapter Forty-Two... 179
    The church's dirty little secret
Chapter Forty-Three... 183
    The pastor and his wife cannot agree on moving. What to do
Chapter Forty-Four.. 187
    Three Big Things to Believe — and One Greater
Chapter Forty-Five... 192
    Ten reasons for the pastor not to resign abruptly
Chapter Forty-Six.. 197
    Our wish for the preacher-killers among us
Chapter Forty-Seven... 200
    The preacher said something I disagree with, so I'm leaving!
Chapter Forty-Eight... 204
    An odd skill pastors need if they are to survive in this work.
Chapter Forty-Nine.. 208
    The best kind of pastor is a broken man
Chapter Fifty... 214
    Pastors need other pastors. That's an iron-clad rule
Chapter Fifty-One.. 219
    Seven prayers of a lazy pastor
Chapter Fifty-Two.. 221
    Get all the education you can. Then, never mention it again
Chapter Fifty-Three.. 225
    Slow down and savor the Scriptures
Chapter Fifty-Four... 230
    Beware the need to be accepted by the world; God intends His
servants to be outsiders
Chapter Fifty-Five.. 234
    The pastor must not ignore the culture around him
Chapter Fifty-Six... 238
    Learn about Submission, Pastor. Or the Consequences Will Be Dire
Chapter Fifty-Seven.. 244
    Pastors will be needing someone to take a bullet for them. Ask God to
provide such a friend
Chapter Fifty-Eight.. 247
    How to preach about America in the worst possible way

Chapter Fifty-Nine 250
    What the pastor search committee is looking for when they visit your
church
Chapter Sixty 254
    What church members have a right to expect of their pastor
Chapter Sixty-One 258
    Last of all, plan to finish strong
About the Author 261

Dedication

I'm the product of several preachers who showed me how it's done. Since they're in Heaven now, asking the Father to "bless them" would probably be redundant. But I'm eternally grateful to Him for Professor George Harrison, Pastor James Richardson, Pastor Morris Freeman, and—well, too many others to count. I am a blessed fellow!

Foreword

A friend said, "Preachers who write books are on ego trips." He had my undivided attention.

"The smartest pastor I ever knew," he said, "never wrote a book. When someone asked why, he said, 'There's no need. Everything I have to say has already been said by people smarter than me.'"

I knew the preacher he was referencing and told him I disagreed. I mentioned several reasons.

I'm not saying ego is not a factor in writing a book, as it is in almost everything we do. I admit it gives me a good feeling to hold the completed book in my hand.

But I wish that pastor (who had refused to write a book) had given us his unique slant on the ministry, on scripture, on biblical stories, and on the churches he pastored. I knew him fairly well and treasured his service to our Lord.

Two of the churches this good brother served mistreated him. I'd love to have his account, as only he could have told it.

The next generation of church leaders benefit from knowing how God's preachers dealt with issues they faced. Paul's First Epistle to the Corinthians is exactly that. If no problems had existed in the church at Corinth, no epistle would have been written to deal with them. Think how much poorer we would be.

I try to write the occasional book. Having been in the Lord's work for over six decades, I have seen a few things during those years, carry scars from several encounters with church people, and have learned some lessons along the way. If nothing else, the scars qualify me to record my story. As Second Corinthians 11 records Paul's account of his scars, wounds, hardships, among other things these enhanced his authority in addressing God's churches.

Ego trip? I certainly hope it's more than that. Some of these books will travel to distant states and even foreign lands, places where I will never venture. And some, I hope, will journey into the future and speak to future generations. Any pastor would love for that to happen.

A line in the Psalms puts it as well as anything I know... *This will be written for the generation to come, That a people yet to be created may praise the Lord.* (Psalm 102:18)

I encourage my pastor friends to write. Write your memoirs, tell us what you have learned, give us your insights into Scripture, share what's bugging you, and by all means, explain what thrills and excites you about ministering in Jesus' name. You have so much to share.

Novelists say that conflict makes a book interesting. No conflict, no book. One novelist taped an index card above her laptop with three words to guide her in plotting her stories: *Things get worse.*

The pastor who writes only about all the glowing successes he has had along the way will soon discover no one wants to read it. The simple fact is it's boring. It's the struggles, the hardships, the trials, the challenges—the conflict! —that makes it so interesting and so helpful. So, pastors will find a ready audience when they talk about the hardest church they pastored, the worst sermon they preached, the most difficult business meeting they moderated, the poorest relationships they experienced in the ministry. I'm not sure why, but the human animal seems structured to learn more from the failures and mistakes of one another than from the successes.

This book is neither an account of my failures or successes, but rather a collection of memorable stories, biblical insights, helpful suggestions and lasting reminders I'd like to leave with those our Lord has called into the pastorate.

What I'm trying to do…

Some years back after my wife and I survived a brutal time in a pastorate, I returned to Psalm 66 which had meant so much to us during the dark days. That's when I saw something I'd missed before….

I shall pay you my vows which my lips uttered, and my mouth spoken when I was in distress (Psalm 66:13-14).

Margaret and I had lived in that Psalm during our crisis and found it to be a source of encouragement. But this was the first time I had thought of making vows as a result of God's blessing.

That day, I made three vows to the Lord. For the rest of my life, I would live simply, give generously, and encourage pastors.

I've tried to keep those commitments.

Consider this book a partial attempt to fulfill the third vow.

In assembling this collection, I have looked back over things I have written in the past and prayerfully selected pieces with a special meaning for God's servants, His pastors.

I hope you find it that.

Each chapter stands alone. While it would be possible for a reader to cover the entire book in a couple of hours, I don't recommend that. I suggest you read a chapter and lay the book aside for a day or two and give the subject some thought.

You will also notice the occasional repetition of scriptures and ideas. This is on purpose. Some lessons need to be repeated again and again for them to "take." It's a great learning technique, one practiced by the Master Teacher Himself.

Now, personally I am not fond of books that are too dense and too technical. The good news is this is not such a book. I want a pastor to enjoy this, to find ideas and encouragement, inspiration and hope. From where I sit, if you find a few good suggestions that make a lasting difference in your ministry, your preaching, your home life, or your health even, I'll be pleased and greatly rewarded.

A word about the editing process, if I may...

Writers will tell you the actual writing was a joy; the editing was a chore. Editing is when the author corrects the typos, makes sure the verbs agree with the subjects, tightens up unwieldy sentences, reconsiders word choices and looks at the punctuation. Entire books have been produced to deal with the hundreds of decisions writers have to make when editing. Italicizing is often a headache for me. Scriptures quoted, we're told, should be in italics. And yet, what about when the page is saturated with scripture? Too much in italics makes the page more difficult to read, it seems.

Most authors rely on layers of editors and proof-readers. But for those of us hunkered over our laptop at the kitchen table and using boutique publishers, we're fairly well on our own.

So, I am asking the reader for leniency here. Every time I go back over even one chapter, I find more things to change. Eventually, you quit that and turn it loose. Sometimes I probably got it right, at other times not. Eventually, one tires of the editing and makes the decision to "send it forth." For better or for worse.

Sometimes when I rise to address a church group, I begin by explaining my lisp, which resulted from the two cancer surgeries on my mouth. People assure me everything is fine, that they can understand me all right.

I suspect that in a way I'm writing with a lisp also. I feel so handicapped trying to advise pastors, many of whom are smarter and godlier than I will ever be. But we do what we can. Blessing pastors is a vow I have made. God help me to fulfill it.

Introduction

The Lord did not call me to preach.

The exact words He spoke to my heart that Tuesday night in April of 1961 were: "I want you in the ministry."

And "the ministry" is a broader category than "preaching." Ministry seems all-encompassing, and since I have served as pastor, assistant pastor, minister of evangelism, director of missions, as well as cartoonist, teacher, adjunct professor in seminary, author, and counselor, it seems to fit.

Only after I had finished seminary did the Lord confirm that I was to pastor churches. Until then, I had several other things in mind—all of which were included in the term "the ministry." But when that word from Heaven arrived—I recall where I was at that moment: on my knees praying in a hotel room in San Antonio—it felt so right. I was so glad.

I love being a pastor.

The best title for a minister, it seems to me, is "pastor." It means shepherd.

As a cartoonist, I love the play on words of pastor and pasture. Sometimes I'll send a note to a fellow pastor where I've drawn horses in a meadow. A billboard in the distance reads, "We who are called to pasture salute you."

Pastor is better than reverend, minister, preacher, doctor, brother, executive, administrator, and even preacher, it seems to me.

Pastor suggests a relationship of trust, like the sheep to the shepherd. Each must trust the other.

Pastor implies a calling, as the Chief Shepherd gives an assignment to an under shepherd. No one goes into this difficult, dangerous work on his own, but is drafted by the Heavenly Shepherd.

Pastor does not come with the baggage of all the other possible titles. It seems to have a certain purity about it.

I am not a big fan of all the modifiers of "pastor," such as senior, lead, executive, administrative, teaching, or even assistant. A pastor is a caretaker, one who protects the sheep and provides for them.

When you say pastor, you've said it all, it seems to me. Call me Pastor Joe. I'm honored.

Chapter One

Be a pastor, change the world.

A preacher I know was on the plane trying to complete the manuscript for a series of Sunday School lessons he had been asked to write. His seatmate wanted to talk. Stuart kept fending her off with short responses.

At one point she noticed his name on his briefcase. He was "Doctor." That intrigued her. "You're a doctor?" she asked.

"Um huh," my friend said, not looking up from his work. "What kind of doctor are you?" she said.

Stuart said, "A Doctor of Theology. I'm a preacher." "Oh," she said. "I thought you were a real doctor."

That did it. My friend laid his books aside and looked at her. "Madam," he said, "If I were a doctor of medicine and did my work well, I might be able to add a few years to someone's life."

"But as a Doctor of Theology—a minister of the gospel of Jesus Christ—when I do my work well, people live forever."

It's a powerful thing this Christian ministry.

It is surely the quickest way to change the world. And the best.

A fellow named Martin Luther went into the same work as you and I and saw the world change right before his eyes. The same thing can be said about John Wesley. John Wycliffe. Dwight L. Moody. Jim Elliott. Peter Marshall. Billy Graham.

And you.

Recently I came across a book called *Give Your Speech, Change the World.* Author Nick Morgan teaches public speaking in numerous formats (universities, as the editor of several publications, and consultant to executives) and has been speechwriter for a governor. Morgan says an old friend of his, another speechwriter, used to say, "The only reason to give a speech is to change the world." Morgan agrees and adds, "Otherwise, why bother?" He answers, "We still need speeches. We need them to move audiences to action…. And lest you think that when I say, 'changing the world' I'm only talking about the big speeches (the ones that CEOs give to shareholders, for example) understand that I'm talking about every speech ever given."

Every sermon you ever deliver, pastor.

Every public presentation you make of any kind. It's that potent.

I'm remembering one Easter morning when I did nothing more than lead in prayer at a community-wide sunrise service and it changed the world. Two families who heard that prayer began attending my church, joined it, and became excellent servants of the Savior. Our church became stronger, their families flourished, and lives were changed. The world changed.

Ministers of the Gospel need constant reminders that this message they preach is potent stuff. It is the power of God unto salvation, said the Apostle Paul (Romans 1:16).

Furthermore…

When you love a child, you change the world.

When you win a soul, you change the world.

When you teach college students, you change the world.

When you pray for someone in need, you change the world. Anyone see a principle here?

What I would love to do, of course, is to elevate the work of the ministry for anyone reading this.

Throughout Scripture we see those who did little potent things for the Lord Jesus that changed the world.

A widow dropped her two small coins into the offering. Over these two thousand years since, her single act has inspired billions of dollars in gifts. The woman literally changed the world that day with two pennies.

A little boy handed his lunch to Jesus and the world was never the same.

Barnabas traveled to Tarsus in search of his friend Saul and millions of people will live in Heaven forever as a result (Acts 11:25).

God said to Moses, "What is that in your hand?" (Exodus 4:2) With that shepherd's rod, the man of God changed the world.

What's in your hand?

What has God given you? What is your calling? What are your gifts, your interests, your talents, your concerns? Will you give these to the One who called you to use as He chooses?

In seminary, I pastored a small church on Alligator Bayou some 25 miles west of New Orleans. When the McCain family visited our church, that week I paid a pastoral visit to their home. Fifteen-year-old Mike, a high school football player, and his little sister prayed with me inviting Jesus into their lives. They and their mother joined our church and I baptized the children. A few years later after I had relocated to another state, I led the father to Christ over long distance. And sometime later—long after I was out of the picture God called young Mike McCain into the ministry. He pastored churches throughout the decades. And now, nearly sixty years later, Mike is retired and still preaching in Wisconsin where he lives.

I had no idea the day I made that pastoral visit to the McCains' that God was using me to change the world. But that is precisely what He did.

Make a visit; change the world.

For three years, as a staff member of a large church in Jackson, Mississippi, I taught the college Sunday School class. We would have two hundred or more in attendance. Three years later, I moved on to pastor in another part of the state. Over the years since I learned that members of that Bible class literally covered the world serving God. Some became medical doctors, other pastors and missionaries, and one became the editor of our foreign mission magazine. No doubt there were others with significant works I know nothing about. By teaching a Bible class of young people, God changed the world.

Did I do it alone? Not even close. As Paul said, one person plants, another waters and cultivates, but the harvest is from God (First Corinthians 3:6).

God will use you, pastor. Believe that. Trust Him. And treasure the labors of fellow servants, because none of us does this alone.

What we must not do is try to judge the results today of what we accomplished this morning.

I like to remind the Lord's people of what I have discovered about the Lord's methodology— When God gets ready to do something great, He loves to start small...

With ordinary people,
Using any method He pleases,
And taking all the time in the world. Only people of faith
Will still be standing by at the end to see what God has done,
And to behold His glory.
All the others have grown impatient and left the field.

One final reminder. In every case mentioned—whether loving a child or teaching a class or knocking on a door or preaching the Word—we will not know what God is going to do with it. This is all of faith.

We do our job and leave the results to Him.

In most cases, we will be in Heaven before we learn what He did with our efforts. If that won't teach you patience, nothing will!

Chapter Two

A special word for those who would help people worship.

The first few chapters of First Samuel have much to say on this subject.

The first rule of worship leadership should probably be stated as Try Not to Get in Their Way.

When people come to worship, if you cannot help them, at the very least try not to interfere with what they are doing.

The sons of Eli the High Priest were nothing but trouble. Hophni and Phinehas—who doesn't love those names! — were wicked men; they had no regard for the Lord or for the priests' share of the sacrifices from the people (I Samuel 2:12-13).

God literally calls them SOBs. Sons of Belial is the Hebrew expression translated as "wicked men" or "corrupt."

Scripture has not a single positive statement about these miscreants.

These men stand as warnings to every kingdom worker to tread humbly and serve honorably. We are stewards and not owners, servants and not lords. Helpers and not directors.

We should encourage worship and not place obstacles and burdens upon the worshipers. We are to help people worship and not divert them into our own purposes.

The people can worship God without you, O thou shepherd of the Lord's flock.

If we cannot help them, do it better, we should back off and remove ourselves from the picture.

Every pastor, every minister of any kind, every support staff, every church custodian, and every denominational worker should be familiar with the first few chapters of First Samuel and heed their caution about worship leaders.

1) The wicked leaders treated those who came to worship with contempt.

(Hophni and Phinehas) were sleeping with the women who served at the entrance to the tent of meeting (I Samuel 2:22). See Exodus 38:8 for information on this ministry of the women.

And you thought lustful ministers were a recent phenomenon.

Through the centuries, stories of ministers preying upon helpless children, vulnerable counselees, and trusting helpers have become commonplace, to our everlasting shame.

2) The wicked leaders treated the people's offerings as their own.

When any man offered a sacrifice, the priest's servant (i.e., those who worked for Hophni and Phinehas) would come with a three-pronged meat fork while the meat was boiling and plunge it into the container or kettle or caldron or cooking pot. The priest would claim for himself whatever the meat fork brought up. This is the way they treated all the Israelites who came to Shiloh (I Samuel 2:13-14).

Deuteronomy 18:3-5 spells out which portions of the offerings belonged to the priests.

Hophni and Phinehas sent servants to take more than what was allotted, and to do so early in the process. While Leviticus 7:31 commanded that the fat be burned on the altar, they wanted their meat raw. Anyone who grills steaks understands that a little fat flavors a steak.

God was not big on barbecuing. He was looking for obedience.

The Lord did not take kindly to their treating His commands so lightly. Their offense was "very severe" (2:17).

3) The wicked leaders treated the Ark of the Covenant as a magic totem.

In I Samuel 4, Hophni and Phinehas carried the ark of the covenant into battle against the Philistines. They were counting on the enemies to panic once they saw the Israelites had "their god" leading the way. But it didn't work out quite that way.

God had said He dwelt above the Ark, between the cherubim. So, for the carnal-minded—Hophni and Phinehas were nothing if not carnal—that was good enough for them. To carry the box into battle obligated God to come along and guaranteed a victory over His enemies.

People are always saying God is obligated to do this or that because "we have His word on it." Maybe we do, but we also have Psalm 115:3. Our God is in the Heavens; He does whatever He pleases.

God has plans He has not told us about and is as unpredictable as the wind (the Lord Jesus told us that in John 3:8).

Instead of intimidating the Philistines, the presence of the Ark actually stimulated them to greater effort. "Boys, we may be in trouble. They have their god with them today. If you ever fought before, you'd better fight now."

So, the Philistines fought, and Israel was defeated. The slaughter was severe–30,000 of the Israelite foot soldiers fell. The ark of God was captured, and Eli's two sons, Hophni and Phinehas, died (I Samuel 4:10-11).

Too late, the priests learned the Lord's presence was no magic guarantee against defeat, that possessing the ark did not automatically mean He was present, and that His blessings could not be manipulated as they wished. In his commentary, John MacArthur says, "…they confused the symbol of the His presence with His actual presence. In this way, their understanding of God resembled that of the Philistines."

Simply stated, for purposes of His own God wanted the Israelites defeated.

Nice little benign history lesson, right? Nothing there for our sophisticated generation of church leaders, right? Bad wrong. There is a world of instruction here.

1) We must honor those who come to worship.

We who lead churches must not abuse them, manipulate them, or see them as serving our purposes. They are not "the attendance." They are not "my crowd" or "our bunch."

These are the people of the Lord. They are "His people and the sheep of His pasture" (Psalm 100:3).

Leaders who abuse and misuse God's children will give account to Him personally someday, and it will not be a pretty thing. Furthermore, those of us who believe that "since I am saved by the blood and 'there is no condemnation,' I will not have to account for what I have done before the Lord" are in for a rude awakening.

Remember you heard it here.

2) We must honor the offerings people bring to the Lord. Every gift is His and not ours.

Among the disciples, it was Judas who loved the offerings more than he should (John 12:6) and who treated the contributions of others as his own.

We should fear for anyone taking Judas as a role model.

22

For those leading God's flock, there must always be financial accountability. Pastors and staffers who live lavishly upon the offerings of the Lord's people should be held accountable. They should be expected to live humbly and faithfully. Churches should insist that just because one pastors a congregation of wealthy contributors does not entitle that minister to an over-sized income and a mansion in which to dwell.

A great number of ministers have not gotten that memo.

Friends in mega-churches tell me the salaries their ministers take home is scandalous. You have to wonder: Just because a church is huge and its weekly contributions run into the millions, why does that entitle the pastors to enormous paychecks? We are not the world. We do not take Wall Street or Silicon Valley as role models.

Every church needs a system of checks and balances, and every congregation on the planet should have an opportunity for members of the flock to stand in a meeting and ask how a thing was decided, who made the decision to buy this or build that. The more distance a church puts between its ministers and the flock, the more abuse it is subjecting itself to.

Moreover, it is required in stewards that one be found faithful (I Corinthians 4:2). If you have not been faithful in the unrighteous mammon, who will commit to your trust the true riches (Luke 16:11)?

3) In all things, we must honor our Lord Jesus Christ.

We must not leave the impression that God is merely a symbol or a good luck charm or that His words are a magic formula. Numerous times through the centuries, the Lord's people discovered the hard way that "God's name on us" did not guarantee them the right to sin, to rebel against Him, to flout His laws or go their own way. In 722 B.C. God allowed the Assyrians to completely annihilate the northern kingdom of Israel. The scattered population would never return, and that nation was never restored. Then, in 586 B.C. God allowed the Babylonians to defeat the southern kingdom of Judah and destroy Jerusalem.

In both cases, many of God's priests were lulling His people into a false sense of security, assuring them "God is with us, so we're untouchable."

If anything, the Lord's people are held to a much higher standard than the world. Behavior that would be overlooked in the world is forbidden to the Lord's saints.

All of us who work in churches and denominations should see ours as a holy calling with a great responsibility and stiff accountability.

Let us honor the Lord's people. Let us respect their worship.

Let us fear God.

The writer of Ecclesiastes shared our concern....

Walk prudently when you go to the house of God and draw near to hear rather than to give the sacrifice of fools, for they do not know they do evil. Do not be rash with your mouth and let not your heart utter anything hastily before God. For God is in Heaven and you on earth. Therefore, let your words be few.... (Ecclesiastes 5:1-2).

Chapter Three

Blind-sided by opposition.

Welcome to the ministry, pastor.

In our experience, most of the Lord's people are wonderful and most of His churches are filled with sincere and godly workers. But once in a while, pastors come upon sick churches led by difficult people who seem to delight in resisting their ministers. When they find themselves unable to control them, they attack. Pity the poor unsuspecting preacher and his family. What follows is written just for them.

"But beware of men, for they will deliver you up to the courts, and scourge you in their synagogues...." (Matthew 10:17)

You and your spouse went into the ministry with hearts aglow, eyes wide open, idealism firmly tucked under your arm, vision clear and focus solid.

As newly minted ambassadors for Christ, the two of you were ready to do battle with the enemy, eager to serve the saints, and glad to impart the joyful news of the gospel.

Ministry was going to be great and noble and even blessed. That's what you were expecting.

You were prepared for the work to be hard, the hours long, and the needs great.

What you did not expect was to be blindsided by members of your own church family—to be slandered by people you counted on as friends when you took a courageous position, and criticized for something you did well. Even lied about.

You knew there would be vicious people "in the world," outsiders who do not believe in God, cannot discern spiritual things, and will not subject themselves to moral absolutes. You were expecting that.

What caught you off guard was finding members of that sweet pastor search committee which brought you to this town with glowing recommendations and high hopes now turning against you, accusing you of misrepresenting yourself to them, blaming you for the ills inside their church family that were present long before you became their shepherd.

Some you loved best are now leaving your church, saying unkind things about you and your family.

You are stunned, puzzled, frightened, and more than a little angry. Questions hound you and rob you of sleep.

Why are they doing this? What is going on here? Why did no one ask for my side of the story but just believe the worst about me? Am I at fault?

What should I do now? How will I support my family?

You made mistakes, sure. Everyone does.

Didn't they know we were human? Were they expecting us to be perfect?

Your wife doesn't want to come to church any more, and if you had a choice about it, pastor, you wouldn't either.

It's not fun anymore.

Welcome to the ministry in the 21st century.

I can say to you categorically, my friend, that as a result of this situation you find yourself in, you are now perfectly placed to do your most enduring work for Christ. I know it doesn't feel like it but take my word. This may well be your shining hour. You are now "walking on your high places," that scary height where the standing is slippery and no one is there to catch you (see Habakkuk 3:19, among other places).

1) These harsh conditions you are facing are not new but have been with us from the beginning.

Some of the First Century Christians loved the Apostle Paul and treasured his teachings, but others despised him, made cruel jokes about him, and ran him down at every opportunity. Read the last few chapters of Second Corinthians and you will find a colleague in your sufferings.

The First Epistle of Peter is almost a handbook for the Lord's workers going through what you are enduring and worse. Believers were being driven from their homes, robbed of everything they owned, beaten, and even killed. The fact that nothing like this has happened to you (we assume) does not diminish the wonderful way these scriptures speak to the Lord's servants suffering for His sake.

2) Not all churches are like this—you will be relieved to know—but sooner or later, most pastors are going to get hold of one.

If you are fortunate, this (ahem) challenging congregation will come as your second or third church, following sweet experiences where the work flourished, and you blossomed for the Lord. If, however, the first pastorate is this mean-spirited one, there is a good chance you and your spouse may decide something like, "We didn't sign on for this; if all the churches are like this, we're out of here," and your first pastorate becomes your last one.

They're not all like this one, you'll be glad to know. But plenty are. So, when dealing with pastor search committees, do your homework and go in with your eyes wide open. Those people need a pastor too, and if the Lord sends you there, you're willing to go. However, do not become their latest victim if you can help it.

3) You would not have been caught off guard and blind-sided if you had paid closer attention to something the Lord Jesus said.

Again and again, our Lord said things like "Blessed are you when men cast insults at you and persecute you…" (Matthew 5:11), "You will be hated of all on account of My name" (Matthew 10:22), and "If they persecuted me, they will persecute you also" (John 15:20).

Jesus told Peter, "There is no one who has left house or brothers or sisters or mother or father or children or farms, for my sake and the gospel's, but that he shall receive a hundred times as much now in this present age, houses and brothers and sisters and mothers and children and farms— along with persecutions—and in the age to come, eternal life" (Mark 10:29-30).

No one can accuse the Lord of failing to prepare His followers for the tough road they were choosing.

At the extreme end of their first missionary journey, Paul and Barnabas decided to retrace their steps and make follow-up visits to the congregations they had just established. They encouraged "them to continue in the faith, and (said to them) 'Through many tribulations we must enter the kingdom of God.'" (Acts 14:22)

They wanted these new converts to know that between here and Heaven they could expect trouble. In Acts 20:29-30, Paul prepares the elders of Ephesus for future attacks, both from outside and inside. He says, "From among your own selves' men will arise speaking perverse things…."

The Lord told you to expect this. Were you listening?

4) This suffering has an expiration date.

Perhaps the Lord will heal this church. Perhaps He will move you to another field. Perhaps He has something else entirely in mind.

Or perhaps He will come again for you. Or take you to be with Him in Heaven. (We had to say that to be completely honest. Anyone reading the Word quickly sees the Lord does not think of a believer exiting the earth and going to Heaven as the awful tragedy the way we sometimes do.)

One thing we know is He will not let this harassment and persecution go on indefinitely.

"This momentary light affliction is producing for us an eternal weight of glory far beyond all comparison...." (II Corinthians 4:17).

5) The Lord is never more with you than when you are suffering for His sake.

Paul said, "At my first appearance (before Caesar), no man stood with me. Everyone forsook me. Nevertheless, the Lord stood with me and strengthened me, that by me the Message might be fully known and that all the Gentiles might hear. I was delivered out of the lion's mouth."

He continued, "The Lord will deliver me from every evil deed and will bring me safely to His heavenly kingdom. To Him be the glory forever and ever. Amen". (II Timothy 4:17-18).

"When you pass through the waters, I will be with you.... When you walk through the fire...." (Isaiah 43:2).

"They will fight against you, but they will not overcome you, for I am with you to deliver you, declares the Lord" (Jeremiah 1:19).

Hold onto Hebrews 13:5-6. "I will never leave thee nor forsake thee. So that we may boldly say 'the Lord is my Helper, and I will not be afraid.' What can man do to me?" What indeed? Actually, a good bit. (For His partial answer to what man can do to you, check out Matthew 10:28.)

6) Remember that the Lord's "crash course for developing spiritual maturity" may include persecution.

Peter told the sufferers throughout Asia Minor, the trying of your faith, being more precious than gold, which is perishable, even though tested by fire, may be found to result in praise and glory and honor at the revelation of Jesus Christ (I Peter 1:7).

He said, after you have suffered a little while, the God of all grace, who called you to His eternal glory in Christ, will Himself perfect, confirm, strengthen and establish you (5:10).

7) You have been given an opportunity to display the character of the Lord Jesus Christ before the watching world and the family of Christ. Don't blow it.

We in America have so few opportunities to "suffer for righteousness's sake." We have freedoms which believers in other lands only dream about.

We can stand on street corners and preach to our heart's content. We can buy all the Bibles we want and go up and down the streets handing them out. We have almost no restrictions on ministry. In fact, many of our elected leaders are outspoken followers of Jesus Christ as well.

That may be one reason we get caught unaware when opposition and ugliness erupt, and we find ourselves caught in the crosshairs of harassment. Nothing had prepared us for this. No one in seminary had told us to expect deacons' meetings to be contests between those who know the Word and a few who wanted to rule. We had not expected the sweet little old ladies who resemble our grandmothers to be gossips who pass along every cruel rumor they hear.

When this happens, when they target you and your family, pastor, as painful as it is, remember these things....

–The Lord is there with you.

–The Lord is up to something in the middle of this.

–You do not know what He is planning to do or how He will use this.

–Your job is to be faithful and do the four basic acts He mentions in Luke 6:27-35 as evidence of your love. We are to do good, bless, pray, and give. These four acts are the evidence of our love, whether we do them to our child, our sweetheart, a neighbor, or an enemy.

When an enemy begins harassing us and robbing ministry of its joy, we are to do good deeds to them, to bless them (i.e., say Christ-honoring things to them), to pray for them (asking God to do His transforming work in them); and to give to them (any tangible evidence of the love of Christ in you).

You knew this was a testing time. What you may not have known is that the test is for you, to see who you are and whether you truly believe.

8) Don't waste this opportunity; you might not get another like it.

Later, you will look back and wonder how you endured it, rejoice that it's over, and be glad you were faithful. But at the moment, you have to get through it.

As one who endured three years of opposition in one church and seven years of harassment in another, I look back and say something my terrific, coal-miner dad used to say about his six children: "I wouldn't take a million dollars for one; I wouldn't give you a dime for another."

9) Someday you will be rewarded, and overwhelmed at what God did through your faithfulness during this tough time.

No one said it better than Peter: "Beloved, do not be surprised at the fiery ordeal among you, which comes upon you for your testing, as though some strange things were happening to you. But to the degree that you share the sufferings of Christ, keep on rejoicing, so that also at the revelation of His glory (that is, at His return) you may rejoice with exultation" (I Peter 4:12-13).

How good is that? You will be so glad you got it right, that you hung tough, and were faithful.

In fact, I'll make a prediction. Remember, you heard it here. At the Lord's return, some believers who were never called on to suffer for Jesus' sake will be envious (in a sort of righteous way, you understand) of all who did. They will wish they had had the opportunity to honor Him in such a strategic way that made such an eternal difference.

That's when you will rejoice that you were counted worthy to suffer for His name's sake. And you will remember Acts 5:41.

10) One final caution, my friend: There is no premium on suffering as a result of your own foolishness, self-centeredness, immaturity, or wickedness.

Peter said, "If you are reviled for the name of Christ, you are blessed because the Spirit of glory and of God rests upon you. But by no means let any of you suffer as a murderer, or thief, or evildoer, or a troublesome meddler, but if anyone suffers as a Christian, let him not feel ashamed; but in that name let him glorify God" (I Peter 4:14-16). If I am rude, angry, and stubborn with the Lord's people and they resist my leadership, I cannot very well run to Jesus and point the finger at them for being mean to me.

Pastors and their spouses should stay in the Word and on their knees. "Let them grow in Christlikeness and maturity, let them learn to serve and give and lead. But let them also learn to take a licking and keep on ticking, to suffer as the Lord did. When He was reviled, He did not revile in return; while suffering, He uttered no threats, but kept entrusting Himself to the One who judges righteously" (I Peter 2:23).

"God bless you, servant of the Savior. Give Him your best. Hang in there. It won't be long, and you will be glad you were faithful. Therefore, my beloved brethren, be steadfast, unmovable, always abounding in the work of the Lord, knowing that your labor is not in vain in the Lord" (I Corinthians 15:58).

Chapter Four

10 foundational truths to remind your people of again and again.

Remind them of these things.... (II Timothy 2:14)

If you have pastored for more than four or five years, or if you are in your second (or more) pastorate, you have learned the hard way that saying something one time to your people does not suffice. Some lessons—the most important ones, particularly—need to be said again and again.

Some of the most foundational messages—such as salvation by faith in Christ, the adequacy of the Word, and the importance of the cross—we continually work into sermons and lessons. These cannot be over-stressed.

Other lessons have to do with how the Christian faith is applied in our daily lives or in the operation of the Lord's church. These too need to be iterated and reiterated.

Each minister will have his/her own list. Here are my top ten principles to stress to your congregation again and again.

I suggest that we run these in the church bulletin, figure out how to get the gist of them onto the sign in front of the campus, print them on posters and post around the church, and speak them repeatedly in committees and classes and sermons.

Eventually, if we say them often enough and strong enough, people will begin to remember them. They might even tease us a little, as though we made these up and no one else in the Lord's work says this. When they tease you, take pride, minister of Christ. You're finally getting through.

1. If you have a problem with change, you are not going to get along with Jesus very well and you are going to be unhappy in this church.

Jesus Christ is all about "making all things new" (Revelation 21:5). He seems not to care much how we did things in the past or how the previous generation did them. He wants people to grow into Christlikeness and that will require radical, on-going change.

If we are wed to yesterday's methods and committed to last year's lessons, we may quickly find ourselves resisting the Holy Spirit.

The church that never changes, that refuses to allow a new song to be introduced, that believes the 1950s were the golden age of ministry, is dying right before your eyes.

Change or die. It's a law of humans, it's a basic principle of all life on this planet, and it's a bedrock tenet of the believer's life.

2. How you treat the church, good or bad, Jesus takes personally.

Our Lord said to the murderous Saul of Tarsus, "Why do you persecute me?" (Acts 9:4) That day, the apostle-in-the-making learned a valuable lesson: what he did to the church, Jesus took personally.

By "church," we mean the Lord's people collectively or any one congregation or any member of the church on mission for Him. (Normally, we would not speak of an individual as "the church," but for our purposes here we will.)

When one blesses the church, Jesus is honored (Hebrews 6:10). A gift to the church is treated as though it were handed to Jesus Himself (see Matthew 10:40-42 and 25:40.)

When one attacks the church or any member of it, Jesus feels the pain and becomes intimately involved (see Acts 7:56).

When the early church was persecuted (Acts 8:1), the Lord went into action and used this mightily to spread the gospel (see Acts 11:19ff).

This theme is found all through the Old Testament as well, as God emphasizes that His Name is on Israel. How they are treated by others, God takes personally. When Israel herself neglected to bring tithes and offerings into God's House, the Lord indicted them for "robbing God" (Malachi 3:8). When the widow dropped her tiny coins into the temple treasury, Jesus implies that God in Heaven is honored by her faith (Mark 12:43-44).

3. The church belongs to Jesus and Him alone. He died for it; we didn't.

No fact is more liberating for a minister than this: You are not on your own out here. The church belongs to Jesus and so do you. You may faithfully hand it back to Him and continue with your work while looking to Him for all resources, guidance, protection, and blessing.

Jesus said, "I will build my church" (Matthew 16:18). Paul told the Ephesian pastors to "shepherd the church of God which He purchased with His own blood" (Acts 20:28).

If your church is hurting financially, tell Jesus. It's His problem. If your church needs to relocate or is dying or is bursting at the seams and you are faced with critical decisions, tell Jesus. It's His church and He knows what He wants to do.

A tiny speech I often give churches where I'm guest-preaching goes like this:

It's not your church, pastor, even if your name is on the sign out front. Deacons, thank you for your faithful service, but it's not your church. Church leaders, we depend on you so much, but this is not your church. Members with seniority, thank you for your faithfulness through the years, but it's not your church. Members who have given the most money, thank you for your generosity, but it's not your church. And, even if the congregation makes the decisions and can do anything it pleases by a vote of the members, it's not the congregation's church either.

The Church of the Lord Jesus Christ was bought with the very blood of God. That's Acts 20:28. If you lose sight of this, nothing else matters; you are on your way to major problems in the congregation.

4. The Lord sends the pastor (and other leaders) not to make the congregation happy, but to make them healthy and holy and to make Himself happy.

Unless the membership understands this, the church is in big trouble and the pastor(s) will soon be under fire for failing to live up to the congregation's expectations.

Many a pastor has been handed his walking papers by a delegation who thought him a failure since the members were unhappy with him. So far have we strayed from the Scripture's teachings for the Lord's people.

A pastor's wife told me a disgruntled church leader pounded on their door early one morning. "Did you know you left that porch light on all night long?!" he demanded. He was concerned about the church's electricity bill.

The pastor calmly reminded his visitor that he paid his own utility bill. Furthermore, he said, their little dog had gotten out of the house the evening before, and they had not found him. "We thought if we left the porch light on, he might find his way back home."

If you think this is atypical and most pastors do not have to deal with such cantankerous behavior from church members with bad mental health, you would be mistaken.

Thankfully, such jerks are a minority in most churches, but almost every church has its share.

The remedy–the cure, the solution, the answer–is for godly and healthy church members to accurately understand the biblical role of the ministers and to speak that to others who don't get it.

And that leads us to the next point.

5. Every leader and each member are charged with protecting the unity of the Body of Christ.

"…endeavoring to keep the unity of the Spirit in the bond of peace" (Ephesians 4:3).

I remind the deacons that they, more than anyone else in the congregation, are charged with keeping the peace. They should move quickly when they observe the congregation's unity threatened by the actions of one or a few church members. Mature and godly (translation: humble and faithful) leaders will know what to do to head off trouble.

A member is loudly criticizing the pastor. He makes no secret of his opposition to the man of God. The question before us is how to deal with it and who should do it?

—The pastor should not have to do this. For him to confront the critic puts him in an awkward position and anything he does will appear self-serving.

—The deacons are the best ones to do this. It will require a certain amount of courage, but if they do not have what it takes to protect the church from troublemakers they have no business being called leaders.

—If the deacons will not act, two or three faithful church members will. They should not make a federal case of this, but simply go together to ask the complainer why he is criticizing the pastor. If the issues are legitimate and can be addressed, they should be. If the critic has a case, the deacons and/or pastor or both can be called in. But if they decide the critic is out of line, they should say so and ask him to stop his harmful actions.

A friend told me his mother's church had run off yet another pastor. "It's a few self- appointed bosses who do this," his mother said. He replied, "Mom! Why doesn't someone stand up to them and put a stop to this?" She said, "Honey, someone has to act like a Christian in all this."

That passive misunderstanding of Christian leadership has resulted in the enemy having a field day in the church of the Lord Jesus Christ.

6. The best thing a congregation can do for the church is to choose good and godly leaders, then get out of their way. Let them do their work.

How does one find "good and godly leaders?" Jesus gave three tests in Luke 16:10-12: 1) how one handles small assignments; 2) how he deals with money; and 3) how he treats things owned by others.

The Apostle Paul cautioned us not to "lay hands on anyone suddenly" (I Timothy 5:22).

Leaders were not to be novices (I Timothy 3:6) and were to be tested before being elevated to service (I Timothy 3:10).

Once the best leaders available are in place, members should get out of their way and trust them to do their work well. There will need to be accountability, but not second-guessing.

They do not need to be subjected to nitpicking or to frequent meetings so typical of small churches in which leaders are harassed about every dime spent.

For good reason small churches tend to stay small. One of the greatest is they tend to select leaders poorly, and then, even when they have good leaders, they do not support them but undercut and second-guess them until they are discouraged and resign in frustration.

In one church, the congregation was preparing to welcome a possible pastor the following weekend. The chairman of the search committee explained the process and laid out the schedule. That's when an unhappy member spoke up.

"That will not give us time to get to know him adequately. How do you expect us to vote on calling him when we have not fully investigated him and gotten to know him?"

My son, a deacon himself, raised his hand to respond to the man.

"We have chosen good leaders," Neil told him. "They have worked long and hard at this and have had many visits and discussions with the prospective pastor. We have continually kept them before the Lord in prayer. Now, let's trust them."

A friend sidled over to me following that meeting. "Guess who Neil sounded just like?" he teased.

He sounded like his father, I'm happy to report. He heard it from me enough: Trust your leaders.

7. Fellowship is the one thing a church offers not available to those sitting at home in front of the television watching their favorite media preacher.

The Greek word translated "fellowship" in the New Testament is *koinonia*, a word having to do with "sharing with each other." In our culture, the word carries a hundred meanings. In the church, fellowship refers to the loving interaction of the family members with each other, as they worship together, work alongside each other, and—for want of a better term— just hang out together.

Tragically, many a congregation sees little or no value in fellowship between its members. If it happens at all, it's an accident. In the average church, members enter, sit, listen, drop something into the offering, and then return home. The next week, they come back to sit and listen and then go home.

A healthy church will be doing a hundred things right, but a primary aspect of the congregation will be strong fellowship between the Lord's people. This has three aspects:

1) they love the Lord, 2) they enjoy each other and spend time together, and 3) they welcome newcomers into their midst.

We've all seen churches or classes where the people seemed to get the first two right but not the third. They were spiritual and they loved one another. But they completely ignored the newcomer. Such groups are not fellowships. They are cliques.

God told Israel in the wilderness how life would be conducted once they settled in the Promised Land. "The stranger who dwells among you shall be to you as one born among you, and you shall love him as yourself; for you were strangers in the land of Egypt; I am the Lord your God." (Leviticus 19:34).

The early church seemed to understand this. "And that day about three thousand souls were added to them. And they continued steadfastly in the apostles' doctrine and fellowship, in the breaking of bread and in prayers…. So, continuing daily with one accord in the temple, and breaking bread from house to house, they ate their food with gladness and simplicity of heart, praising God and having favor with all the people" (Acts 2:41, 46-47).

8. Love often has an emotional element. But love itself is not an emotion; it's far more than that. Love is an action. Love is something you do.

No teaching of the Bible is more needed today than this. People in the pews tend to think of love as an emotion, a feeling, which is sometimes present and often lacking. To do a thing without that emotion, some actually say, would be hypocritical.

This is entirely backward. To do a loving thing without the emotion of love being present may be the very essence of faith.

No one can command their emotions. We cannot force ourselves to feel angry or fearful or loving or hateful.

Therefore, for God to command that we love–as He does from one end of the Word to the other–must mean we are to do something other than "feel." Love is something we do. Love is an action, not an emotion.

"But I say to you who hear: Love your enemies." That's Luke 6:27. The entire passage of Luke 6:27-35 spells this out in greater detail.

The Lord is not requiring us to feel all gooey and sentimental toward those who are fighting us. He is asking us to do loving things toward them which He will then use as a strong and faithful witness to them.

What loving things?

The passage which follows that command contains four actions our Lord wants to see in His people when they are attacked and opposed. Do good to those who hate you, bless those who curse you, and pray for those who spitefully use you.... Give to everyone who asks of you. (See the entire passage, Luke 6:27-38)

The four most basic acts of love, whether we are talking about loving our neighbor, other disciples, our mates, our children, or our enemies, are the same: do good works to them, bless them with our words, pray for them with the Father, and give good gifts to them. (Note: This little teaching will be repeated throughout this book for good reason.)

"My little children, let us not love in word and in tongue (only) but indeed and in truth" (I John 3:18).

9. Nothing we do demonstrates faith better than praying.

How many times are we commanded in the Word to pray? It must be in the hundreds. Luke 18:1 is one of my favorites. And He was telling them a parable to show that at all times they ought to pray and not to faint. At all times: that's the imperative of prayer. Fainting is the alternative to praying.

We do a lot of things to demonstrate our faith in the Lord Jesus, but nothing more than praying. After all, we do not see the One to whom we pray, and we may never see the answers to most of the things for which we pray.

Today, I prayed for a child having brain surgery in a local hospital. The request came over the internet from a mutual friend. I am praying for the president of the United States. I'm praying for missionary friends on the other side of the globe. I'm lifting my children in prayer.

In most cases, I will never know to what degree or in what way my prayer was answered. To persevere in prayer means to demonstrate faith that the

Lord in Heaven hears that my prayer means something to Him, and that my prayers are making a difference in the world.

For most people, that alone is reason to quit praying. When we do not see the One whom we address and never know whether it made a difference, "fainting" becomes the norm.

There is no way to know exactly, but many leaders believe a large percent of people calling themselves Christians no longer pray except in emergencies.

Praying requires faith. "Lord, give us faith to pray consistently and fervently and to continue faithfully!"

10. Every church needs a little conflict now and then.

Churches seem to run to extremes here: either they are constantly in conflict, or they never have any and when they do, members panic and feel it's the end of the world.

It helps to note that the early church dealt with one kind of conflict or other from its inception. In Acts 3-4, the problem is with the Jewish authorities. In Acts 6, it was members bickering among themselves. In Acts 7-9, it's persecution from outside.

If to be a New Testament church is our desire, then we should be ready to accept persecution and inner turmoil and respond to it promptly and faithfully.

I once moderated a church business meeting in which the congregation terminated the pastor. The reasons, such as they were, were miniscule. The leadership simply did not like the man or the way he did ministry, in my judgment. That night as I left the building, an elderly member said, "This is the fourth minister in a row we have run off."

That is a church that does not know how to handle conflict. It reminds us of marriages in conflict where all the couple knows is to get a divorce. There are other alternatives, far better ones.

A little conflict from time to time is a sign of life for a church. A dead body experiences no conflict; a growing organism may know constant conflict.

A little conflict from time to time keeps the leadership on its toes. It reminds them the enemy is out there, "walking to and fro, seeking whom he may devour" (I Peter 5:8).

A little conflict gives the church leadership experience in how to deal with the more serious variety which crops up occasionally.

At a pastors' conference, the leader asked each person to introduce himself and talk about his work. One old gentleman told us his name and added, "I'm over here at Shiloh. You know there's always a mess going on at Shiloh. But that's all right. Where there's no friction, there's no traction!"

I said, "Whoa! Let me write that down." It was worth remembering.

All these principles are worth remembering and reminding your people of again and again. In fact, that's the only way they will ever learn them.

Do it right, pastor, and long after you have moved on to other fields or to glory, your people will still be practicing principles of healthy church management which you have drilled into them through your faithful service.

I can hear them now. "We used to have an old preacher who told us frequently that…."

You'll be in heaven. Literally.

Chapter Five

What's a pastor to do when his biggest competition in town is another preacher?

Sometimes a pastor finds a neighboring pastor is sucking all the air out of the room. The new preacher is dynamic and exciting, and crowds are flocking to his church. He's a media star. He's pulling people out of the other churches.

Sound familiar? It's not a new phenomenon.

"Now a certain Jew named Apollos, born at Alexandria, an eloquent man and mighty in Scriptures, came to Ephesus" (Acts 18:24).

Sometimes you're Apollos, sometimes you are Paul. Early records indicate Paul was short and bald, nothing much to look at. And some said he wasn't much to listen to. See 2 Corinthians 10:10.

Apollos, on the other hand, was something else. A real champion.

What do you want to bet Apollos was gorgeous to boot. A real hunk. Articulate in the pulpit. Probably wore these cool suits and had a trendy haircut.

Named for Apollos–a god of both Greeks and Romans, the champion of the youth and the sharpest thing on Mount Olympus! –this preacher would have made a great television evangelist. He made an impact wherever he went.

What's more, he was good. He was spiritual and godly and not shallow at all. Not a flash in the pan.

Which just made it harder on his neighboring pastors of the local churches. They could not in good faith dismiss the guy as unworthy or a superficial rock star.

"Being fervent in the spirit, he spoke and taught accurately the things of the Lord..." (18:25). "He vigorously refuted the Jews publicly, showing from the Scriptures that Jesus is the Christ" (18:28).

They couldn't fault his preaching. Apollos was a good preacher and what he said was dead on. Christians were impressed and his opponents distressed. But still...Something was missing. "He knew only the baptism of John" (18:25).

So, there was something lacking about his doctrine, although we'd be hard put to know exactly how that played out. As John MacArthur puts it, "Despite his knowledge of the OT, Apollos did not fully understand Christian truth."

It turns out Apollos was humble, too. (Is this guy frustrating or what? We keep thinking there has to be a major flaw somewhere but find none.)

"When Aquila and Priscilla heard him, they took him aside and explained to him the way of God more accurately" (18:26).

The guy was teachable.

Then, Apollos left for Greece (19:1). Down in Corinth, they loved him (I Corinthians 1:12 and 3:4).

Okay. Let's pause here and talk about this phenomenon.

The new preacher comes to town and suddenly, he's all the rage. Ever been there?

In the 1970s Dr. John Bisagno took Southern Baptists by storm. At the First Baptist Church of Del City, Oklahoma, he began baptizing hundreds every year and caught the attention of our denomination. Then, Houston's First Baptist made him their pastor. There, he would baptize a thousand people annually and eventually lead them to relocate to the interstate with a zillion-dollar campus. By any measurement, he was a flaming success.

Brother John was a powerful preacher. He was handsome, funny, and personable. What else? He played the trumpet. Oh, and his wife was gorgeous. They were nice people.

Soon Dr. Bisagno was on the program of every pastor's conference and evangelism conference around the country. And he was wonderful. He connected with the audiences and was a stem-winder. A powerful and eloquent preacher. Crowds raved.

I remember the day John Bisagno was speaking to our state's annual meeting and was followed on the program by Dr. Ken Chafin, head of our denomination's evangelism ministry. Dr. Chafin was no slouch in the preaching/communication department, but not in the same league as Bisagno. As he began his message, the buzz from Bisagno's appearance still lingered in the air. So, Dr. Chafin addressed that.

"You fellows in Mississippi love Johnny Bisagno," he said. "But let me ask you a question. "How would you like it if he were pastoring in your hometown? You've been telling people for years churches can't have revival anymore. That people just don't respond to the gospel like they used to. And then, this preacher shows up and starts winning thousands to the Lord and packing them in to the rafters. How would you like that?"

Chafin said, "You love him because he comes to your convention and delivers this rousing message, then gets on the plane and flies back to Texas. And you don't have to compete with his great success."

As things happened, within a year or two, Dr. Chafin himself became pastor of South Main Baptist Church in Houston, not far from Dr. Bisagno. The two churches were vastly different and the preaching styles of these two men as unlike as it's possible to get. As far as I know there was never any competition or ill will between them. But Chafin had made a great point.

What if that happens in your town? What if the young Apollos arrives and begins pulling in the crowds and charming the city and buying airtime on the television station? What if you begin noticing some of your people missing from their pews, and soon your office receives letters asking that their membership be transferred over to Apollos' church?

How would you feel? What would you do? How would you handle it? Scripture addresses this subject, as it does almost everything, we can think of.

The church members at Corinth began choosing their favorites. Some said, "I prefer Paul." Others, "It's Apollos for me!" And still others, "Cephas (Peter) is my man!"

And some in the congregation stuck their noses in the air and said, "We're of Jesus' party!"

One was as bad as the other.

So, Paul addressed this cliquishness which afflicts carnal church members and torments the rest of us pastors.

"Who is Paul? And who is Apollos? They're only ministers (servants) whom you believed, as the Lord gave to each one. I planted, Apollos watered, but God gave the increase" (I Corinthians 3:5-6).

He continued; we are God's fellow-workers. You are God's field, God's building.... I laid the foundation, and another built on it... But Jesus Christ is everything. (My paraphrase of I Corinthians 3:9-11.)

We're all in this together. We are team members. We each need the other. Sometimes we are the darling, sometimes we're the one left on the sideline.

When you are the star, the Apollos of your town...

You're young and excited and the new pastor in town. All the churches around you are being led by older men, settled, perhaps a little boring. The field belongs to you, and you eat it up. Crowds flock to hear you preach, teens adore you, and you're asked to serve on the Chamber and speak to the civic clubs and join most of them.

You're tempted to believe their acclaim. To think there's no one else like you. That the other pastors are failures, and you alone are faithful.

Take a deep breath. It's a passing fancy. Soon, the crowd will move along to the next flash in the pan. Your balloon will burst, and you will stand on the sidelines watching your members chase after the next ministerial attraction.

Read Acts 14 and take a lesson from Barnabas and Paul. After healing a man in Lystra, the crowds made these two apostles their champions. "The gods have come down to us in the likeness of men!" they cheered. As they brought animals to sacrifice before them and garlands for their heads, it was all Paul and Barnabas could do to stop this madness. It wasn't to last.

An hour later, troublemakers from the last town Barnabas and Paul had visited arrived to attack and slander them. The same crowd that wanted to worship them now gathered stones to kill them. "They stoned Paul and dragged him out of the city, expecting him to be dead" (14:19).

So much for the adulation of the crowd. Fickle is hardly strong enough a word.

So, when they make you their idol, don't let it go to your head. Do your work. Keep your eyes on Jesus. It'll soon pass. Never forget that the crowd that cried "Hosanna!" to Jesus on Sunday was calling "Crucify Him!" by Friday afternoon.

And if you are the pastor on the sidelines watching the new darling take your town by storm...

Pray for him. Speak well of him. Be very careful not to appear jealous or small-minded.

Do not envy him or resent him. Appreciate the good he's doing. Look for things to compliment if you can. Put in a good word for him with the other pastors, some of whom may be seething with envy or suspicion or resentment.

Do your job. If you are losing members to the new guy, keep telling yourself (and your leaders who may be panicking at the empty pews and low offerings), "This is not about us, but about the Lord Jesus. And if they're doing a better job over there, then let's pray for them and encourage them."

"A million years from now, all that will matter is that we all were faithful to Jesus."

Let his success spur you and your team on to greater effort. Make sure you're doing your very best for the Lord, that you have not been lulled to sleep.

Drop the new pastor a note of welcome and appreciation.

Invite him to lunch and bring along two or three other pastors. Try to guard against discussing the phenomenon of his church pulling away your members. This too will even out in time, and the craze will pass. Get to know him and accept him into your group. You will likely find out that he is a little surprised and overwhelmed by the reaction of the community.

He may end up becoming one of your best friends. I've seen it happen.

If he happens to be one of those pastors who is a loner, who ignores your overtures toward friendliness, do not be discouraged. Keep your eyes on the Lord. Pray for him and speak well of him when you can do so honestly. If you watch his sermon on television and were blessed, drop him a note to say so. And do not be discouraged if you get no response. You are a servant of the Lord Jesus Christ (see Romans 14:4).

Teach your people the principles of I Corinthians 3 at a time when this is not an issue. That way, they are prepared for when it becomes one.

How does the old joke go? Sometimes you're the bug and sometimes you're the windshield.

Chapter Six

Preachers are different. You've noticed? Here's why.

Someone asked, "Why does my preacher not weep at funerals? Not even at his own mother's.

By the time we laid my wonderful mama to rest, I was in my early 70s and she was nearly 96. She was so ready to go. If it's possible to be ready to give one's beloved mother back to Jesus, we were. And yes, we still miss her every day, and it's been several years.

But there's another reason for the lack of tears. Starting early—my mid-20s—I began doing heart-breaking funerals, one after another, the kind that will tear your heart out and stomp that sucker. Do enough of these, and after a while you run out of tears.

It's not that you do not care, do not love, or cannot feel. It's just that you care and love and feel without tears.

Furthermore, by this time, the preacher has come to terms with the message of Christ and has settled once and for all that this is true, this is what I believe, and I commit my entire life to it.

The young preacher proclaims this stuff more by faith. In time, he comes to know it and as John said, to know that he knows. Knowing that the gospel of Jesus is true means he will see his mother again, and that's she's doing just fine today.

So, don't be surprised if he cries very little.

"Why does my pastor seem detached from the joys of our wedding or the sorrow of our funeral?"

I'll tell you my story. On a Saturday afternoon we held a one o'clock funeral for Susan Edmondson at the Methodist church down the street because our sanctuary was decorated for a wedding two hours later. Susan had grown up in our church, was a popular and well-loved young woman, the youngest child of older parents, and had been the victim of a bizarre accident. Working alone in an art store in New York City, that day she had moved a huge piece of art—a heavy column or something—by "walking" it back and forth. As she turned to walk away, it fell on her, crushing her skull. She never knew what hit her. We were all devastated.

The church was packed with heart-broken friends and family. I recall none of the details of the funeral but will never forget the anguish I felt trying to be the family's pastor that day.

Then, returning from the cemetery, we gathered in our church sanctuary to unite Nathan Wright and Susie John in marriage. We did everything we could to rejoice with them.

It was one of the hardest afternoons I've ever had. When it was over, I went home and had trouble sleeping. The next morning, Sunday, I was expected to get up and function as usual, preaching in two morning services and another that night. But my heart had been ripped out.

I knew then why some people turn to liquor or drugs.

After a pastor does this a few times, he learns to cope by not entering so deeply into the pain or rising so high with the joys.

It's what a pastor does. It's a survival technique.

"Why are all preachers nuts?" That's the title of what follows handed me by the pastor who wrote it.

Explanation: He and I were discussing this. When he asked me to write such an article, I suggested he write his story and send it to me. I've edited it only slightly.

"What I'm about to share is no different from 95 percent of all pastors. However, I believe the events we experience shape who we are and what we have become. If a pastor doesn't have the ability to compartmentalize, he won't last long. Here we go...

My first funeral was for a lady named Violet Barr. She was a senior adult confined to a wheelchair. She died in a house fire. Her only relative was a niece. The niece's fiancé died trying to save Violet. I had been a pastor all of 4 months. I stood in the labor and delivery room and watched a mother hold the lifeless body of the child she just delivered. I had the funeral two days later. Over the years I have done countless funerals for babies. Too many to remember. I recently attended a funeral for brothers who drowned over Labor Day weekend. The boys were young enough to be buried in the same casket. I did the funeral of a man who was an invalid and died in a house fire. Seems to be my specialty. Drove to a church member's place of work and stopped him from committing suicide. I had his wife stay on the phone with him till I got there. Took the gun away from him and took him to the hospital emergency room.

By the way, I've done many funerals for those who have taken their lives. Some included overdoses......usually teenagers. Was at a social event for

46

junior high and high school students when we learned a popular student had been shot in a hunting accident. I was asked to tell the kids. Following the attacks of 9/11, the local school called and requested we come and counsel the students. Over the years, been called upon to talk to students following some tragic event such as the death of a student. Our church served as a shelter following Hurricane Katrina. We housed over 300 people in our family life center. This required organization and volunteers. I still have flashbacks of the people we helped. Could have been the most stress I've ever endured. Had to check my preaching professor from NOBTS into our shelter.

"In 2004, the day before Easter, my father-in-law died unexpectedly at the age of 60. Had to tell my wife. I preached the next day and a few days later conducted his funeral. The next year, the day before Easter, my dad died, preached the next day, and conducted his funeral on the Tuesday. I did a funeral two days later for a church member's father. Like many pastors, vacations, holidays, and days off have been interrupted by church needs. I've done funerals on Thanksgiving Day, Christmas Eve, and the 4th of July. One Wednesday, I went to two funerals in the afternoon. The last was at 5:00pm. I preached the Wednesday night service at 6.

"I've done two funerals and one wedding on the same day. I've had to go to the home of a church member and tell the wife her husband was killed in an automobile accident. I've helped identify bodies. I've had to tell countless family members their loved ones have died. I have counseled a family about a sexual abuse situation concerning a father and his 12-year-old daughter. Father was arrested. Have also helped young ladies who have been raped. Along those lines, have helped families deal with teenage pregnancies.

"During my first six months at my last church, my mother died. I preached at her funeral and then preached the next Sunday. My staff accused me of grandstanding. My wife was so sick she couldn't get off the couch and ultimately had to have surgery. My oldest daughter had an emergency appendectomy on Saturday. I preached the next day. My youngest daughter's car basically blew up. And my new staff didn't like the way I conducted staff meetings. Made for an interesting year. It never got better.

"I have had to say goodbye to friends as we have moved to other churches and I've conducted funerals for not only other family members, but real, real close friends. I have been in the room of many people and watched life leave them, including my own Dad. I've helped funeral directors load up lifeless bodies and stayed to minister to grieving families. I have also stayed at the hospital with a dead body countless times till the funeral director could get there. I haven't even touched on church politics, and counseling sessions. There are too many to list. Been called a dictator, visionless, son-of-a-bitch, and a bastard. Was told one day by a man who deals in lumber, "You're the strongest man I've ever know!" As Forrest Gump would say, "I don't know about that!"

Chapter Seven

The pastor will sometimes feel like a failure. Sometimes he is.

"For not he who commends himself is approved, but whom the Lord commends" (2 Corinthians 10:18).

"Did I fail?"

Every man or woman who ministers in the Kingdom of God is quickly struck by two realities:

The perfection of God (and thus the desire to present to Him worthy offerings of worship and service) and the imperfection of mankind (meaning anything we offer Him will be flawed, even at its best).

As a result, we are often tormented with feelings of inadequacy and hounded by the reality that our efforts have not been enough, our devotion has been too weak, and our ministries a far cry from what we had hoped.

"I feel like a failure."

Those words and that feeling are voiced not just by those who literally are failures. Some of the (outwardly) most successful pastors and spiritual leaders on the planet deal with the same sense of futility.

"It's never enough."

—We leave church on Sunday knowing that the sermon we delivered was nowhere near as wonderful as the one we received from the Lord in our study. What happened between the study and the pulpit?

—The vision we had for our church soon ran into the reality of a thousand foes: our own self- doubt, the skepticism of certain members, the honest inquiry of our friends and supporters, and the ongoing needs of the congregation. This project started out to be far better than it turned out. What happened?

We were laboring, planting seed and cultivating, and expecting our efforts to produce a banner crop. When little fruit appeared, we naturally felt that we have been the reason.

We have failed.

Here is our best counsel to the hard-working laborers in the Lord's field who find the reality at weighing-in time to be less than they ever envisioned when they headed into the field at the beginning of the day....

1) "Stay in the ministry long enough and you will learn you can do everything right, but there are still a hundred and one other factors that influence the result."

We do our best and leave the rest with the Lord.

2) "You have been faithful. That more than anything else is the standard."

"Moreover, it is required of stewards that one be found trustworthy" (I Corinthians 4:2).

3) "Some seeds take years to produce. Continue waiting before the Lord and see what He's up to."

"Be not weary in well doing, for in due season we shall reap—if we don't quit!" (Galatians 6:9).

4) You are not your own judge.

As Paul said (in our text above), even if you give yourself a passing grade, it's meaningless. The "Grader" is the Lord and no one else. "To his own master (a servant) stands or falls" (Romans 14:4).

It's almost comical the way God's preachers rush to and fro seeking approval from one another. I've known of pastors starting colleges to award their friends honorary doctorates with the expectation that the favor will be reciprocated.

When I was 40 years old and serving as a trustee of one of our denomination's ministries, I saw that my family and my church needed more from me than I was giving. So, I refused a second four-year-term in order to stay home. My reasoning went something like this: "When a preacher dies, no one cares what boards he served on. What matters will be his family and the churches he led."

A few years later, I attended the funeral of a well-known denominational leader. As they recited the many boards and agencies, committees and commissions, the deceased had served on or led, I glanced around the room. People were bored. No one seemed to care. Now, I'm a realist and know a) someone had to lead these works and b) we do them for the Lord, not for public acclaim. But it confirmed to me that what matters most to a father and a pastor are the major assignments the Lord hands him. For me, that was leading my family and my church.

Let the pastor be faithful where God has assigned him. Paul told Timothy, "Fulfill your ministry" (2 Timothy 4:5).

Some pastors spend too much time on the golf course, reading novels, working on their farms, pursuing their favorite hobby, watching television, playing on the computer, or a thousand other diversions that may not be bad in themselves in moderation, but which sap their energies and dull their brains and interfere with the work God gave them to do.

Let the pastor wake up, look around, and take stock of his situation.

Let the pastor pull aside with the Lord for a time of confession, cleansing, and redirection. Let the pastor pray to be reassigned to the Lord's calling. Then, let him get up and go to work.

Should he confess to the church? Probably not. Just tell the Lord and seek His guidance and blessing. Then let him rearrange his schedule, get the support of his spouse and one or two co-workers, and get on with it.

His ministry time may be evenly divided between sermon study, administration, and personal ministry. (The last mostly means to get out of the office and touch lives for Jesus!)

Should the pastor tell other ministers about this change? Not for a year. He should show the Lord, the church, and himself he is serious about this redirection before mentioning it to others. When he does share it, he will want to ask the Lord when and how.

Keep telling yourself, pastor, that you are "more than a conqueror through Him who loved us." You can get this right.

One final thing. Guard against the perfectionistic ideal which keeps insisting that nothing you do is acceptable since it is imperfect. That standard, which appears so noble on the surface, is your worst enemy.

Keep Psalm 103:14 before you. He Himself knows our frame. He is mindful that we are but dust. God is under no illusions about you and me. Were He expecting perfection from any of us, He would have given up in disgust a long time ago. He knows He got no bargain when He saved us. When we sin, the only one surprised is us.

But serve Him anyway. He is a God of grace and mercy. Every day of your life, give thanks for that!

Chapter Eight

Should the pastor confess his doubt?

If I had said, 'I will speak thus,' behold, I should have betrayed the generation of Thy children (Psalm 73:15).

Some questions need to be handled in private and not made public.

A friend who had not been to church in a while ventured back recently only to be slapped in the face by the sermon.

The guest preacher chose the Noah story from Genesis 6-8 for his sermon. My friend said, "He informed the church that he does not believe that story. He said it was impossible for Noah to have carried food on the ark for all those animals for a period of 90 days. And imagine the waste those animals would have produced!"

"He said the story was made up by old men to teach people that God punishes those who do not obey Him."

One wonders what conditions prompted the leadership of that church to invite the enemy to fill the pulpit. That is precisely what they did and it's who he was. Anyone undermining the faith of the Lord's people in the Holy Scriptures is no friend.

On the other hand, let's give the guy the benefit of the doubt and suppose that he was having trouble reconciling that story with what he knows about life. Most of us have been there and done that with various teachings of Scripture. At one time or other, we have struggled with the Virgin Birth, the miracles our Lord performed (or other miracles throughout the Bible), the Atonement, and of course, the "biggie," the resurrection of our Lord.

As a matter of fact, the Lord does not mind our wrestling with these matters. He who is The Truth has nothing to fear from honest inquiry.

But that's not the point.

God can use such struggles to strengthen us as we work through the doubts to arrive at solid answers. In my own life, areas which used to torment me are now my strongest convictions. And, from what my pastor friends say, that's fairly typical. That's how God works.

However, while the minister is working his way through his doubts and questions, he should keep it to himself. Better yet, let him share with a few close friends and mentors who can assist him as he digs his way out of the hole of despondency.

Whatever you do, do not preach your doubts.

This is the point of Psalm 73, a favorite of so many wise people through the years. Anyone unfamiliar with it should pause now and check it out.

That Psalm counsels us not to stand before the congregation and tell God's people "I have doubts about this," "This is a contradiction with (such-and-such) and I cannot reconcile them," or "Surely this did not happen the way the Scripture presents it."

Do. Not. Do. That. Ever.

But let's say you do. Call it being "transparent" or "intellectually honest" (give me a break!) or however you choose to tag it.

Suppose you do share with God's people the issues you are dealing with, and then later find where you were wrong and get straight on these things. That is, you find the answers— as you usually will if you wait before the Lord and continue to seek His Truth.

Then what will you do?

Retracing your steps and apologizing to the people you misinformed along the way is out of the question.

You can never reassemble that congregation again.

Over my lifetime, being somewhat normal, I have questioned various teachings in God's word and then in God's good timing, received answers and assurances. As a young minister, I had questions about the Lord's bodily, physical resurrection and in time became convinced of the "infallible proofs" of Acts 1:3. At one time or another, I have questioned many basic doctrines and tenets of the Christian faith, but as I continued seeking and praying, studying and listening to the Lord, almost every question has received a divine settling. And, as the saying goes, I am stronger in broken places.

What if I had spoken of my doubts and questions?

"Oh, I must be honest with my people," some pastor says. In his sermons he tells them the Bible stories of which he has doubts, the doctrines which he questions, and the promises of God which he disbelieves. He calls this transparency.

Such a preacher is an egotist of the first order. He thinks his assignment is to preach to himself.

A minister who preaches his questions and peddles his doubts has no business in any pulpit in the land. As he sows doubt instead of faith, gives questions but offers no answers, he is a troublemaker and not a friend. He is the equivalent of a medical doctor who enters a plague-riddled village to announce that the vaccine being offered by the missionary doctors is flawed. Unless he has something better to offer, let him stay home.

Preachers and teachers who plant doubts and encourage unbelief will stand before a holy God and give account for the damage done to hearers, as well as upon people whom they in turn influence. Unbelief can be passed on just as surely as faith can.

"Let not many of you become teachers, my brethren, knowing that as such we shall incur a stricter judgment" (James 3:1).

As faithful shepherds of the Lord's people, let us speak faith to them and not our fears. Let us guide them to safety and not push them further into lostness and deeper darkness.

Sheep are skittish enough from feeding off one another's fears; shepherds should lead them in paths of righteousness to green pastures and still waters. When he is no longer able to do this for whatever reason, let the appointed shepherd hand over the care and feeding of the flock to one who will be loyal and faithful.

"I solemnly charge you in the presence of God and of Christ Jesus, who is to judge the living and the dead...preach the word" (2 Timothy 4:1-2).

Chapter Nine

An effective minister must learn to say 'no' sometimes. Want to hear my tales of woe?

It's hard for us people-pleasers to say 'no' when going-along to get-along would cause fewer waves.

By people-pleaser I do not mean as opposed to doing the will of God, but preferring the people around me to be happy if it is in my power to make them so.

"Why can't we all just be happy?" Smile, please. Many of our readers are in that boat. And some of us need to step out and take a stand on solid ground.

My theory is that writing about mistakes made in my ministry of sixty-plus years is of more interest to the general reader and of greater value to the young pastor who wants to know where the potholes are in order to avoid them. Even as we all learn from our mistakes more than from our successes, I suspect we benefit more from hearing of the failures of others than of their victories and successes. It certainly makes for more interesting reading!

I'm thinking of two instances in particular when I should have put my foot down and said, "No, absolutely not" and held my ground. As it was, I meekly went along with what others around me wanted—always wanting the people around me to be happy—and have lived with the memory of that ever since.

The first time, I was 30 years old, and concluding my third pastorate.

This was to be my final service in that church where I had labored hard for three and a half years. I had a sermon prepared, some final things to say to the church, points I felt would be helpful and encouraging, and a fellowship honoring our little family was scheduled afterwards.

That Sunday afternoon, the chairman of the deacons who also was chairing the pastor search committee, phoned. "Pastor, Brother Martin is in town, and we would like him to preach for the church tonight. Otherwise, we will have to bring him back from the Gulf Coast and it might be several weeks before that can happen."

Hugh Martin was a seminary classmate and a good man. In fact, four years earlier, it was Hugh who had given my name to this church. I owed him a lot. What I did not owe him was my final service with my church. (Of course, the problem was not with him but with my chairman.)

The rest of this story—after I agreed (meekly, I might add, and against my wishes)—was that that night when time for the sermon came, Brother Hugh Martin stepped up to the pulpit and began to preach. That's when the chairman of the committee leaned over to me.

"Pastor, we want to vote on him tonight."

I said, "Wait a minute." Yes, we're having this conversation on the fourth row, right in front of the guest preacher who is midway through the introduction to his sermon.

I said to the deacon, "Sir, this is a holiday weekend." It was New Year's. "You have members out of town, and they hardly know the search committee has started looking for a pastor. They are not going to like returning home to discover the church has already called a new one."

The chairman—a good man, but completely used to getting his way in everything—said, "The committee is agreed on this, preacher." Translation: He had told the members of the committee and they had meekly—there's that word again! —gone along with it. They would not have protested if they had learned I was against it.

What I said was, "Well, I'm leaving. You can do whatever you please." What I should have said was, "No. This is not right. And you cannot do it." And he wouldn't have.

Of course, three hours earlier, I should have told him this is no way to present a new pastor. Wait two or three weeks, then bring up Hugh and Jean Martin from Gulfport and let them have the full weekend getting acquainted with the church. Had I done that, the chairman would have acquiesced and done it, and good things would have happened. The congregation would have appreciated it, the new pastor would have started off on a good note instead of bearing the resentment of several over the way this was handled, and my final memory of that church would not have been spoiled.

I don't sit around regretting this. It is, however, permanently fixed in my memory.

The second instance, I was thirty-four. and in my first year of a new pastorate.

I'd been at this large, influential church for only a few months. We had just added to our staff a friend who has recently finished seminary. As my assistant, Tom would work with high school students. Soon after arriving, he asked me if the church could have a "youth revival."

The term "youth revival" can mean many things. What it meant to me—remember, I'm hardly out of adolescence myself—was a full week of meetings with an excellent speaker. In time I was to learn that a youth revival could also involve only the youth and take place over a weekend.

Tom had a seminary classmate he wanted us to invite. "He was voted the outstanding graduate last year," Tom said. They were great friends.

Now, I did not know the guy and had never heard him preach. But on the strength of the recommendation of my young assistant, we invited him and gave him a major slot on the church calendar: Sunday morning, Sunday night, and each night through Wednesday.

Sunday morning, he preached before 800 people, which included perhaps a hundred college students. The television cameras were live.

And he goofed royally.

Somewhere in the sermon, this young preacher pontificated about the Lord Jesus in what was full-out heresy.

What he said was, "When Jesus was praying in the Garden before going to the cross, there is evidence that He did not know he would be raised from the dead."

I'm sitting in the front row. You may believe that I came awake in a heartbeat.

"Did he say that? Surely, he didn't say Jesus did not know he was going to be raised from the dead!"

But he did say it.

I thought of the times the Lord Jesus had said, "Destroy this body and I will raise it again on the third day." "As Jonah was in the belly of the fish three days and three nights...." and so forth.

Then, the young preacher repeated that statement. And did so one more time later. Three times. There was no getting around it, I was going to have to address this.

For the rest of the sermon, I'm sitting there thinking, "All right, pastor. What are you going to do now? You cannot let this stand. It's full-blown heresy. He's contradicting the plain teaching of Scripture."

To address his statements in this service would humiliate him in front of this crowd as well as family members who had driven in from Missouri to support him.

On the other hand, if I waited until next Sunday to address it, we would not have this same congregation back. In fact, common sense says we could never assemble this exact crowd again.

So, at the end of the service, I did it.

I called attention to what the young preacher had said and cited some scriptures that said otherwise. I hated doing it and could only imagine how he must be feeling. But he had brought it on himself, I felt.

Later, I found out that he and my young assistant had fed off each other's anger toward me and that the guest had considered canceling the rest of the meeting. "That would have been all right," I told him. We went forward with the revival through Wednesday night, although it had lost its luster for me.

In the next deacons meeting, I addressed this and explained to the leaders what had happened. The chairman had one sentence for me. "Pastor, you're being too free with your pulpit." That's all he said. And he was right.

A hard lesson well learned.

In the first place, I wish I had said 'no' to a youth revival—or a meeting of any kind—with a preacher whom I did not know and had not heard. And, I wish I had had the gumption to end the revival after the first meeting instead of prolonging the agony.

As a result of these two painful episodes, I eventually developed a little more backbone and the skill to say 'no' to people I loved and respected. And, as you may have noticed, I survived.

You will too.

Chapter Ten

I urge pastors to read constantly.

Read for sermons, read for insights, read for enjoyment, for relaxation, for inspiration.

Since it's a truism that we are what we read, the pastor's reading material is important. I like to read widely and recommend it.

At this moment, in addition to the wide range of biblical material on my shelves, I have several sections filled with books on Abraham Lincoln, books on Winston Churchill, books on the Civil War and the Second World War, and another section of books on comic strips and cartoon characters. I read a western novel almost every week.

Read what interests you is about as good advice as I know how to give. One advantage for the pastor reading very old books of sermons is picking up insights and illustrations you can be fairly certain no one else is using. So, if you use one of the three Leslie Weatherhead stories below, it's a sure bet that no visitor will approach you after the service to say his pastor told the same story last week.

Leslie D. Weatherhead, well-known British pastor, served London's City Temple for many years. In 1945, he published a collection of the sermons he had delivered to his people during the war that had just concluded. Only the first sermon had this as its title, but the entire book was named *The Significance of Silence*.

A story about ingratitude

Weatherhead repeats a story Prime Minister Winston Churchill had recently told in a speech, about a sailor who dived into the waters of Plymouth Harbor to rescue a drowning child. Not long after, the sailor bumped into the little boy and his mother in the streets of Plymouth. The child nudged his mother, and she stopped the sailor. "Are you the man who pulled my little boy out of the water?" The sailor was glad to acknowledge that he was and thought possibly the mother might have in mind some kind of reward. "Yes, madam," he said proudly.

"Then," said the mother, with fire in her eyes, "where's his cap?"

A story about what's really important in life

"I sat with another minister in the home of a charming and wealthy layman who was entertaining us both. The talk turned on Wordsworth's poetry, and our host said, 'You two make me jealous talking that way. I have always thought I would like to read a lot of poetry, but I have never had time. When I have made my pile, I shall take it up.'

"He was quite sincere about it, but he never did take it up. A sense of values is not a thing you can switch over, like turning the dial of a radio. You cannot engineer an interest in it, let alone attach dynamic purposefulness to it. It becomes harder and harder, as the years pass, to direct your life by a new star. If you spend fifty years with the dominating aim of making money, you can't suddenly say to yourself, 'Now I will like poetry.' You lose your taste for lovely things, or, worse still, they don't seem worth so much.

'He who stays in bed on Sunday morning,' said Dr. Selbie of Mansfield College, Oxford, 'may not be committing a great sin, but his sense of values is being filched from him. He is putting the value of comfort higher than the value of self-discipline and worship.'"

A story about the homegoing of the faithful

We are not here to be happy, Weatherhead asserts in the sermon "Is It Really Good to be Alive?" He writes, "We are here to glorify God in a character which has been schooled in such a way that it finds its joy in communion with him."

He tells about his sister who had died of cancer some years earlier.

Weatherhead had bumped into an old friend who said, "I wonder if I ever told you of what your sister's ministry meant to me. She would be astonished if she knew (perhaps she does). I often went to see her during her long illness I can never forget my last visit. It was about a fortnight before she went. We had two hours together, and she was full of fun and laughter and wonderful anticipation. I could repeat today some of the very words she said. She was like a child going home for Christmas! I never knew anyone who more completely and literally 'ran up with joy the shining way.' Her influence has lived with me all through the years."

This prompted Pastor Weatherhead to think back to his visit with his sister just after she had received word that her recovery would be, humanly speaking, impossible. "She was in a Liverpool nursing home. It was a dark, dull November afternoon, but when I went into her room, I could only say that it was just as though someone had lit a beautiful lamp.

Nobody had really done so, but the glory in her face seemed to illumine the whole room. I suppose she saw the dismay in my own, because she said, 'Don't be troubled at the news.

Everything that you preach is perfectly true.' And then she added a sentence that is written on my heart in gold forever: 'I am proud to be trusted with cancer.' Now, what do you make of that? 'I am proud to be trusted with cancer.' Not that she did not fight it. Cancer is not the intention of God. .... God did not will it, but God had allowed it, and that was enough for her.

By the time it had won a victory over her body, her soul was more than conqueror through him who could use even cancer to bring her where he wanted her to be, to make her soul greater than ever, and to express his own glory in a human life."

That's why I love old books, particularly ancient books of sermons. At this moment, on the shelf just behind this chair where I'm sitting, you'll find books of sermons by Robert Murray McCheyne ("Sermons of Robert Murray McCheyne," 1961), by Helmut Thielicke ("Out of the Depths", 1962), by Harry Emerson Fosdick ("A Great Time to Be Alive,"1944), by Martin Niemoller ("Dachau Sermons," 1946), as well as a biography of Martin Niemoller, "Hero of the Concentration Camp," 1942.

And a couple of old comic books, but don't tell anybody.

Chapter Eleven

High standards are great but lose perfectionism.

It sounds so right: "I expect nothing less than perfection from you. We have the highest standards in this church (or company or family)."

I was married for fifty-two years to a perfectionist. Oddly, she did not apply that standard to other people but accepted them as the imperfect humans they all are. She applied perfectionism to herself and to me. In both cases, it was disastrous.

Many years ago, Psychology Today magazine ran an article titled "The Perfectionist's Script for Self-Defeat." It was one of the most practical and helpful things I had ever come across.

Well, okay, I didn't "come across" it. My wife did. She was the subscriber to that magazine which this Baptist preacher rarely had time for. But she came upon the article which proved to be of great help to us both.

According to the writer, the perfectionist is licked before he starts. Since he cannot be perfect, anything he does, even his very best efforts, will be lacking.

Here's how that works out...

Take a woman on a diet. She has done well for two weeks now, avoiding the danger foods, eating only the prescribed meals. She has lost seven pounds and can already feel the difference in her clothes. One day in a moment of weakness, she eats three potato chips.

Just three. But she is so overwhelmed by guilt and the knowledge that she has broken her diet; she gets discouraged about the diet and goes on a binge. By the end of the day, she had consumed three bags of chips and a half-gallon of ice cream.

Anything wrong with eating 3 potato chips? Not at all. The problem was the unrealistic standard she erected for herself and the impossibility of living up to it.

A pastor said to me, "When I begin at a new church, I say to the staff, 'As far as I know, you are the best at what you do in the world. I expect the highest standards from you. If I ever find otherwise, you will be the one who convinces me.'"

That sounded noble, I suppose. However, the pastor was setting himself and these staff- members up for a disappointment. He was expecting fallible, frail humans to live up to an impossible standard.

He was right to affirm them and correct to encourage them to set high standards. A pastor recently told me the staff he inherited at his new church had grown lazy and unproductive and desperately needed to be motivated to do better. That is often the case. My point here is that setting an impossible standard for oneself and for one's employees is not the answer. You're dooming yourself and the others to failure.

We've all heard the line that "anything worth doing is worth doing well." A friend jokingly said her philosophy is "if it's worth doing, it's worth overdoing."

However, let me suggest a variation, one that might not sound right at first.

If it's worth doing, it's worth doing poorly.

That little backward-sounding ditty has a lot going for it. On the surface, it appears to encourage shoddiness, and we're not proposing that. But take another look and it says something stronger, that if a project is worth doing, just because you cannot do it perfectly does not mean you shouldn't try. Give it a shot. Pretty good is better than not at all.

Here's a guy who refuses to sing a solo in church because he does not sound as good as fill in the name of your favorite singer here. The fact is, he sounds fairly good. Not great. No one is going to be calling from Nashville offering him a recording contract. But for our church, he would do fine. But no, he won't even try, and that's a real shame. He could bless a lot of people and do himself some good by taking the plunge. Even if it's not of professional quality, if it's the best you can do, go with it.

Bob refuses to give a talk in front of his church. Long ago, in the eighth grade, he was delivering a memorized speech and halfway through forgot his lines. The memory of that embarrassment still lives and calls the shots inside Bob to this day. He will make any sacrifice not to repeat that humiliation and so refuses to even try to speak in front of a small group. We assure him he'll be talking about something he knows very well his own testimony of faith in Christ, and he can do it any way he pleases. But because he knows his delivery will not be smooth and flawless, out of the fear of failure, he refuses to even try.

If God used only the perfect among us, no one would be doing anything. "All have sinned." "He Himself knows our frame; He is mindful that we are but dust." (Romans 3:23 and Psalm 103:14)

So, loosen up. Give yourself permission to fail. But more than that, allow yourself to give the Lord your best even when it's not up to the standards you'd like to offer.

Likewise, lighten up on others. No one can live perfect sinless lives and we should relieve them of the burden of our out-of-sight expectations.

Someone asks, "What about that verse in the Sermon on the Mount where Jesus says, 'Be ye therefore perfect, even as your Father which is in Heaven is perfect?'" (Matthew 5:48) A good question, one that deserves a good answer.

Author and seminary professor Craig L. Blomberg writes that "perfect" is better translated as "mature" or "whole". "Jesus is not frustrating his hearers with an unachievable ideal but challenging them to grow in obedience to God's will to become more like him." He quotes J. Walvoord who said, "While sinless perfection is impossible, godliness, in its biblical concept, is attainable."

The best biblical evidence I see for that is the 20th chapter of Exodus, where we find the Ten Commandments. After revealing these commands to Moses and the Israelites as His standard, God turns right around in the same chapter and gives them provisions for an altar. It's as though the Lord was saying, "Here is My standard and it is unchanging. However, I'm aware that you are frail and prone to failure. Therefore, because I know you will fail to live up to this standard, here is an altar. This is my provision for you to receive forgiveness for 'falling short' of my standard."

Every such Old Testament altar points to Calvary. That's the source of our eternal forgiveness, the place where God ultimately dealt with sinful human beings.

No wonder we make so much of the grace of God. As the perfect God deals with imperfect mankind, He does so with a complete understanding of who we are, how we are, and what He may expect from us.

"He Himself knows our frame; He is mindful that we are but dust" (Psalm 103:14).

Since the God of perfection knows who we are and does not expect perfection from us, we would do well to cut ourselves and our friends a little slack also.

Showing mercy and grace to those around us always blesses people.

Chapter Twelve

The worst kind of Christian faith

I know what it is to bore myself with my own preaching.

It's not putting words into His mouth to say that one thing the Living God utterly despises is limp, weak-as-tea ministry rendered by insipid, bored disciples who would rather be doing anything in the world than that.

I have been guilty of this. And if you have been in the ministry for any length of time, my guess is you know something about this kind of failure also.

"You possess endurance and have tolerated many things because of My Name and have not grown weary. But I have this against you: you have abandoned the love you had at first" (Revelation 2:3-4).

The church at Ephesus was doing a hundred things right and one big thing wrong: they had lost the heart for God they had at first. They preached and taught, they ministered and served, they prayed and witnessed. But their heart was not in it any longer. And to God, that negated the entire thing.

"Remember how far you have fallen; repent and do the work you did first. Otherwise, I will come to you and remove your lampstand from its place, unless you repent" (Revelation 2:5).

If you think that sounds like what the Lord said to another church down the road a few miles, you would be correct. "I know your work, that you are neither cold nor hot. I wish that you were cold or hot. So, because you are lukewarm, and neither hot nor cold, I am going to vomit you out of my mouth" (Revelation 3:15-16). Lukewarm religion. Passionless Christianity. The worst kind.

If being passionate about Jesus Christ means to care most deeply for the Lord, to focus on Him completely, to be willing to devote great amounts of time and energy to pleasing Him, then what would passionless Christianity look like?

A lukewarm, passionless faith in Jesus Christ is characterized by half-hearted devotion directed heavenward, powerless ministry rendered passively, thoughtless prayers offered mindlessly, and worthless offerings given begrudgingly. It cares little for the Lord and nothing at all for people.

This kind of Christianity is the curse of the modern church. No one is drawn to Christ by its display. There is no magnetism, nothing that attracts, and plenty to repel.

Passionless Worship.

In the final days of the Old Testament period, God was angry at His people for the sorry state of their worship. The prophet Malachi told them their sickly offerings were an insult to Him (Malachi 1:7) and the wickedness of their personal lives were polluting His altar (1:12). The character of their worship sickened the Lord and repulsed outsiders (2:8-9). Their mournful prayers were shams (2:13) and the priests' sermons were dead on arrival (2:17).

God had had it up to here. He was sick and tired of it.

"Therefore, this decree is for you priests: if you don't listen, and if you don't take it to heart to honor my name," says the Lord of Hosts, "I will send a curse among you, and I will curse your blessings. In fact, I have already begun to curse them because you are not taking it to heart" (Malachi 2:1-2).

Take it to heart. Did you get that?

Our Lord Jesus told the people of His day, "Hypocrites! Isaiah prophesied correctly about you when he said, 'These people honor me with their lips, but their heart is far from me.'" (Matthew 15:7-8) He was quoting Isaiah 29:13.

The heart. It's all about the heart. "Put some heart into it," we say. We mean energy, enthusiasm, that something extra that makes the difference.

You can tell preaching that is only going-through-the-motions from the kind that originates in the heart, is inspired by the Spirit and driven by compassion. You can tell singing that wells up from the depth of one's being from the kind that is professionally performed but without warmth or caring.

God wants the hearts of His people in all we do in His name.

A Heartful Worship

Our word "enthusiasm" comes from the Greek "en" meaning "in" and "Theos" for "God." To the originators of this word, God Himself provided that extra something that made a speech divine or a gift eternal or a touch heavenly.

Jesus called for us to "love the Lord your God with all your heart, with all your soul, and with all your mind" (Matthew 22:37).

He didn't invent the concept of loving the Lord with all our hearts but took it from the prophets. Samuel told Israel of his day, "If you are returning to the Lord with all your heart, get rid of the foreign gods and the Ashtoreth that are among you, dedicate yourselves to the Lord, and worship only Him" (I Samuel 7:3).

"Abijam walked in all the sins his fathers had done before him, and his heart was not wholly devoted to the Lord his God like the heart of his father David" (I Kings 15:3).

"(Jehoshaphat) did what was right in the Lord's sight. However, the high places were not taken away; the people had not yet directed their hearts to worship the God of their fathers" (II Chronicles 20:33).

"(Amaziah) did what was right in the Lord's sight but not with a whole heart" (II Chronicles 25:2).

Partial obedience. Going through the motions. Half-hearted ministry. Lip service.

Such service to God does Him injustice, bears a negative witness to the world, abandons those who come to us expecting to be helped, and delights the enemy of all that is good and holy.

The preacher James, half-brother of our Lord, called this "double mindedness" (James 4:8). He said, "An indecisive (double-minded) man is unstable in all his ways" (James 1:8).

The Apostle Paul knew it to be the powerless thing it was. "(In the last days, people will be) holding on to the form of religion but denying its power" (II Timothy 3:5). He described the Christianity of a sizeable portion of the church membership today.

Recognize yourself in any of this? I do.

I have prayed prayers that did not rise beyond the ceiling. I have given offerings that were more from duty than love.

I have preached sermons long on scriptures and short on compassion.

I have shared my faith out of a legalistic sense that I would be in trouble if I didn't.

I have attended meetings and counseled people and studied the Bible when my heart was on another planet.

I have been convicted by Scripture which commands us: Whatever you do, do it enthusiastically; as something done for the Lord and not for men, knowing that you will receive the reward of an inheritance from the Lord.

You serve the Lord Christ. (Colossians 3:23)

We know the source of such passion.

At the risk of oversimplifying the matter, I'll just put it point blank: when I spend time on my knees, when I daily and consistently yield myself to the Lord, when I bring everything in my life under the Lordship of Jesus Christ, then, when I rise to go forth to serve the Lord, the passion is present.

The passion—the enthusiasm, the spirit, the energy, the caring; the zeal, the unction, the power! —arrives when I obey and not before. If I sit in my recliner waiting for a liberal outpouring of the Lord's Spirit to energize me to get up and go forth, I will never rise.

It is in the obeying, in the going forth, that the Lord empowers.

It will surprise everyone except the preachers among us to know that many ministers do the work of the Lord in the flesh. They study without asking the Father. They pray without really connecting with God and remaining long enough to receive His answer. They counsel from their own wisdom, give from their own resources, help from their own strength.

I have been there and done that.

I once confessed a period of backsliding to the church I pastored. I told them, "Some of you wonder how I could have preached when my heart was in rebellion against God. I did not say a thing I did not believe; I said a great deal I did not feel."

God wants your heart in it, preacher. And He is the source of a new heart.

That's what David prayed for. "Purify me…and I will be clean; wash me, and I will be whiter than snow. Let me hear joy and gladness; let the bones you have crushed rejoice. Turn your face away from my sins and blot out all my guilt. God, create a clean heart for me and renew a steadfast spirit within me…. Restore the joy of your salvation to me and give me a willing spirit. Then I will teach the rebellious your ways and sinners will return to you" (Psalm 51:7-13).

Chapter Thirteen

The most striking thing about leaders

"The most striking thing about highly effective leaders is how little they have in common. What one swears by another warns against. But one trait stands out: the willingness to risk." (Larry Osborne, quoted by John Maxwell in "The 21 Indispensable Qualities of a Leader," p. 40)

Now, we know the leaders were all different, but it's good someone finally said it.

We get so tired of this one-size-fits-all standardized formula for making effective leaders. One of the most hopeful things I've found about leadership is this:

"If you look at the lives of effective leaders, you will find that they often don't fit into a stereotypical mold. For example, more than 50 percent of all CEOs of Fortune 500 companies had C or C- averages in college. Nearly 75 percent of all U.S. presidents were in the bottom half of their school classes. And more than 50 percent of all millionaire entrepreneurs never finished college." (Maxwell, "21 Indispensable Qualities," p. 83)

Now, when John Maxwell cited those statistics (he didn't give his source), he came to a different conclusion than the one that occurs to me. He said, "What makes it possible for people who might seem ordinary to achieve great things? The answer is passion. Nothing can take the place of passion in a leader's life."

Far be it from me to argue with John Maxwell, the guru of leadership. And I certainly do not dispute the importance of passion and focus.

For instance....

One Saturday morning, for four hours I sketched people at the Riverwalk in downtown New Orleans as a part of the Muscular Dystrophy Association's annual outing. As often

happens, someone stood by my right shoulder as I worked and made an occasional comment or asked questions. Saturday, it was a little girl, perhaps 12 or 13 years old. She said, "So, Mister Joe, how long did it take you to learn to draw like this?" I said, "Honey, I've been doing this all my life. I cannot remember a time I wasn't drawing."

The person I was sketching at the moment happened to be a cheerleader for the New Orleans Saints, a member of what they call the Saintsations.

I said, "It's like Samantha here. I'm guessing you have danced all your life from the time you were a little child." She said, "Exactly right."

That's passion, and I'm all in favor of it.

More than passion

But there's more to be said than just passion about the high percentage of leaders who did poorly in school or never finished college.

On the surface, we might conclude this is just more evidence that our schools are teaching the wrong subjects and poorly preparing people for the real world. There is some justification for that point of view.

But take another look and see if you don't agree that real leaders often tend to be late bloomers. They didn't hit their stride in the third grade or even in high school, and so teachers and parents failed to see their potential and relegated them to some lesser status in life. Winston Churchill was so pigeon-holed by his father, who concluded that since Winston could never be a lawyer, he'd have to settle for the life of a soldier. He missed that by a country mile.

Leaders have always tended to come from outside the mainstream of the culture. They are outliers, says Malcolm Gladwell.

These late bloomers are the ones who thought differently in school, were bored in class, and saw things in ways not taught in textbooks. In many cases, teachers considered them troublemakers.

Late bloomers who keep growing.

And one more: leaders keep growing. That to me is the great lesson of Maxwell's "50 percent" statistic. Doing poorly in school was not the end of the world for them, but just the beginning. They found a subject they were interested in and threw themselves into that, leaving all the other stuff for generalists (who usually end up teaching. Hey, I'm a teacher who is married to a teacher. So, I know. I admit to being a generalist and sometimes even pride myself in it.).

In the decade after the death of President Kennedy, I read several biographies of the man. A college classmate named Red Fay said, "In college, I was ahead of Jack Kennedy. I was a better student than he was. But the big difference is, he kept growing and I quit."

Don't ever stop growing.

I say that about my wonderful dad, who as the oldest of twelve children quit school after the 7th grade to work in the coal mines. He had a mind as sharp as anyone in town and, even though he was sentenced to the next 35 years inside the depths of the earth cutting out bituminous coal, he kept growing. He learned all he could about the coal business, learned everything he could about his labor union, and read every magazine that came to the house. At one point when he was in his middle 50s, he took a correspondence course in becoming a detective. He had no plans to be one. He just wanted to learn.

When Dad died in November of 2007 at the age of 95-plus, a half-dozen magazines were regularly coming to the house, everything from Fortune to the Reader's Digest. As was said of a mountain climber lost in the Alps, "He was last seen going up."

George Shinn, at own time the owner of an NBA team, grew up in the small town of Salisbury, North Carolina, the only child of a single mom who took in sewing to pay the bills. George graduated dead last in a class of over 250 students. (He told his story at my daughter's high school graduation and made a lasting impression on those students, particularly those who had done poorly in high school.) Yet, he kept growing. He attended a business college, then became a recruiter for them, and when the school was in danger of going under, assembled some investors and bought it. Later, he bought more business schools, and the rest, as they say, is history.

Occasionally, I encounter students who obsess over getting all A's in school. Or to be exact, they fret about the possibility of not getting an A. Now, I'm in favor of good grades. But straight-As are over-emphasized in our society and the students often pay a heavy price for this dubious achievement.

The bottom line about all this is simply, if you did well in school, fine, but keep growing. And if you did poorly in school, okay, put it behind you and keep on growing. There's no penalty for being a late bloomer. Einstein was, we're told.

The dumbest television commercials I have ever seen have to do with training your infant baby to memorize facts and learn numbers and identify presidents and such. What foolishness.

Let them be kids. Let's not ask them to compensate for our own failures to study and apply ourselves.

There will be plenty of time for the children to learn to read and study academic junk. Until then, put them in the swing and sing songs to them. Get down on the floor and wrestle with them. Take them to the park and let them feed the ducks. Enjoy them and let them enjoy life.

And while you're doing that for your child, try it for yourself.

Chapter Fourteen

Things the pastor cannot do.

Ed was emphasizing to his church leadership why having a pastor's residence next door to the church is not necessarily the best thing. They replied that they had always enjoyed the luxury of having the minister on the premises, and they would hate to relinquish that blessing. That's why, when the hurricane destroyed the pastorium and the congregation had to make a decision about rebuilding, Pastor Ed thought this would be a good time to move the pastor's residence.

"Let me ask you something," Ed said to the five men and women seated around the table. "How many of you have ever taken a vacation and stayed at home?" Every hand went up.

"Well," he said, "that's something a pastor can never do. If he's at home, and everyone in town can see he's at home, he's always on call."

The good folk seated at the table admitted they had never thought of that before.

"And it's not just the church," Ed emphasized. "The community comes knocking, too. And I love that, don't get me wrong. It's just that sometimes it gets wearisome."

As his area denominational leader, I complimented Pastor Ed on explaining that to them. When lay leaders understand the uniqueness of the pastor's burdens, often they can be counted on to do the right thing and help to ease them.

After hearing Pastor Ed's account of this meeting, I began to reflect on other things a pastor cannot do as a result of his unique position in the church and community, things which "normal" people do without a thought.

A pastor cannot decide to skip a Sunday and take his family to the beach. Other people do it as a matter of routine.

After prayer meeting and choir practice, my son and his wife took their three children and drove four hours to the beach, arriving at 1 a.m. They stayed until checkout time from the condo on Sunday morning and got home in the middle of the afternoon. They are faithful church members, good givers, and steady Sunday School workers, so this represents nothing in the world except the need for a few days of rest.

But it's a luxury denied to a pastor, almost always.

The only way a minister can pull up at the last minute and head to the beach and miss Sunday services is by using valuable (and usually scarce) vacation time. No matter how hard he works during the week, to the congregation Sunday is his primary workday and he is fully expected to be there and to do his best work.

And frankly, because of the call of God upon his life, the pastor would not have it any other way. Only, he wishes the congregation was more aware of that fact.

A pastor can't allow himself a break from reading the Bible, tithing his income, and attending church. Whether we call such an interlude a time of backsliding or a little needed rest, the one person in the church for whom this is forbidden is the man in the pulpit. He must spend time in the Word each day and bring well-prepared sermons each Sunday. It is expected he will set the example for the congregation in all matters of the Christian life, from witnessing to the unchurched to tithing his income to reading the Bible each day to loving the unlovely wherever he finds them.

A pastor can't pick and choose the people he will greet and spend time with. Everyone owns stock in him and can pick up the phone and ask for a portion of his time.

Even though he might like to, most pastors cannot choose a best friend or two in the congregation, believing that it's not a healthy thing for the rest of the members to observe. So, either they end up with no close personal friends, or their best friends become pastors from other towns or members from churches they previously served.

A pastor cannot tell a church member off, or, as my mother used to say, "he cannot bless him out." He is expected to maintain his Christian control and behavior at all times. He loves the unlovely and controls the fleshly impulse to respond to unkindness with harshness. He returns good for evil and love for hate.

There are so many pastors who cannot do which "normal" church members do with hardly a thought. But they wouldn't have it any other way.

After all, there are far more wonderful things a pastor can do which most people in the congregation do not have the freedom to do.

Unless he is bi-vocational, a pastor can devote all his time to the service of the Lord. Part of his actual duties is sitting at his desk reading the Word of God and studying his books or driving across town and calling on the sweet old people in the retirement home. Just think—he gets paid for that!

The first time I was able to quit my outside job and receive a full paycheck from my church, I felt almost guilty over the joy I was experiencing from getting paid to do what I loved best.

A pastor is given a great honor by the Lord and the church that calls him as its shepherd. True, there are restrictions upon his behavior and some limitations upon his freedom, but in almost every case he wouldn't have it any other way.

Pastor Ed's church is still trying to decide where to locate the pastor's residence. If they asked me, I'd tell them to give him enough money to purchase his own home so he can build equity and eventually own it. Many a pastor has come to retirement time and found himself without a home of his own. That happens to lay-people also, I'm confident, but it's not recommended for anyone.

Chapter Fifteen

The promise Jesus has made to the obedient

One of the ways I know the Lord is sending me a message is when I'm reading a familiar scripture and suddenly, something I'd never seen jumps off the page and grabs my attention. That happened Thursday morning of this week.

In a passage where our Lord is urging His audience to turn their focus from the rich and well-to-do toward the needy and helpless, Jesus says, "When you give a party (reception, banquet), do not invite those who can return the invitation. Instead, invite the poor, the crippled, the lame, the blind." These people do not have the means to repay you, Jesus says, however, "you will be repaid at the resurrection of the righteous."

That line stood out in bold print: You will be repaid at the resurrection of the righteous.

All the bells went off inside. What a great promise. Jesus looks into the distant future and sees a time when debts will be paid, when rewards will be handed out, when the faithful will receive the recognition God has promised.

The line from Proverbs comes to mind: He who gives to the poor lends to the Lord and He will repay him for his good deed (Pr. 19:17). Jesus is foreseeing that precise moment when God pays the debt in full. It's a thrilling thought.

Later that morning, a pastor friend in Kentucky emailed me about his work with a commission charged with curtailing gambling in that state. They also deal with other moral issues, including the control of alcohol and drugs. He sent some disturbing statistics, enough to discourage many a volunteer in this line of work.

I replied that he must not get discouraged, that anything he can do to protect children and families from these scourges is a great work. That's when Luke 14:14 came to mind. "You will be repaid at the resurrection of the righteous." I said to him, "You may never know this side of the judgment just how many lives you save, how much good you do, how many children you bless." He agreed that it means working by faith, knowing you're doing the work of the Lord and trusting Him to use it.

That's tough, as we both know so well.

We live in an age of instant gratification. We want our rewards now. Tell the average person to do a good deed now and they will be repaid at the judgment, and you might as well promise them they will be repaid ten thousand years from now. It does not compute.

Anything short of next month is out of the question for most people.

"The just shall live by faith," declares both the Old and New Testaments. That meant one thing to Martin Luther, namely that the way of salvation is by faith in Christ not in man's good works. However, it also conveys another line of thought: anyone who obeys the Lord is going to be doing a lot of things simply because he believes in the Lord, meaning by faith. Not because of the immediate payoff, not for the good feelings or public acclaim or fruit that he sees borne from it.

He will do it by faith.

Later that same day, I sat at a table with several colleagues in ministry. As we shared prayer requests, one of the men said he was speaking that evening to a group of college students about a mission trip to Africa.

I said, "I have the text for your message tonight."

I called his attention to Luke 14:14 and its promise to the faithful: "You will be repaid at the resurrection of the righteous."

He laughed, "Talk about delayed compensation!" True enough. It may be delayed compensation, but it is also guaranteed remuneration, backed by no less than the Word of the Lord Himself.

All of which raises several questions for anyone in the service of the Lord Jesus Christ:

1. Is that promise good enough for you?

2. Is that motivation sufficient to get you up and into the fields, to do what He said?

3. Are you willing to work today for a payoff that does not come until Judgement?

4. Can you invest yourself even when you see no visible results, knowing that God in Heaven sees and counts, that He knows and blesses and has promised to repay?

In this culture we're mostly like day-laborers who need their payment in cash at the end of the working day. Retirement benefits even thirty years from now hold little interest to the average employee. We want the latest model in everything from cars to televisions to kitchen appliances. We are members of a materialistic society where consumer goods are newer and brighter and more interesting and often cheaper every year, and we feel entitled to them. Save for the future? Not hardly. We want what we want, and we want it now.

Into that mindset, our Lord says, "If you invest yourself in helping others, you will be repaid—at the Judgment."

Can we wait? It's all about faith in the Lord Jesus.

Our world wants to see results now. We watch a young preacher, seemingly energized with some kind of secret anointing, erect a steel building on an interstate and within six months, run five hundred in attendance and in two years five thousand at numerous locations. It happens so often; we begin to feel that should be the norm. However, go into a difficult area and begin a new work, then a year later have only a handful of converts and your supporters start looking for a better place to invest their mission dollars. In their minds, God is not blessing your efforts.

Scripture promises us results for our labors, but not necessarily today. "Be not weary in well- doing, for in due season you shall reap, if you do not quit" (Galatians 6:9).

Can you work? It's all about faith in God's Word.

Our culture wants proof, not promises; it wants money-in-the-hand, not the word of One who lived thousands of years ago. This generation does not do long-range planning or down-the-road investing. Leave people to their own devices and they will rebuild a house in a flood plain because, "What are the chances it will flood here again in my lifetime?" In California, they rebuild on earthquake faults and unstable hillsides. In Central America, on the sides of active volcanoes. In New Orleans, in reclaimed swampland that lies below sea level.

Will you be wise? Will you believe Christ?

If you are willing to walk by faith, to work today and leave the results to the Lord, to wait on His timing for the rewards then I have good news: You can be an effective disciple of the Lord Jesus Christ.

Chapter Sixteen

What you need to know about those celebrity pastors

I know a few of those (ahem) big-shot pastors. And I know a few things about them, they don't advertise.

That said, here is my list of what celebrity pastors are experiencing on a daily basis that might surprise you. As always, these are generalizations, of course, and do not fit all megachurch pastors. However, you might be surprised to know how many it fits!

1) A sense of inadequacy.

It goes like this: "All the usual indicators say we're doing a great job, but if that's the case, why do I feel like a failure, as though I'm missing something as clear as the nose on my face? Maybe what I'm doing with God's call is not such a good idea after all. But what about all those people who depend on me for their livelihood and those who say they look to me as their pastor?"

2) A nagging sense of failure, even though the numbers (attendance, budget, etc) are in the stratosphere. The pastor feels there has to be more, "something we are missing."

Not only does the mega-pastor feel inadequate, but frequently he feels the ministry is missing something huge. Are we really changing people's lives? Are we making disciples of Jesus or just friends? What else should we be doing? What should we begin and what should we cancel?

3) A fear that all this acclaim will dry up, and then who am I?

In one church, I was friends with a mega-pastor who told me what he was experiencing. I had mentioned something about wanting to know why people sometimes left my church for another. He said, "Not me! Man, I can't handle it. I do not want to know why they left. Just go!" We laughed, but I found it revealing.

4) A sense of guilt, which takes many forms.

He worries that he is being idolized instead of Jesus.

He worries that his huge church is siphoning off members from the smaller congregations in the area, and while his ego once fed on that, these days there is this nagging feeling that something about this is not right. Some of those people were active in the leadership of Shiloh Number Two, but now that they have joined Big One, they simply occupy a pew.

He feels guilty when people call him "Pastor" since, while he preaches to thousands, he actually shepherds very few people.

Some of these pastors hate the acclaim they are receiving. And yet they are addicted to it. It's a no-win situation.

5) A strong urge to set things right in next Sunday's sermon.

Perhaps he can say something this Sunday that will correct the imbalance or restore the ship to the proper channel. Alas, that rarely happens since he has events to promote, expectations to fulfill, funds to raise, leaders to satisfy, and a thousand items on his agenda which interfere with a major overhaul of his ministry. Besides, he wouldn't know how to come clean with the congregation, to clear off the slate and start over.

So, he keeps on keeping on, somehow hoping what he's doing is acceptable to Christ and that the Lord will use it.

6) A sense of being swept along by the current instead of controlling it.

People envy the freedom he enjoys as pastor of "that huge church on the interstate." He himself knows freedom is the very thing he has little of. He is at the mercy of his celebrity, his advisors, his staff, his schedule, and his public. Everyone needs a little piece of him—

sign this, speak here, lead this, go there, appear on this show, solve this problem, start that movement.

He sometimes thinks back on the time when he and his wife were newlyweds and just starting in ministry, when they lived in an apartment and ate spaghetti on Monday nights at the neighborhood cafe, and Sunday was the highlight of their week. Those were the days.

7) A craving for anonymity and privacy.

How nice it would be to sit in a restaurant with his wife and have a quiet evening without strangers coming over to have their pictures made with him or telling him how wonderful he is or calling him "Doctor." They pull at him, asking him to visit this person, call that one, speak in this church, advise that church. Which is why the pastor and his wife usually stay home or eat in the homes of members or in private clubs.

He remembers when he ate that up and lived for that kind of acclaim. But long ago he saw how empty that all is. Now, in his heart of hearts, all he wants is to serve the Lord Jesus and be used of Him.

And yes, he envies the pastor of Shiloh Number Two.

8) A nagging sense of hypocrisy.

People think he is holier than they are, that pastoring that huge church somehow has elevated him to a super-Christian echelon. What if they knew he and his wife argue, that sometimes he goes days without opening his Bible or an entire day without praying?

What if his members should find out he's a lot like them?

9) A need for a few good friends.

Everyone needs friends, the kind of people who know you as you are and with whom there is no pretense and no need to impress. But these pastors have an intense need for a few such friends. Good or bad, it seems the mega-pastors end up gravitating to pastors of similar churches for the simple reason that they're all living the same lives and struggling with the same burdens. They get it.

10) The need to be loved for who they are.

Just like everyone else on the planet.

One final word. Sometimes even pastors will fawn over the celebrity preachers and treat them as rock stars. Not a good thing. Respect them? Sure. But it should be the same honor we bestow on any servant of the Lord who is faithfully doing his job, regardless of the size of his church or the scope of his acclaim.

In fact, we would be doing them a favor if we cut through all the trappings of their celebrity to call them "Brother" (as opposed to "Doctor"), to pray for them the same way we appreciate being interceded for (without telling them you're doing it), and to send them a note of appreciation if and when their ministry touches you.

Treat them the same way you would anyone else who is faithfully serving the same Lord as you.

Chapter Seventeen

Everyone fails from time to time. Learn to fall forward.

Want to hear a story about my great embarrassment? I thought you might.

As the new pastor, I had invited Adam to lunch to speak to him about his relationship to Christ. His wife appeared to be an active Christian and their two daughters were full participants in our church's youth program. Perhaps Adam just needs a little encouragement, I thought.

I asked Adam to choose the restaurant. "How about Jimmy C's," he said, and told me where it was. Since I was new to the New Orleans area, I hardly knew one restaurant from another in this city noted for great eating. We would meet at noon on Thursday.

We greeted each other, were seated in a booth, and gave our orders to the waiter. I went straight to the subject on my mind. "Adam, can I ask you about your relationship to Jesus Christ?" He was friendly and open and did not mind at all telling me his thoughts. Somehow along the way, he had studied under humanist teachers who had provided a steady diet of atheistic reading for his young vulnerable mind. It was my assignment, it appeared, to try to counter some of that.

The waiter brought our lunch, I said a short blessing, and we dived in. That's when the young woman showed up at our table.

She was dressed or undressed might be closer to the truth in a flimsy, see-through shortie pajama thing that showed far more of her than it ought. I would not have been more stunned if she had walked down the aisle of my church dressed like that. Glancing around the restaurant, I saw she had company. Other barely clothed young ladies were visiting at the tables and chatting with diners.

Adam and I visited Jimmy C's on the day of their weekly lingerie show.

It's hard to witness a fellow whose eyes are straying and whose mind is on other things, particularly while you yourself wish you were somewhere else on the planet. But that was my task, and I did it as well as I could. When the meal was over, we parted amicably, and I drove back to the church office.

My preacher friends (to whom I have told it) have had a big laugh at that, but at the moment, it was a nightmare.

I never made that mistake again. In the future, I would know something about a restaurant before making a reservation to take a friend there.

It would be easy to obsess over that embarrassment. If my mind were unhealthy, I'd probably attribute Adam's failure to believe in Christ to "what the devil did that day." But not liking to give the devil credit for what is not his, I refuse to dwell on that. Christians need to remind ourselves from time to time that our three foes the unholy trinity they're called are—a the world, the flesh, and the devil. I think we're safe in saying a lingerie show is all about the flesh.

Don't Park Here is the title of a paperback a friend gave my wife years ago. I'm not sure what use Margaret made of it, but I've dog-eared it and built a dozen sermons around its concepts. The point which author C. William Fisher was making was that we should not camp out at the point of our handicaps, failures, fears, sufferings, or resentments. Repent of them, give them to the Lord, learn from them, accept the Lord's mercy, then get up and get back in the game.

In the chapter on "parking by your failures," Fisher tells stories of a woman who parked by a broken marriage and never recovered, a pastor who parked by a failed pastorate and left the ministry, a writer who parked by a rejection slip and never penned another word, and Christians who park by failures to live up to the Lord's expectations and walk away from the church.

Garson Kanin, the playwright, once said, "If you want to succeed, you must prepare to fail." It seems to be one of the rules of success, that somewhere along the line everyone must fail. My own observation is that one learns far more from failure than he ever does from success.

The legendary author of Western novels, Louis L'Amour, claimed to have collected several hundred rejection slips before selling his first short story. In later years, he would speak of the lessons he learned from all those failures. Had he been a success too early, he would have quit learning and growing. Each rejection made him try that much harder.

Someone has called failure God's back door to success.

Everyone fails. Not only does God know that about us, but He made plans for our failures from the beginning. In Exodus 20 where He gives the Ten Commandments, immediately afterward He instructs Moses on plans for altars. Altars were to be made of dirt or stone, He said, and not prettied up by the hammer and chisel. An altar is an ugly place, a place of death, where our sins are atoned for. My impression is that people read that chapter and rush right on by without considering why God put those two instructions back-to-back. The juxtaposition of these two sections—the commandments and the altar—is fascinating. It means that God was building into the system a means for our forgiveness even from the first.

Up front, God gave us His standard. These are my commandments. "Do these and live." Then, knowing we could not keep them perfectly and would fail, He gave us the way back into His fellowship. What a thoughtful Lord!

"He himself knows our frame," David said in Psalm 103. "He is mindful that we are but dust." God was under no illusions about what Jesus' death on the cross was buying. He wasn't getting much for the price He was paying, and He knew it. "We are but dust." "We have this treasure in earthen vessels," Paul said in II Corinthians 4.

One wonders if the angels in Heaven shook their heads when they found out the cost that would have to be paid for the redemption of mankind. "Too much," they might have said. "They're not worth it."

The love of God has always been a wonder, even back in the dim origins of time. Nothing speaks of the love of God better than His willingness to forgive those who refuse to live according to His standards.

There are two extremes to be avoided in this matter, as there are with practically every other issue on the planet. We can be blase' about our sins. "Well, I'm just human. We all sin." A popular, but shallow spiritual song from the 1950s had this line in it: "Though it makes him sad to see the way we'll live, He'll always say, 'I forgive.'" This goes by the name of cheap grace.

The other extreme is in believing God is so harsh, He would never forgive sin. Once we have failed Him, it's all over and we can quit trying to please Him.

Both are lies from the father of lies, Satan himself.

"Pastor," Thea said, "One of these days, I need to talk to you about something." I was the new, fresh-from-seminary pastor of Thea's church and had already heard the gossip about her. Before I knew what was happening, my secretary had blurted out that a year earlier,

Thea had had an affair with a man she worked with at the department store. "She doesn't think anyone knows," the secretary assured me. I thought to myself, "Leave it to you and soon everyone will know."

"Anytime," I told Thea, "I'm here to do anything I can for you."

Thea was in the hospital with a bleeding ulcer and was in great pain. I pulled a chair up to her bed and made small talk until she decided to pour out her heart and tell me the awful tale of her sin. She would have died on the spot had she known I already knew about it.

At the end, I said, "Has God forgiven you for this?" She said, "I really believe He has." She hesitated a moment and said, "I just can't forgive myself." I said, "You have higher standards than God, is that it?" She reacted quickly. "The very idea! Why would you say such a thing?"

I said, "Listen to yourself. Oh sure, God can forgive me. But I have higher standards. I can't let myself off that easy."

She said, "Then tell me what to do." I said, "Believe that Jesus Christ paid the penalty for that sin on the cross, the same way He did all the rest of our sins and failures. And He says, 'Their sins and iniquities I will remember no more.' He says, 'As far as the east is from the west, so far have I removed their transgressions.' So, now, it's time you started believing Him and got up off the floor and got on with your life."

One year later, I received a note in the mail. "It was a year ago," Thea wrote, "that you told me just exactly what I needed to hear. I am a healthy person today. Thank you."

Repent of it. Give it to Him. Learn from it. Then put it behind you and go forward. Everyone fails. Just don't park there.

Evangelist and former all-pro defensive end for the Cleveland Browns football team, Bill Glass, often told of a lesson he learned in junior high. "When I first started playing football," he says, "I thought when you got knocked down, that was a good time to get some rest. But I soon discovered that you get stepped on and fallen on when you're on the ground. Then I noticed that in pro ball, most of the tackles are made by players who were either knocked down and got back up or knocked off balance and kept on going."

Glass uses that lesson for a principle about life. "When the devil knocks you down with temptation, he wants to keep you on the ground. He plays on your guilt by saying, 'Some Christian you are. What if the people at church could see you now? What would they think?'"

He points out that Scripture gives us John 1:9 as a means of getting back to our feet. "If we confess our sin, He is faithful and just to forgive our sin and to cleanse us of all iniquity." So, Glass urges, when you get tripped up, don't stay there. Get up, confess your sin, and believe in the Lord that He has forgiven you. Then get back into the game. It's great advice from one who knows.

Chapter Eighteen

Some preaching is a waste of time.

I love some of the specialized channels on Sirius XM satellite radio. At one point, they replaced the channel playing big band music of the 1940s with one devoted to Billy Joel's music. At first, that sounded all right. I enjoy several of his great hits. The problem is he also recorded a lot of junk.

To get to the occasional hit, you have to endure all the mediocre stuff.

Same with novelists. Our favorite writers can turn out some real bombs. You wonder why they don't write only bestsellers.

The answer, of course, is that they have no way of knowing. If, as Paul said, "we see through a glass darkly," it's also true that we write books and compose songs without a clear idea of how it will be received.

When I was young in the ministry, I spent three years on the staff of a large church and got to see up close how things are done in the megachurch. Most of it was great and educational; all of it was interesting.

On more than one occasion, I chauffeured our pastor—a young man himself and probably a mite too impressed with his accomplishments—on short trips where he would address a group of ministers in some nearby town. I can still hear him saying, "Why am I wasting my time doing this? That bunch is never going to do anything."

Now, I disagreed with him then—and said so, leading to some interesting conversations—and do so to this day.

Now, it's true that some preaching to such groups is a waste of time.

Likewise, some preaching on Sundays is pointless and worthless also, for all the good it does.

The problem is we never know.

If a farmer knew which field was going to produce and which would do poorly, he could save himself a lot of time and trouble. If an investment counselor knew which stocks would flourish and which were disasters, he would be hailed as a genius.

We don't know.

The writer of Ecclesiastes had this very thing in mind. "Sow your seed in the morning, and at evening let not your hands be idle; for you do not know which will succeed, whether this or that, or whether both will do equally well" (Ecclesiastes 11:6).

Don't try to judge the soil and conditions and make predictions; just sow the seed.

A preacher goes forth like a farmer, sowing down all the fields he possesses. Some will bring forth fruitfully and some sparingly. But his job is to sow the seed and leave the production to the Lord.

Our Lord Jesus put it this way: "A farmer went out to sow his seed. As he was scattering the seed, some fell along the path and the birds came and ate it up" (Matthew 13:3ff.)

Had the farmer known he was wasting his time there, that the birds would steal his seed, he could have saved himself some trouble.

In our Lord's parable, other seeds fell on rocky places where they sprouted and sprang up, but soon withered under the heat of the sun. Some seed fell among briars which choked off this new life. Fortunately, some fell on good soil, "where it produced a crop of a hundred, sixty, or thirty-fold."

A farmer was showing a visitor around his farm. The city fellow pointed out that the last rows around the edge of the field had smaller plants and didn't seem to produce much. The farmer said, "Yes. The last rows always produce poorly." The guest said, "Then I suggest you not plant the last rows. I'm surprised you haven't thought of that."

On our family farm in north Alabama, we would sometimes walk across fields broadcasting soybeans. Months later, the field would be cut and baled as hay for the winter months. By "broadcasting," I mean it literally. We cast broadly. (Which, of course, is where the term originated.) We threw the seed in every direction. No doubt the birds got some, and some did poorly for other reasons. But all in all, the soybeans produced well, and the animals got the benefit.

A farmer lives and works by faith as much as any preacher or missionary ever has or ever will. Christians could learn a lot from living on a farm for 12 months.

The Apostle Paul said our efforts in this world fall into two groups, wood, hay, and stubble and gold, silver, and precious stones. (That's I Corinthians 3:12.) The first includes work produced in the flesh, using carnal methods and for unworthy motives. It doesn't last. The second is what the Spirit within us does for the glory of Christ. This is permanent fruit, the kind that glorifies the Lord and blesses mankind forever.

In this life, we do have a degree of control. We may abide in Christ and work in the Spirit and thus produce good work which is characterized as "gold, silver, and precious stones."

Even then, however, much of the work we do and the preaching we deliver will fall on deaf ears. Some will seem to have been a waste of time. But we leave that all with the Lord.

He alone knows. And nothing is ever wasted when done for Him and unto Him.

Chapter Nineteen

Humor is good, when done right.

I was 27 years old with a new seminary degree and ready to take on the world. We had driven up from the bayou country of Louisiana to Greenville, Mississippi, to visit Emmanuel Baptist Church for a trial weekend. If we liked them and they liked us and if we all agreed God was "in this," then I would become their new pastor.

I had pastored two small churches before, but this was my first "trial weekend." Those are well named as they are trials for everyone concerned. That's why I did what I did that Sunday morning.

I told three jokes in the sermon.

During the worship service, someone introduced Margaret and our two sons and presented me. I walked to the pulpit, smiled at the expectant congregation, and opened my mouth to speak. Up until then, I had done fine.

First. "This is my first time preaching in Mississippi. I'm delighted to be here, and particularly glad to see you're all wearing shoes."

Okay, not a joke, but I meant it as one. They actually laughed, which was all I wanted. They knew I was teasing them about the reputation for backwardness Mississippi has.

Second. "Preaching here today and you and I looking each other over reminds me of the country preacher who was in the same situation I'm in today. He said to the congregation, 'There is a powerful lot of wonderin' goin' on here today. You are wonderin' if I can preach, and I am wonderin' if you know good preachin' when you hear it!'"

Again, it got some laughter. It's not a knee-slapper, but a pleasant bit of humor. Up until now, I was okay. This was the time to move into the sermon. But I didn't. I had another joke, the best one yet, I thought.

Third. "Flip Wilson, popular African American comedian, was portraying a Black preacher in this same situation on his television program. You know how the congregation answers the preacher in their churches. He looked out at the people and said, 'If I's called to be pastor of this church, this church is going to WALK!' The people called back, 'Let 'er walk, boy, let 'er walk!'"

"The preacher said, 'If I's called to be pastor of this church, this church is going to RUN!' They said, 'Let 'er run, boy, let 'er run!'"

"The preacher said, 'If I's called to be pastor of this church, this church is going to FLY!' They said, 'Let 'er fly, boy, let 'er fly.'"

"The preacher said, 'If this church is going to fly, it's going to take MONEY!' They said, 'Let 'er walk, boy, let 'er walk.'"

(Hope I don't offend by printing the joke in dialect, but that's how he said it and it's the only way to tell it. The teller has to raise his voice in the appropriate places to make it work, too.)

It was a funny story. They laughed, and I went into my sermon. Oddly, I have long ago forgotten what the sermon was about but will never forget those three little things. The reason I remember is what happened afterward.

Monday morning, my family was having breakfast in the home of some church members before driving back to New Orleans. Lawrence Bryant, chairman of the church's deacons as well as chair of the pastor search committee and the leading layman of the congregation, arrived at the home.

"We have a little problem, preacher," he said.

The problem was those jokes I had told. "I've heard from some of the congregation," he said, "and they were put off by that bit of foolishness." Then he turned to two passages in Paul's epistles to Timothy in which he urged the young pastor to "avoid vain babblings."

I had been rebuked, big time. And this by a man who scarcely knew me during our church visit. Nothing about this bode well.

The next Sunday morning, the church voted on calling me as their pastor. In a congregation of 140 on Sunday morning, around 30 voted against the recommendation. When Deacon Bryant phoned to tell me, I turned him down. "That's too many," I said, "so I'll just say 'no.'" But he was a wise man and gave some good advice.

"Preacher," he said, "I have to go to a service at the county jail this afternoon and I'll be back home about 4 o'clock. Why don't you think about it and pray, and then I'll call you when I get back." Fair enough.

I got up from the lunch table—we lived in a small apartment in the back of the church—and walked around to the little sanctuary. I closed the door and knelt at the altar and began praying. Within five minutes, I knew the Lord was leading us to Greenville. A few weeks later, we loaded a truck and made the transition. We stayed there for three years and two months and saw God do some phenomenal things. It was so obvious He had led us to that town and that church.

I had almost sabotaged the matter by overdoing the humor.

Once I got to know the church, I found that my predecessors had been rather humorless individuals and the congregation had grown uptight and overly serious. Anyone who knows me will not be surprised to learn that we soon got them out of that! Before long, they were a happy, rejoicing bunch who found laughter coming easily to their hearts.

I believe in humor. Humor is good, when done well and appropriately.

I appreciate the statement from Sarah, the wife of Abraham, after she gave birth at the age of 90. She said, "God has made laughter for me" (Genesis 21:6). I tell congregations, "The Lord has made laughter for you, too. And some of you are not getting your recommended daily allowance!"

Laughter is beneficial for more reasons than I can count. It helps the health, calms the spirit, changes the mood, eases the tension, defuses anger, and unites people in joy.

There's nothing wrong and everything right about joy and laughter. However. Jokes and humor are not appropriate for every situation.

I was studying Paul's Epistle to the Romans for two reasons. I would soon be teaching it, and I was illustrating it with a series of cartoons. In one cartoon, this fellow says that Romans would be a lot easier to understand if Paul had inserted a joke here and there. That of course was a tongue-in-cheek remark referring to a) the difficulty of this book and b) how a lot of people want everything overly simplified.

A joke or even a humorous remark would be completely out of place in a serious work like Romans.

Knowing when to tell a funny story and when not to is a sign of maturity.

As a student of history, I read a lot of Abraham Lincoln books. (And yes, there are a lot!) As great a man as he was, he was constantly criticized for the jokes he told. So out of place, some said. Others said they were unneeded. And more than one said some could not be told in mixed company!

Bible students will recall the story of Abraham's nephew Lot who lived in the ancient city of Sodom. When the angels warned Lot of the coming destruction of that wicked city, Lot did the natural thing and rushed to alert his family members. But there was a problem. He appeared to his sons-in-law to be jesting (Genesis 19:14).

The biblical writer does not explain that cryptic comment, so we are left to analyze it on our own. To me, it means only one thing: Lot must have been such a joker that when he tried to get serious, no one believed him.

Somewhere I read of a clown who ran onto the stage of a playhouse to announce that the theater was on fire. The audience thought it was part of the act and roared with laughter. But he was serious. Dead serious.

As a young preacher, if I thought of a funny remark that fit the point, I would tell it right in the middle of the sermon. I cannot begin to remember the times friends would approach after the service to lovingly rebuke that trait. "You were at such a great place in the message...and then you spoiled it by making the joke."

What was going on there? Who knows? Insecurity, lack of discipline, fear. Something. It took a long time and a lot of prayer to get over that, to where I could say 'no' to the impulse to add a humorous remark to the most serious point.

The best kind of humor, of course, is the natural kind that arises spontaneously without planning. I'm not against the other kind either. The pastor heard a great story that week which he thought the congregation would enjoy. If it works, use it.

At a men's breakfast at our church early one Sunday, a Gideon speaker began his message with a funny story. As I recall, it did not pretend to illustrate anything; it was just a great story. Two hours later, I was preaching in a friend's church and when I rose to the pulpit, I said, "Would it be all right if I told you a great story, I heard this morning?" They nodded their heads, I told it, they enjoyed it, and then I went into the sermon. Anything wrong with that? Not a thing. In fact, the mirth bonded us together just a little.

"Like apples of gold in settings of silver, is a word spoken in right circumstances" (Proverbs 25:11).

I'm not sure what the point of golden apples laying on beds of silver is all about, but the "word spoken in right circumstances" surely applies to a great joke or funny line. When well-chosen and rightly timed, there's nothing better. Otherwise, skip it altogether.

Chapter Twenty

Lazy, uninspired preaching is an insult to the Lord of Heaven and earth!

On Facebook I posted a note concerning a Ralph Compton western novel I was reading. Apparently, his main character was riding a super horse.

The novelist has him leaving New Orleans heading toward "Indian Territory "which must mean Oklahoma and by the end of the first night, he beds down below Shreveport at Winnfield, Louisiana. "Wait just a cotton-picking minute," I thought and checked the map.

From New Orleans to Winnfield is 250 miles. Can a horse carry a rider that far in one day? The author had them arriving at their destination in two more days.

Whatever was he thinking?

A few friends opined that this is a novel, it's fiction, and the author can do anything he pleases. It's called artistic license. But not so fast, I insisted.

We do require a little verisimilitude (been looking for a chance to use that word!) even in novels. This means it must look real at least on the surface, and that did not. Not even close.

In a Civil War novel some guy gets off the train in Birmingham. At that point I stopped reading and threw the book away. Birmingham did not exist during the Civil War, was incorporated around 1870, and carried the nickname "The Magic City" for the speed with which it sprang up and grew. (I know Birmingham fairly well. Went to college there and lived there six years.)

In another book, author Ralph Compton has the same rider as above in New Orleans "enjoying the cool breezes off the Gulf." Had the writer bothered to look at a map, he would have seen that New Orleans is a hundred miles north of the Gulf of Mexico. (And I lived in metro New Orleans for thirty years, so this geography I know also!)

A friend commented that this is why he preferred the western novels of Louis L'Amour. I did not tell him that Mr. L'Amour, celebrated for his realism and accuracy, may have been no better at getting the details right. In one book, he has a bad guy killed, then later in the story that same fellow is alive and active. When asked about the discrepancy, L'Amour said, "My readers don't care about that kind of thing."

I beg to differ. In the first place, even though I read practically every book of his when he was alive, I do not consider myself one of "his readers," but a customer. I bought his books and read them and enjoyed them for a time, until he became lazy and preachy and repetitive.

In the second place, Mr. L'Amour was dead wrong about what "his" readers expect. Even readers of western novels want the author to get things right. What L'Amour should have said was that he—and not his readers—did not care about that sort of thing. And that, L'Amour customers will recall, is directly contradictory to the biographical stuff at the end of his books claiming that everything he says is accurate. "If he says there is a stream there, there is a stream there." Apparently not.

To be sure, all of this is hardly important in the grand scheme of things. But I'll tell you what is...

People have a right to expect our leaders - government, political, educational, and ministerial - to speak the truth. To get their facts right. As they say, "You're entitled to your own opinion, but not to your own facts."

In the campaign for president, after each debate we may expect reporters to give us fact checks, in which the claims and positions of candidates are examined and shown for what they were. Rare is the candidate who deals carefully and conservatively with statistics and quotes.

Those of us who support political candidates must be careful in considering what to believe and what to repeat.

As a pastor, I'm far more interested in preachers getting these things right than politicians or novelists.

We are representatives of the One who said, "I am The Way, The Truth, and The Life." If we cannot speak the truth when we stand in the pulpit, we should stand down.

I'm personally grieved by preachers who deliver slanderous attacks on people from the pulpit. When it turns out they had their facts wrong and simply did not know what they were talking about, they tend to blame someone else. "Well, I got this from Evangelist So-and- so." "I read it off a flyer." "I heard it in the news."

Too many of our churches are being overseen by vultures. They love to feast on dead carrion, on the rottenness in our society, on the failures of our leaders.

93

When I have called attention in social media to preachers attacking celebrities or political leaders from the pulpit, some have responded that John the Baptist confronted King Herod over his adulterous marriage. Nathan confronted King David. Even our Lord called Herod a "fox." I respond that God has called us to be New Testament preachers of His good news, not Old Testament prophets.

The pagans once said something interesting about Paul. In Acts 19, when Paul and his companions were arrested in Ephesus because of the success of their evangelism which was hurting the pagan silversmiths' business, the town clerk quietened the mob. He said, "Everyone knows how important Ephesus is to the worship of Artemis (or Diana), so we have nothing to prove. Now, you have brought these men here who are neither robbers of temples nor blasphemers of our goddess."

Don't miss that.

When on trial, no one accused Paul of slandering the pagan idol. I read that and am amazed. He surely had a lot of negative thoughts about that idol. But he kept them to himself. And God honored him for it.

I cannot stop careless preachers from violating this or from using sloppy data and inaccurate information. The one thing I can do is to make sure I get my facts right.

For Jesus' sake, I will maintain a high standard of faith and faithfulness.

I may not please the crowd that wants all the dirt on celebrities in my sermons, but I can please the One who sent me. And any preacher of the gospel would a thousand times rather do that.

Chapter Twenty-One

Pastor, make your people think!

...and in that law, he meditates day and night. (Psalm 1:2)

In his book *Eat This Word*, Eugene Peterson tells of something his dog did in the Northwest woods where they were living. One day the little mutt dragged a huge bone up to the house.

Clearly, it came from the carcass of an elk or moose, he said, and the dog had certainly not brought that animal down. But that pup gnawed on the bone day after day, eating it away little by little. Sometimes, he would bury the bone in the leaves and later dig it out and resume the process of ingesting that huge bone. Eventually, he consumed the entire thing. When scripture instructs us to meditate on the word, Peterson said, that's the idea.

We are to consider it from every angle, take in all we can today, then lay it aside and bring it out later and gnaw on it again. We do this until it becomes part of us.

In every church there are those who enjoy being prodded into deep meditation on scriptures. Likewise, there are those who insist that their spiritual food be predigested so it goes down smoothly.

My observation is that only the first group will grow spiritually. The unthinking group is content to remain spiritual infants.

The unthinking Christian demands simple sermons, easy lessons, no gray areas, all Scripture interpretation to be neat and orderly with no room for differences of interpretation, and no challenges to his beliefs, his position, his world. Run the Word through the blender.

The believer unwilling to think has a difficult time with Jesus. Our Lord refuses to give in to our shallowness, just as He did with every other lazy group He encountered in the First Century.

The pastor's challenge is to move members of the second group into the first category—to excite them with the delights of reflecting on God's Word, to provoke them into thinking about His message, and to encourage them to study their Bibles, until they learn to incorporate God's truths into their lives.

Consider this example.

"Now there were some present at that time who told Jesus about the Galileans whose blood Pilate had mixed with their sacrifices. Jesus answered, 'Do you think that these Galileans were worse sinners than all the other Galileans because they suffered that way?'"(Luke 13)

The Lord promptly answered his own rhetorical question with a "No, but unless you repent, you too will all perish." Clearly, He wanted them to think about this.

Then, to stress the point, Jesus told them of a similar tragedy with an identical application. "Or those eighteen who died when the tower in Siloam fell on them–do you think they were more guilty than all the others living in Jerusalem?" (Luke 13:1-5)

Well, Lord, pardon me, but...well, you see...we don't actually like to think about these things. Can you just lay it out there in black and white and we'll simply believe you and run along. Sorry. He refuses to give in to our laziness, to cater to our inertia.

This Luke 13 passage is one that answers those who wish to turn every tragedy—earthquakes, tsunamis, hurricanes, epidemics—into God's judgement on people's wickedness.

The book of Job also shoots down this shallow thinking and carnal theology. However–and this is the sticking point–many who call themselves followers of Jesus do not want to study God's word, do not want complexities in their theology, and do not want to be told they're wrong.

A church member said to me one day, "I don't know what the Bible teaches, but I know what I believe." And she seemed proud of this, as though she had attained some kind of mature status.

I told her she had just ended the conversation.

What is a pastor to do when his people want everything cut and dried, when they insist that God's truth be simple, stripped of all complications and alternate interpretations, or they will reject it all together?

I've heard preachers quote that line from Revelation, "He who has an ear to hear, let him hear," as evidence God intends everything in the Book to be crystal clear. To them, if one doesn't understand even the complicated Book of the Revelation, Satan has befuddled your mind.

What they intend, of course, is that we should accept their interpretation as the norm and reject all others.

Such preachers and teachers are part of the problem. Such wrong-headed proclamation is one reason many in the pews have given up trying to understand the Bible at all. They mistakenly decide that the Bible is restricted to trained scholars only and that they are out of their element when they dare enter such a theological minefield.

God gave us a miraculous thing in the Holy Bible. Much of Scripture is available to the 7-year-old who learned to read only last year, while at the same time there are depths which the best theological professors still have not fully plumbed.

It's a wonderful thing, this Bible you own.

To say that we should don our thinking-caps when we open the Word is not to imply it's too difficult for the average believer or inaccessible to the layperson.

Nor is it to imply it's simple or easy. Some is hard; much isn't.

From time to time, we'll hear well-meaning believers state their theology of the Scriptures as: "God said it, I believe it, that settles it."

Invariably, someone tops that with, "Hey, friend, God said it. And that settles it whether you believe it or not."

Both statements are woefully lacking.

God said a lot of things. And in many cases He did not intend for His people to simply utter an "Okay, got it!" and run along.

Many statements from the mouth of Jesus as well as from the Father Himself delivered through the prophets were meant to provoke the hearers into thinking matters out.

Jesus Christ often played the role of a provocateur. He was given to saying things you were free to take the wrong way in order to force you to think. If you didn't get His nuance and dismissed Him with no more thought, that was your problem. A case in point is John 6 where Jesus is telling hearers they will have to eat my flesh and drink my blood. The disciples said, "This is a difficult statement; who can hear it?" In His response, our Lord explained, the words that I have spoken to you are spirit and are life. And, as you notice, He seems not to have explained what that line meant either!

Mark 10 contains numerous such instances.

Jesus said, anyone who does not receive the kingdom of God like a little child will never enter it (Mark 10:15).

Note that He did not elaborate. Over the years, I've heard a hundred

97

possible interpretations on what it means to receive the kingdom as a child. I probably manufactured fifty of them myself. Maybe all are true. More than likely, the Lord left that statement open-ended in order to encourage us to take it from there.

To the rich young ruler who called Jesus "Good Teacher," He said, "Why do you call me 'Good?' There is no one who is good except God alone" (Mark 10:17-18).

Was Jesus good? Undoubtedly. And was He God the Son? To be sure. So, what was going on here? Clearly the Lord wanted the young man to think through what he was saying. When he gave honor to Jesus, he should know what he was saying. Jesus was both good and He was God. But not everyone "got" that.

A bit later, as the crestfallen young man walked away dejectedly, the Lord observed, it is easier for a camel to go through the eye of a needle than for a rich man to enter the kingdom of God (Mark 10:25).

The disciples were stunned. If that's the case, then the people they thought of as God's favorites, those who had a leg up on everyone else—well, if they can't make it, then we're all in trouble!

They muttered, "Well, who then can be saved?"

Jesus: "With man this is impossible, but not with God. All things are possible with God" (Mark 10:27).

Clearly, when we speak of the salvation of one soul from sin, from the grasp of the unholy trinity (the world, the flesh, the devil), and from a fate of eternal hell, we're in the realm where God alone rules supreme.

Then, as if the disciples didn't have enough to tax their brains, the Lord said, "No one who has left home or brothers or sisters or mother or father or children or fields for me and the gospel will fail to receive a hundred times as much in this present age….along with persecutions, and in the age to come, eternal life. Many who are first will be last, and the last first" (Mark 10:29-31).

No one who heard that walked away saying, "Okay. Got it!" This was another stunner requiring the full use of all their faculties. What did He mean, how did that apply to them, what does He require from us, when will these rewards come, and why in the world did He add persecutions?

Throughout this dense and loaded tenth chapter of Mark, the Lord said many things that challenged the minds of His followers, but nothing more than this.

"We are going up to Jerusalem and the Son of Man will be betrayed to the chief priests and teachers of the law. They will condemn Him to death and will hand Him over to the Gentiles who will mock Him and spit on Him and kill Him. Three days later, He will rise." (Mark 10:33- 34)

The disciples were stunned. What could this mean? How could this be? What if we did something to stop it? Isn't the Lord caving in to the enemy? What will become of all His prophecies for the future? What will become of us? Were we wrong in who we thought Him to be?

The disciples had the answers to none of these questions. In fact, if what Mark reports as happening immediately afterwards occurred in real time, it's clear they refused to think about what He had said at all.

James and John, two of His closest apostles, approached and asked for the choice seats "in your glory." (10:37)

Jesus said, "You don't know what you are asking."

There! They had not thought through any of this. They were merely guessing what it meant.

They might as well have been asking for "what's behind door number one as opposed to two or three." It was all guesswork.

Our Lord said to all the disciples, "Whoever wants to be first must be slave of all." (10:44)

We're satisfied that none of them got that, either. Not then, they didn't. Later, they were to learn all too well what it meant to give one's life in service to others.

Jesus: the thinking person's Savior.

Those who refuse to think often dismiss Him with a toss of the head.

I have read (I cannot vouch for its authenticity) that Oprah Winfrey said she turned away from the Christian faith when her pastor emphasized that God is a jealous God. A jealous deity was unworthy of anyone's devotion, she felt.

As though we have a choice in Gods.

Had she done a little Scripture study on her own—and not limited her grasp of the Christian faith to what one very fallible preacher said—she would have seen God is jealous for His children, not of them. Big difference. Every responsible parent is jealous for their children, wanting only their best and striking out against anything that could hurt them.

Her refusal to think about this has great consequences for herself and the multitudes who look to her for inspiration.

In his novel *Elmer Gantry*, Sinclair Lewis had a preacher leaving the ministry because, as he explained to a colleague, there are too many contradictions in the Scriptures. In Matthew 5:16, he pointed out, Jesus tells us to "let your light so shine before men that they may see your good works and praise your Father in Heaven." Then, in 6:1, He says, "Be careful not to do your acts of righteousness before men to be seen by them."

The fictional preacher said he was tired of trying to reconcile such contradictory statements, of which the Bible is saturated.

He wanted his theology easy, his doctrine pre-digested, his comprehension of salvation requiring a minimal effort.

Any ten-year-old can see that these do not contradict at all, that the Lord is talking about a matter of focus. However, the preacher in the novel— and we suspect Sinclair Lewis himself—did not want a religious faith that would require actual thought on his part.

One more word to the pastor

What is a pastor to do when his entire congregation does not want to think, when they demand the sermons to be of the most elementary kind requiring nothing from them except what generates a continual chorus of 'amens'? (That problem, incidentally, has been with us from the beginning. I refer you to Hebrews 5:11ff.)

Such a pastor must lead them to want more than they have been getting. Studying the Word of God and looking deeply into its teachings comes naturally for some but is an acquired taste for others.

Let the pastor drop a piece of red meat into a devotional sermon from time to time. Let the people chew on it and learn to savor it. In time, many will never want to go back to Gerber's again.

I can hear a preacher say, "But my people won't chew on red meat. They will choke on it." True enough. Some will.

You might have to start with a smaller group, pastor. In a Bible study class, most members expect to receive deeper insights and challenging truths.

Involve them in considering some of the Lord's "think about it" statements from the gospels. What did the disciples understand this meant? What are we to make of it in our lives? How does this compare with other statements on the same subject in Scripture? Are there denominations that take another interpretation? What would an unbeliever say about this?

Give them a nugget or two (or if you like other metaphors, "red meat to chew on" or "a bone to gnaw on") to take home with them and reflect on during the next week.

Jesus said we were to love the Lord God with all our heart, soul, mind, and strength.

He said "mind" and meant it. We shouldn't have to check out minds at the door when entering God's house.

Of course, neither should we go too far in the opposite direction and turn the sermon time into a seminary classroom. Insights from the Greek or Hebrew should be used sparingly if at all in a Sunday sermon. They may work well in small groups, however.

A friend of mine was suffering from brain exhaustion. The preacher evidently thought he was addressing a bunch of professors, judging from the depth of his sermons and the big words he used. My friend had taken just about all the nuggets/red-meat/bones-to-gnaw-on he could stand.

"Pastor," he said, going out the front door, "May I remind you the Lord said, 'Feed my sheep.'"

The pastor replied smugly, "That's what I'm trying to do, my friend."

"No," he said. "You misunderstood him, pastor. He did not say 'Feed my giraffes!'" Good one to end on.

Chapter Twenty-Two

Help someone find their calling in life. Scripture calls that 'discipleship.'

In my early 30's, I was a staff member at a large city church. My pastor was frequently invited to speak out of town and sometimes he would invite me along to drive. On one of those occasions, he said something that has stayed with me ever since.

"See that little church," he said as we traveled down a country highway. "Often the pastor of that little church can preach just as well as or better than the pastor of the big, influential church. But the difference is that he can't turn loose of jobs. He insists on doing everything himself. The other guy, however, puts people to work. He matches the right person to the right job, and everyone wins. They get satisfaction from doing their job in the church, the work gets done, the pastor is freed up for other things, the church grows, and the Lord is honored."

The secular world calls this delegation; scripture calls it discipleship.

One pastor sees a task that needs doing and starts thinking of who has a gift or the aptitude or at least the willingness for this and he enlists them. The other pastor sees a job and does it. Both are godly, dedicated men of the Lord, but only the first is being fair to his people.

Along about the same time as that conversation with my pastor, I attended a national conference on church management in Atlanta. There were 700 of us packed into the auditorium of that downtown hotel. In the middle of the opening session, as our host was presenting the schedule of the week, a hotel employee approached the platform pushing a vacuum cleaner and proceeded to clean all around the speaker.

At first, the speaker ignored him. Then the employee said, "Sir, can you move over here and let me clean under your feet?"

Our leader was visibly perturbed. He said, "Buddy, could you do that some other time? We're trying to have a meeting here."

The employee said, "No, I'm sorry. This is the only time I have to clean this room."

The leader said, "I'm going to have to speak to the manager of the hotel about this." The worker said, "I'm the manager of the hotel."

"You? You're the manager of the hotel and you're vacuuming the carpets?"
"Right."

"Could you tell me why, if you're the manager of the hotel, you have to do the carpets. Don't you have other people who can handle this?"

The manager said, "We do, but I vacuum better than anyone else."

That's when everyone knew it was a put-up job. The "worker" was actually a member of the professional team presenting the program, making a point about management to the hundreds of church leaders sitting before them.

Just because you do a job better than someone else does not mean you should do it. You may be robbing another person of a great opportunity to grow and serve. By taking away their task, you are hurting them and needlessly increasing your own workload.

Sitting there, I thought of something I had done in my seminary pastorate. When I arrived as pastor, I discovered the Sunday bulletin was being typed and reproduced rather poorly by an older lady in the congregation. As a veteran professional secretary before coming to seminary, I knew I could improve on it. I could type rings around this lady. I would make the printing more legible and the bulletin more attractive.

She quickly agreed to let me handle it. I'm confident the precious lady was glad to be free of the task.

I was taking a job away from a church member and adding to my own chores. Not really smart.

It's called delegating upward.

In the early New Testament church, a fellow by the name of Joseph was found to be such an encourager of other people, the congregation renamed him Barnabas, which roughly translates to Son of Encouragement. One of my professors called him "Mister Encourager." Here is a rough outline of the record on Barnabas.

Acts 4:36-37 He sold some land and gave the money to the church.

Acts 9:26-30 He stood up for the newly converted Saul of Tarsus when no one else would trust him.

Acts 11:22 When a revival broke out among the Gentiles of Antioch of Syria, the Jerusalem church sent Barnabas "Mister Encourager" up to check on it.

Acts 11:25 Barnabas realized the situation in Antioch was the very need for which Saul of Tarsus had been called by God. And, since Saul had returned home to Asia Minor, Barnabas went after him. In matching the man with the job and the need, he was providing a perfect role model for God's people.

Acts 13:2 The Holy Spirit calls out "Barnabas and Saul" as the first missionaries. At first Barnabas is the leader and he decides they will minister first in his home area of Cyprus.

Acts 13:42 Paul's preaching ministry in Cyprus became so successful, the two are now referred to as "Paul and Barnabas." The relationship has completely reversed. We notice there is not one glimmer of resentment from Barnabas. His disciple is outpacing him, and he loves it.

Acts 15:36-41 Paul and Barnabas decide to retrace their first journey and check on all the disciples they've made and the churches they started. However, they fall into a disagreement about John Mark, the nephew of Barnabas, who had accompanied them part of the way on the first journey, then dropped out. Paul had marked him off his list, but Barnabas was willing to give him a second chance. So, in the time-honored way of God's people through the years, they split up and went in two directions. Paul and Silas headed directly to Asia Minor, Paul's stomping grounds, while Barnabas took the young man John Mark and headed for Cyprus, his own home.

Some years later, we find Paul speaking of John Mark with great respect (II Timothy 4:11), and of course, we have the Gospel According to Mark, the product of this young man's faithful service.

Good job, Barnabas, putting your arm around the young vulnerable man and giving him a guiding hand.

That's all delegation is: helping someone find their right place of service.

"Follow me," Jesus said to a group of fishermen one day, "and I will make you to become fishers of men." Later, He said to them, "Go into all the world and preach the gospel." What was He doing but delegating His work to the disciples, matching them up with the assignments He had for each. "Feed my sheep," Jesus told the Apostle Peter.

The specifics of His call where each one should go, what he should do, would be the work of the indwelling Holy Spirit. That's still the plan for God's children. When I was serving in New Orleans, ministerial students at our seminary would visit my office regularly to talk about the possibility that God might want him or her to serve a church in our area. Ultimately, the discussion centers around God's will, finding it and being in its center.

Someone asked me one day, "Do you believe God has a place of service for every believer?"

I said, "I certainly do. Where do you work?"

He named one of the chemical plants upriver from New Orleans.

I said, "Does your director of human resources ever put someone on the payroll, then send him over to the plant manager and say, 'See if you can find a place for this one?'"

He laughed. "Oh no. If they put you on the payroll, they have a job for you. They're pretty efficient."

I said, "More efficient than God?" He said, "Hmm."

Since Scripture makes it clear that every believer receives spiritual gifts for ministry and service (I Corinthians 12:4ff.), it's not a stretch to believe the Father has a task in mind for each of His children.

Jesus encouraged His followers to "pray the Lord of the harvest to thrust forth laborers into the harvest" (Matthew 9:39). Since the Lord is the finest Director of Human Resources ever, it all comes down to a matter of prayer for His leadership. We might go so far as to say the Holy Spirit is the most effective practitioner of Management Principle No. 1—delegation—in the universe. He's always matching us up with the role that is just right for us.

Every church nominating committee struggles with finding people in the congregation to fill all the vacant slots in the organization. Rather than stressing out over the huge task and the unwilling members, what if they decided to seek the Father's will in prayer, then fill only the jobs for which He supplies the workers. That would end the "any-warm-body-in-this-slot- syndrome" and elevate the meaning of service to the Lord and the church.

After all, better to leave a position vacant than to fill it poorly.

And far better to fill the position with a person whom the Lord has chosen and called.

Chapter Twenty-Three

Mediocrity is so easy, comfortable even. But we can do better than that.

"...you are lukewarm, neither hot nor cold..." (Revelation 3:16)

Mediocrity is a warm blanket.

Mediocrity is satisfied with pretty good.

Mediocrity is the head in the sand when the storm is raging around us. Close your eyes until it all blows over.

Mediocrity is the coward's way out when critical decisions need to be made. "Well, let's give this some more thought." "Let's not be too hasty here." "We don't want people to think we're extremists."

There's safety in mediocrity. We're like everyone around us. We don't stand out. No one criticizes us. They don't even see us. We blend into the landscape.

The word mediocre comes from two Latin words, *medi* meaning "halfway," and *ocris* meaning "mountain." Somewhere there must be a list of every mountaineer who made it to the crest of Mount Everest. But no one ever bothered to note those who got halfway up and turned around for home.

As a pastor, I'm tempted to criticize people who choose mediocrity rather than daring, who play safe and avoid risks. Yet I often live that way too. In my personal life and church leadership, something inside me wants the conservative, safe way. The outcome I fear is not so much failure as criticism. I've refrained from writing to the editor on a controversial subject for fear of becoming the focus of criticism. My ego was too fragile. I felt I could not take it.

Or possibly I'm judging myself too harshly.

Perhaps the caution I feel is actually maturity advising me not to squander hard-earned trust on a cause not worth the price. We've all seen foolhardy people rush in where angels fear to tread, when they should have been quiet and stayed at home. It's not always easy to know.

Shamelessness, the antidote for mediocrity

"...and standing behind Him at His feet, weeping, she began to wet His feet with her tears, and kept wiping them with the hair of her head, and kissing His feet, and anointing them with the perfume..." (Luke 7:38)

So many people in Scripture demonstrated a wonderful shamelessness in Jesus' presence. The men of Capernaum tore open the roof of a house to get a friend into Jesus' presence.

The woman of Bethany wept openly in a hostile surrounding, so intent was she on worshiping Jesus. The woman called Syro-phoenician would not take 'no' for an answer as she begged the Lord to help her child. The blind beggar of Jericho kept calling on Jesus when people tried to silence him, until the Lord heard and healed him. The tax collector of the same city climbed a tree to see the Lord, then publicly confessed his salvation in Jesus' presence. Then, there was the blind man of John 9 who grew increasingly bold and fearless in his allegiance to his Lord. The women of Galilee followed Jesus, contributing to His support and remaining near the cross.

Just as remarkable, from our vantage point, is the number who pulled back from the Master lest they be embarrassed. Those who would not confess Him "for fear of the Jews." Peter who denied Him in the high priest's courtyard. The disciples who followed Him from afar.

Joseph and Nicodemus who waited until it was safe to go public in their allegiance.

We can tell a lot about ourselves by what it takes to embarrass us. Paul says even speaking of what some people do is shameful. Then he says, "But I am not ashamed of the gospel of Christ."

So many church members speak easily of shameful practices, but "blush to speak His name." Something is bad wrong. We should fear silence and shrink from disobedience.

We can decide to live another way. There is no spiritual pill that will end the problem of mediocrity. There is no one-prayer- solves-all for this malady. It's an everyday thing, work, a discipleship.

The solution involves choices I make day after day, from the moment my eyes open in the morning until I lay my head on the pillow at night.

It starts with acknowledging my shallowness, my love for convenience, my preference for the easy way out, my fear of criticism, my desire for easy answers and comfortable choices.

I will never completely conquer this, not in this lifetime. So, the prayer for faithfulness and the will to excel for Jesus' sake must always be kept current.

Am I a soldier of the cross, a follower of the Lamb? And shall I fear to own His cause or blush to speak His name?

Must I be carried to the skies on flowery beds of ease? While others fought to win the prize and sailed through bloody seas?

Are there no foes for me to face? Must I not stem the flood? Is this vile world a friend to grace, to help me on to God?

Sure, I must fight if I would reign. Increase my courage, Lord. I'll bear the toil, endure the pain, supported by Thy word. (Isaac Watts)

Chapter Twenty-Four

Preaching is easy. Unless you want to do it well.

Not that we are adequate for these things. But our adequacy (sufficiency) is of God (2 Corinthians 3:5).

If you want to be a preacher and are satisfied with what R. G. Lee called "sermonettes by preacherettes to Christianettes," then you can do that easily enough.

Prepare sweet little devotionals around interesting Scripture verses you have come across. Add some cute stories and raise your voice at least once in the 15-minute presentation (to convince the more discerning that what they're hearing is really preaching) and you can stay at that church a long time.

However.

If you are a God-called messenger who believes that the sermons should speak to the culture and address issues people sitting before you are actually dealing with, sermons in which you bring the light of God's eternal Word to shine upon the decisions people make, if you truly want to make disciples of Jesus Christ and not just church members, then you have a problem.

You're not smart enough. You are not holy enough. You are not courageous enough.

My longtime friend Rick Lance says, "You don't have the morality, the mentality, or the maturity to do this yourself."

You're going to have to go to the Lord and find out how He wants this done. "Faithful is He who called you and He will bring it to pass" (I Thessalonians 5:24). There's a good reason for this promise.

If you do not go to Him and ask, then wait before Him for His instructions, but decide that anyone can see what needs to be done and set about planning your preaching ministry the way you "just know" it needs, your head will soon explode.

The demands are too numerous, the needs too great, the pressures beyond your ability to withstand.

You are not adequate for these things. Think of it this way ....

A pastor in the 21st century needs to be well aware of...

1. The message of the entire Bible. (Good luck with that!)

2. The changing culture of the country, as it moves more and more off the grid before your very eyes. What was acceptable and reasonable a generation ago may now be illegal; what is normal today within another generation will get you attacked as a right-wing reactionary and possibly a terrorist. God help us.

3. The religious alternatives to the True Faith. It's not enough any longer for a pastor to proclaim that "Jesus is the Way, the Truth, and the Life" and "No one comes to the Father except through (Him)" (John 14:6). These days a faithful pastor needs to know some of what those alternative faiths are teaching and why they are forbidden and be able to address them intelligently. To some degree, every pastor needs to be an apologist.

4. He needs to keep up with the daily news, at least on some level. The Middle East, China, all of Asia, the Third World Countries the list of countries challenging our nation seem endless.

5. What about immigration into this country?

6. What about people in the pews living together as husband and wife but without marriage? And the changing view of the world toward homosexuality and trans-gendering.

7. What about the youth ministry? What does the pastor want from the new staff member who is assigned to reach students? Are there guidelines and no-no's? Are there dangers?

The list is endless.

When the Lord called me into the ministry as a college senior, only the first ("know the entire Bible") was on the list. The Middle East was another planet, sexual deviation was just that, and youth ministry consisted of rallies on Saturday night to sing choruses.

The young adult beginning a pastoral ministry today can easily be overwhelmed by the expectations and demands upon him in daily service and particularly in his preaching.

That's why he has to do these five things as a regular, consistent routine....

1. Live on your knees. A pastor's constant prayer is "Lord, show me what you would have me to do; then help me to be able to do it."

2. Live in the Word. A pastor should have a room with a table where he

can leave his Bibles and sermon study materials and know they will be there waiting for him tomorrow morning when he enters the room. He reads and studies and lives in the Word all week long.

3. Cut yourself some slack. You're not going to get this right all the time. Do the best you can and expect to come up short from time to time.

4. Attend the best conferences. Ask around. Other pastors will tell you the meetings they found most beneficial. Do not waste your time on the others. Urge your church leadership to set aside money in the budget for your continuing education.

5. Have a team of brethren who are your soul mates and a few veterans who are mentors. You are all redeemed by the blood of the Lamb, you are all called by God into the ministry, and you are all finding it impossible to do perfectly. So, you pray for each other and encourage one another, and periodically you gather for talk and prayer and fellowship.

God bless all pastors. Particularly the young ministers who will someday look back on this as a simpler time when the issues were more sharply defined, and the expectations were lower.

"Lord, bless your servants. We claim the promise that 'Faithful is He who called you and He will bring it to pass."

"Bring it to pass, O Father. Whatever is Thy will. Amen."

Chapter Twent-Five

One question we in ministry are not allowed to ask.

"Sow your seed in the morning, and do not be idle in the evening, for you do not know whether morning or evening sowing will succeed, or whether both of them alike will be good" (Ecclesiastes 11:6).

You do not know which will succeed.

You do not know if both will bear fruit.

Or if perhaps neither will succeed.

You may not see the fruit in this lifetime.

Perhaps, if we stick around long enough, we will know which of our efforts made a difference. But not often.

"Was it worth it?"

Ah, that is the question.

And the answer? God knows.

Disciples of Jesus Christ must never try to calculate the cost/benefit of an act of ministry. Our assignment is to obey. To be faithful.

It is His responsibility to make of it something special.

We have no idea how God will use something we do, whether He will, or to what extent He will. We obey Him, do what He has assigned to us, then leave the matter with Him as we move on to our next assignment.

We are His servants.

Every veteran pastor will identify with the following scenario....

A family member in your congregation is facing critical surgery in another city. You get up at 3 am and drive the distance, arriving at sunup. You have prayer with the patient just before the patient is wheeled into surgery. You sit with the family and do whatever you can (prayer, conversation, witness, sharing Scripture—or none of these things, depending on the circumstances, on the prompting of the Spirit). Then, you drive home. You may have devoted your entire day to this one act of ministry.

Invariably, someone will ask a critical question. "Was it worth it?"

Was this the best investment of your time? Should you have done this?

Perhaps it was your spouse who asked. It could have been a colleague or a friend. Or just as likely, your own accusing heart raised the issue.

You answer, "God knows."

As indeed He does. Only He does. And He's not telling.

Ever since my youth, I've been a sketch artist. I draw people wherever I go. When I preach in churches, the host will usually encourage people to come early and/or stay late so I can draw them. They set up a table and provide chairs for me and the subjects. The drawing takes two minutes or less, and I sometimes go three hours without a break. Occasionally, I will drive long distances to draw only and not to preach. A few times each year, I'll do wedding receptions and conventions which take several hours each.

What am I accomplishing with all this drawing and sketching? It's a valid question.

Honestly, I don't know.

I know, I know. You would think I had answered that a long time ago. But I haven't.

A family member used to observe me dragging home late at night after a full evening of driving, sketching, and speaking. Expressed or not, the question was always there: "So, why do you do this if it makes you so tired?"

In most cases I was too tired to answer. But in my mind there flashed an image of my coal- miner father lumbering up the West Virginia mountain after a full shift digging coal. Did he enjoy his work? That was beside the point. It was his job, and he did it.

It's my job. I do it.

Now, in truth, some possible answers to that question might include I love doing drawing people, it seems to bless people, they pay me (often, not always), and if afterwards I get to preach God's message, those I've sketched seem to listen well. The personal connection established at the table seems to bond us and cause them to want to hear what I have to say. I take full advantage of that.

From time to time, I present high school programs I call "Lessons from drawing 100,000 people." In the auditorium or gym, I'll sketch the kids before and after the program, then during the session draw the principal and coach and deliver my 12-minute presentation. Often, a few classes want me to come by and sketch or talk to the art students about cartooning. After several hours of this, I am so fatigued the host pastor may have to take me by the hand and lead me out of the building and toward a restaurant for nourishment. And what did we accomplish through all of this?

There is absolutely no way to know.

But here's the thing: I don't need to know. It's who I am; it's what I do.

I do it because God has gifted me with this love for people, a talent for sketching them, and a delight in using the gift.

Is that reason enough to do it?

Perhaps what we accomplish is nothing more than to add a smile to someone's day. A little joy. Or, to build a memory into their lives, when they find the sketch years from now. And was that worth it? Again, I do not know. I do not need to know.

But I will keep on doing this as long as the invitations keep coming in, the fingers keep working, and the eyes and brain don't give out. The occasional bout with arthritis is a problem, but thankfully it's rare and light.

As I write this, I'm nearing my 84th birthday, and still drawing, and preaching, speaking to seniors, teaching deacons, still working. So, blessed.

None of us know.

Preachers could ask the same questions about the sermons we preach and the ministry we give. What was accomplished? Was it worth the many hours of study and prayer and work? The many miles driven. God knows.

And we're good that. Scripture commands: "Do your work heartily, as for the Lord rather than for men, knowing that from the Lord you will receive the reward of the inheritance" (Colossians 3:23-24).

Whether we render a solo in church, serve a meal at the nursing home, preach a sermon in the jail, or sketch a few people in the mall, we do this "unto the Lord," and leave the results with Him.

My wife Bertha bakes loaves of delicious banana bread and crochets beautiful Afghans which she gives away throughout the year. Jim, a deacon and longtime friend, walks about the church handing out chewing gum, thousands of pieces a year (the sugarless kind, he is quick to point out). Our friend Stephanie takes her violin into nursing homes and hospital rooms and plays for people.

When someone asks, "Was it worth it?" or "Why did you do that?" we may simply smile, but what we are thinking is a variation of: "Ask the Lord who told me to do it. It was for Him."

"When the Son of Man comes," Jesus said, "will He find faith on earth?" (Luke 18:8)

Those who serve Him in ways large and small without knowing what He will do with their efforts know the answer to that question.

"Be thou faithful unto death," said our Lord, "and I will give you the crown of life" (Revelation 2:10).

Chapter Twenty-Six

For the young Timothys entering the ministry

Now, if Timothy comes, see that he is with you without cause to be afraid; for he is doing the Lord's work, as I also am. Let no one therefore despise him. But send him on his way in peace, so that he may come to me; for I expect him with the brethren (I Corinthians 16:10- ll).

Few people are more vulnerable in the ministry that a beginning and very young pastor. He marches forth into the work of the Lord with all the essentials, he thinks—a love for Jesus, a great testimony of His salvation, a confidence in the Word (the part he knows), and convictions about the gospel.

What he does not know—and is about to learn—is that lurking just ahead in the various churches will be people of good intention and equally strong convictions who are poised to reject him because of what he does not have: age, experience, a polished style, and a treasury of wisdom on what to do in various situations. His voice sounds unsure. His mannerisms are not steady. He uses leftover expressions from his teen years that grate on the ears of the older generation.

This is going to require patience from everyone. The young preacher must be patient with the people who are slow to accept him. The congregation must be patient because their pastor has a world of growing to do. They can help each other. But to pull that off, each will have to give the Lord their frustrations and hopes. They will have to decide whether they believe in Jesus Christ or not.

Some will not measure up, sad to say.

The fact that time will take care of everything people are finding objectionable about the young minister matters little to his critics. Many will reject him out of hand and turn a deaf ear to him simply because he is younger than their youngest grandchild and lacks experience.

Unless someone helps this young shepherd, he's not going to make it.

Now to our text.

What was going on with Timothy? Why should he fear to preach to the Corinthians? What would cause God's people—good Christian people, presumably—to "despise" him, to "look down on him," as some translations put it?

Aren't the men and women in the pews the best people on earth? Aren't they redeemed of the Lord, indwelt by the Holy Spirit, and commanded to love "even as I have loved you"?

Haven't they been instructed to "obey those who have the rule over you in the Lord"? (That's Hebrews 13:17)

True enough. But there's one more thing going on here which the young pastor must not miss: The people in the pews are still very human. And they didn't quit being human after the Lord saved them.

In fact, for some of them, their "humanity" just got stronger than it ever was. That can be bad or good.

Everyone in the Lord's congregations—and in the pulpit too, we might add—is a blend of the carnal and the spiritual. If after reading Paul's discussion of carnal and spiritual people in chapter two of First Corinthians you got the impression that the demarcation between the two is clear and deep and distinct, you would be wrong. Often, someone is spiritual today and carnal ("in the flesh") tomorrow. The best evidence of that is yourself.

You and I are that way, and it's a safe bet that everyone else in the congregation is too.

The young Timothys among us are going to need some advocates. They will need someone who can address the bullies in the church who are in danger of ruining this young ministry's usefulness in the Kingdom and can also pull the young preacher aside and talk straight to him.

In his First Letter to Timothy, Paul tells him, "Let no one look down on your youthfulness, but rather in speech, conduct, love, faith, and purity, show yourself an example of those who believe" (I Tim. 4:12).

Paul is saying, "You're going to have to work not to give these people something to criticize. Work on your speech, your behavior, the way you love them, your faith in Christ, and your personal purity. Do this and you will be making yourself a role model for everyone in the church, including the bullies."

Timothy must silence the critics with his godly conduct.

The British commentator William Barclay writes, "The Church has always regarded youth with a certain suspicion, and under that suspicion Timothy would inevitably fall."

Later, in his Second Epistle, Paul tells Timothy, "God did not give us the spirit of timidity, but of power and love and discipline" (II Timothy 1:7). We come away thinking this young pastor has a problem with shyness.

Paul adds, "You therefore my son, be strong in the grace that is in Christ Jesus." (II Timothy 2:1)

Clearly, Timothy–like all young pastors–needs a mentor, someone who will stand up for him before others, counsel him in private, and pray for him without ceasing. He needs an advocate, but one who will speak directly to Timothy as well as for him.

He had such a friend in Paul. How blessed he was.

This is not just about youth. Every pastor of every age and level of experience needs a friend or two or three who will speak truth to them, in love and courage.

The kind of friend I'm talking about is one who can tell you the following...

– "That sermon was terrible. It's clear you had not really thought through the concepts you were trying to convey."

– "You eat like a slob. I suggest you get your wife or some good friend to help you with this. And I don't mean next week."

– "Your nose hairs need clipping. They are embarrassingly long. I cannot believe your barber hasn't told you this." (Or your ear hairs.)

– "Your choice in clothing works well...for a 15-year-old. But you're an adult and ought to dress like it." (Variations: "The way you dress is right out of a fashion magazine–the 1955 issue. Spend a few dollars and get some current clothing." "Get someone to show you how to dress. You really need help.")

– "Pastor Bob, why are you so angry in your preaching?" This is what a friend does, if it needs doing.

A lesser friend would keep silent because they do not occupy a position of sufficient trust to enable them to do it effectively and live to tell the tale.

Proof: Let a new friend say any of the above to you and you are shocked, then offended, then humiliated. Even if you went immediately and acted on their counsel–and benefited from it–you would still hold that

118

individual at arm's length and dread future contact with him. "Clearly," you would say to yourself, "that guy thinks God has sent him to straighten out the world."

It's just human nature.

This is why most of us keep our mouths shut when we see a colleague in the ministry— someone we like and respect—violate some decent standards and know that we could be of help to them. We don't do it because it would be presumptuous, we would offend them, and the hurt we might cause would not be worth the good we might accomplish.

This is precisely why I kept my mouth shut when a friend's nasal hair and another friend's sloppy eating habits were all I could see during our visits.

Proverbs 27 contains a number of helpful insights about the kind of deep friendship people in the ministry need to give and be able to receive....

"Faithful are the wounds of a friend, but deceitful are the kisses of an enemy" (27:6). Such a friend will tell the truth even when it hurts. And because he/she is your friend, you take it, benefit from it, and the relationship grows. In time, you may be able to return the favor (for favor is what it is).

"Oil and perfume make the heart glad, so a man's counsel is sweet to his friend" (27:9). A true friend will not limit his comments to the negative. He/she will want to encourage you in the areas where you are doing well.

"He who blesses his friend with a loud voice early in the morning, it will be reckoned a curse to him" (27:14). There is a time for everything, for praise as well as for criticism. Choose your time well, friend.

"As iron sharpens iron, so one man sharpens another." (27:17)

For good reason you and I need a friend or two or three, the kind who can tell us our sermon stinks, that we are slobs, our personal hygiene needs attention, and that we are dressing like a teeny bopper. They do this to make us sharp in the best sense of that word.

Life has a way of taking the edge off everything, including our finest sermons and most profound insights. Going up against a good friend in a friendly sparring match—which is what happens when longtime buddies get together—can prod us to introspection, prayer, and study.

We must not leave Proverbs 27:17 without noting something. When iron sharpens iron, that process will be accompanied by friction, heat, noise, and flying sparks.

Two stories....

First. A pastor friend recalls vividly the day his best friend walked out of church in the middle of his sermon. Thinking he might be ill, the pastor called him that afternoon. "Hey, are you all right?"

"Yeah," he said. "I'm fine. I just couldn't take it anymore." "Take what? What are you talking about?"

The friend said, "Listen, you did not say a thing I disagree with in your sermon. But you say it with such anger. Who are you mad at? I'm just tired of listening to you harangue the people as though they're all convicted criminals!"

That stung. The pastor didn't sleep a wink that night. And the next morning, as he prayed over the matter, still reeling from the pain his friend had inflicted, the Holy Spirit suggested he listen to a recording of his sermon. That's when he heard for himself the hostility he was inflicting upon his people.

It changed forever the way he preaches.

Second story. At the age of 27, Milton became worship leader for one of the great churches in his state. Over two decades, he built a powerful ministry involving hundreds of people. I was surprised to learn that when he was a college student, a church had fired him for being too young and too inexperienced.

It was a small church, but Milton told me he had loved leading the worship there and directing the choir. But for some reason, an old gentleman in the congregation seemed to detest him. The man never missed an opportunity to let Milton know he was a failure as a leader and simply did not have the personality or ability to lead this church in worship.

The man's criticisms hung like a dead weight on this young minister long after he had left that church.

Some years later, a colleague in another state was bringing his senior adults to Milton's church for a concert. Milton invited the entire group—two busloads—to his home for breakfast. That morning, as the buses arrived, Milton walked into his front yard to greet everyone.

He was not prepared for what happened next.

The first man off the bus was his old nemesis. The old fellow who had given Milton so much trouble, who had tormented his mind for decades, now stood before him. Amazingly, he wore a smile as big as Montana. He stepped up to Milton, threw out his arms for an embrace, and said, "I always knew you had what it took, my friend!"

Milton was speechless. And completely baffled. The old fellow seemed not to have a clue the pain he had inflicted on this servant of God.

There's a moral in there somewhere, young Timothys.

Most of the older critics in your church are oblivious to the pain they are causing and the harm they are inflicting on your ministry. If you can love them anyway, and if the Lord will give you a sheltering older friend to speak up for you and get you over the hump, in time they will get past this.

Until they do, keep the faith.

Chapter Twenty-Seven

Perhaps the hardest thing a pastor will ever have to do.

Speak to the current moral dilemma facing the country (or dividing your community) without making matters worse.

That has to be one of the most difficult minefields a pastor ever has to tread. One misstep and he's a goner.

In the decade of the 1990s, it was President Clinton's infidelity that was dividing the country. At about the same time, it was the O. J. Simpson trial. Twenty years later, the issue was sexual harassment (or any of its various manifestations: sexual molestation, intimidation, assault, etc.) by men in positions of power. Every age has its issues.

For our purposes here, let's take an issue that everyone is familiar with....

A man runs for public office, and someone stands up and says, "He attacked me." Or molested me. Touched me inappropriately. Took advantage of me. Assaulted me.

Sexual harassment is an issue that will not ever go away, it appears.

The media flocks to the accuser and stories are written. Sleuths check out her story and some corroborate it while others trot out family members who say she is a chronic liar or family members of the accused to say they've never known him to do anything like that.

Then, next step. Other women step up and say, "He treated me the same way."

Quickly, the matter becomes page one across the country. Leading the nightly news. Fueling talk shows. Dividing everyone on Facebook. Splitting families.

Defenders are enraged. Supporters of the accusers are offended by the way their friends have accommodated themselves to the culture and forgotten Jesus' call to defend the helpless and bless the children.

Soon, the pastor decides this matter must be addressed in next Sunday's sermon. A hundred questions filled his mind.

Should he do it? And what exactly should he do? How can he speak to this business without taking sides? And if he takes sides—either side—what good will he accomplish? And what price will he pay? Or maybe he should just preach the biblical story he had been studying and leave the current issues alone. No one will get angry with him from preaching on Joshua or Moses.

The question: How can he speak about the controversial issue of the day without further dividing his congregation?

There are two mistakes a pastor can make...

He can fail to mention the controversy at all. This will confirm to many the irrelevance of the pulpit, that pastors do not live in the real world.

Or he can assume that the congregation is all of one mind on this and take a firm stand on one side or the other. In the more liberal churches (sorry for the label, but the reader will understand), the pastor may assume everyone is energized by the accusations of the women and agree the accused should go away quietly. In the more conservative churches (i.e., conservative in doctrine, practice, and politics), the pastor might assume everyone is angry at the accusers and supportive of the man. Both assumptions would be in great error.

Almost no congregation is monolithic (all of one kind). Even in the most conservative of churches, there will be Bible-believers who are more socially liberal. Also, every church will have members who were victimized but kept silent, and while they will never speak up and identify themselves, they will forever lose confidence in a pastor who is quick to brand the accusers as liars.

The poor pastor. What is he to do? I'll take a stab at answering that.

One. Let the pastor spend much time on his knees asking the Father that very question.

This requires a willingness to do whatever the Lord says. Otherwise, there's no point in asking.

Two. The pastor may decide that "I have no word from the Lord on this matter."

It would be in order to say that to the congregation in the service. This will not satisfy everyone. Many in the typical church will have their own view as to the "clear moral position" and no patience for anyone on the other side. But most people will appreciate a pastor with the good sense to wait on the Lord and not run ahead of him.

Three. When and if the Lord directs him, the pastor might want to do some or all of the following....

–Recognize that good and sincere believers will take opposite sides of many of these issues. So, he could speak to both sides.

–Address the issue in prayer, asking God to direct, to give wisdom, to be glorified in these matters, and to bless America.

–Speak about the moral issues involved while not addressing the specific details happening at the moment.

–Find biblical principles involved. In many cases, those principles will apply to both sides of a controversy.

–If the pastor has a great story that sheds light on the issue, this is the place for it. But that too is risky. A wise pastor will try out the story on a few trusted advisors, starting with his spouse. Does it work? Does it help? Does it speak to the issues? Does it suggest something we should do? And perhaps most importantly, "If you were me, would you tell this story?"

–Does the story of Joseph and the wife of Potiphar in Genesis 39 speak to the current issue dividing us? Or the matter with David's sons Absalom and Amnon and their sister Tamar?

In every congregation some will need reminding that you are not violating Matthew 7:1's instruction: judge not. That scripture refers to condemning, not decision-making. We make similar choices about "judging" all the time. Can I trust this teen to watch my children?

Can I believe this politician enough to vote for him/her? You made a similar decision about joining this church: Is it wise, right, safe, godly?

This is about discernment, not condemnation.

–Call for love. We are to be known to the world by our love for one another, said our Lord (John 13:34-35). And not by our political unity or social philosophies. If we love only those who agree with us on controversial issues, what have we done? Even lost people do that. (See Luke 6:32-34)

"Lord, give wisdom to the leaders of your flocks, please. And give them courage to speak out faithfully on difficult issues. May they do so with wisdom and love. Thank you."

Chapter Twenty-Eight

Think God can't use you? Think again.

"And Moses said, 'Who me, Lord? I've not been to seminary. I didn't even finish college. The other preachers won't respect me. Pulpit committees won't have anything to do with me.

There's a bounty on me back in Egypt. I stutter a lot and tend to freeze up in front of groups. You've clearly dialed a wrong number, Lord."

"And God said, 'Shut up and listen.'" (My rather free version of Exodus 3-4.)

"The Lord can't use a nothing nobody like me."

Ever heard that? Ever said it?

Repent, sinner. You underestimate God! (And you might be overestimating your own importance in the equation.)

The Lord delights in taking nobodies and doing great things with them.

I heard the testimony of the fellow who was working on the Graham dairy farm in Charlotte, NC, in the 1930s, the worker who took Billy Graham to the Mordecai Ham crusade where he gave his heart to Christ. He said, "I know you think Billy Graham must have been a unusual teenager for God to have done such great things with him in his adulthood. But you'd be wrong. In fact, if you had seen a hundred teenagers in that town, and tried to pick the one who was going to be used of God to touch millions for Christ, you couldn't have done it."

Billy Graham was a normal, typical teenager.

As a 16-year-old working on the dairy farm, Billy was interested in one thing and one thing only, the man said. Nope, not girls. "He wanted to drive the farm truck." And that's how the farm worker—I regret I've forgotten his name—got Billy to the crusade. "I told him, if you'll go with me tonight, you can drive the truck tomorrow."

Two of Paul's epistles are addressed to Timothy, his son in the ministry. Timothy served Paul in many ways and pastored the church at Ephesus for a while. He was clearly a major player. But, if anyone could have begged off for lack of ability, eloquence, and a hundred other things, it was he.

Question: Have you ever looked at a young person with extraordinary

125

talents and gifts—looks, presence, brains, personality, and eloquence—and thought, "God is going to do great things with him?" Or her.

If so, you have fallen into that trap. It's our nature to think such a person with such assets will be used in extraordinary ways in life, as well as in the kingdom. The only way this is true, however, is for one to bring all those gifts and talents to the cross and give them to the Savior. Then, as He pleases, they may be picked back up and used as instruments for the Kingdom. But until this happens, all those positives can be impediments to usefulness in the Lord's work.

Back to Timothy....

Timothy was physically weak, according to I Timothy 5:23 where Paul refers to his "frequent ailments."

Timothy was personally timid, according to 2 Timothy 1:7 where Paul reminds him that "God has not given us the spirit of fear, but of power and love and a sound mind."

Timothy was relatively young, according to I Timothy 4:12 where Paul urges him to "let no one look down on your youthfulness...."

Timothy was emotionally fragile, according to 2 Timothy 1:4 where Paul recalls his tears.

Now, let's say you're looking for a champion for Christ, one whom God can use for mighty things. Here we have a too-young man, one who is physically weak, rather timid, and fragile emotionally. Would you consider him? Probably not. And definitely not, if there were other prospects with better resumes.

If I Corinthians 1:26ff is not a part of the fiber of your tissue, may we suggest that it should be. It will explain a thousand things about how God works: whom He chooses, whom He passes over, whom He rejects, whom He blesses, etc.

"You see your calling, brethren—that there are not many wise according to the flesh, not many mighty, not many noble.

"God has chosen the foolish things of the world to shame the wise; God has chosen the weak things of the world to shame the things which are strong; and the base things of the world and the despised, God has chosen, the things that are not, that He might nullify the things that are."

Why did He do this? "That no man should boast before God." (I Corinthians 1:26-31)

And so, if you are a Fortune 500 executive, if you are wealthy beyond our imagination, if you were ever a Miss USA or a Mr. Olympia or a national champion or Olympic gold-medal winner in anything, God can still use you. However, it will be in spite of all those things.

No flesh should boast in His presence.

It's all of grace, my friend.

"Not that we are adequate to think anything of ourselves, but our adequacy is of God" (2 Corinthians 3:5).

Running out of excuses, aren't you? (Smiley-face goes here.)

When God calls, do not waste your time or try His patience by enumerating all the reasons you are unqualified. You are indeed unqualified, but that's not the point.

The Father delights in using those judged as unusable by the world. You will recall that "the stone which the builders rejected has become the chief corner stone" (I Peter 2:7).

Now, what were you saying about being a nothing nobody?

On a mission trip to Argentina, our minister of youth Bryan Harris stopped at a market stall where a craftsman was carving out matte' cups from blocks of wood. Customers were allowed to choose the block from which he would fashion their cup. Bryan reached down into a bucket at the man's feet and pulled out a piece of wood. The man protested, "These are rejects, senor. You do not want a cup from this." Bryan said, "This is exactly what I want." And while the worker carved his cup from that block, Bryan spoke to him about "the stone which the builders rejected" becoming the chief cornerstone. And he led the man to Christ.

If you are feeling rejected by bosses, lovers, friends, the world, anyone—lift up your head, friend. We have a Savior who specializes in great things through despised instruments.

Chapter Twenty-Nine

Bogged down in minutia: the occupational hazard of ministers.

"I feel like I'm being eaten alive by a school of minnows."

"I felt like I was being stoned to death by popcorn."

Ask any pastor.

My observation is the pastor of the medium-sized flock has it hardest.

The pastor of the tiny church has one well-defined set of jobs and the leader of the mega- congregation another entirely. The first has a few clear and well-understood roles while the latter has a vast team of helpers allowing him to focus on a few huge responsibilities.

It's the pastor in the middle who has little say-so about what he will do today.

The pastor-in-the-middle, which is the shepherd of the church running, say, one to three or four hundred, depending on a thousand things including resources and available helpers, will always have more on his plate than he can get to.

This pastor is the administrator of the church. He is the boss of the employees. He gives directions to everyone who works there. He deals with problems and headaches. He is the counselor for the congregation. He is the hospital visitor and does all the funerals and weddings. He is a member of every committee in the church and as a rule, if he doesn't call the meeting and attend, nothing gets done. He is the go-to person for every question.

He dictates all the letters, and likely types them himself. He follows up with the visitors and prospects, phoning or visiting them. Meanwhile, he preaches all the sermons and even some of the Sunday School lessons. Add to this one overwhelming fact...

He's married. He has a wife and children, and they need him. He loves them dearly and is constantly torn because he is not giving them what they need.

Everyone owns a piece of him. Every church member feels he belongs to them, and each has a right to call on him. He has no personal time, no days blocked off when he is unavailable.

The denomination needs him to attend area meetings and sometimes to serve on committees. As a member of the community, he meets with other pastors and leaders from time to time.

His mama needs him. His extended family is calling. Grandpa is in the hospital, Grandma is laid up and unable to look after herself, and the siblings are of little help. So, he's torn by the younger and the older generations of his family.

He has trouble sleeping because of all the nagging needs which will not leave him alone. When his head hits the pillow, he can think of calls needing returning, sermons needing attention, and problems needing addressing. Meanwhile, his wife has been waiting for this time to communicate to the man she loves.

Oh my.

Sound familiar?

The tyranny of the urgent

This needs your attention now. Mrs. Jones is on the phone and needs her pastor. The secretary informs the pastor that she has made four appointments for him today, a day he had hoped to hide in the study and prepare Sunday's sermon. That article needs writing this morning, the mail goes out at 10 and his letters need to be in it, and that ministers' meeting starts at 11:30.

Now. Here. You. Urgent!

Mark chapter 1 has something for us on this subject.

In the early morning while it was still dark, He arose and went out and departed to a lonely place and was praying there. Simon and his companions hunted for Him, and they found Him, and said to Him, 'Everyone is looking for You.' And He said to them, 'Let us go to the towns nearby, in order that I may preach there also; for that is what I came out for.' (Mark 1:35-38).

Do not rush past this. It's the precise lesson we need today. The Lord had spent a tiring evening healing and helping people (1:32-34). Finally, exhausted, He went to bed, then next morning got up early to walk in the hills and talk to the Father. When the disciples managed to run Him down, you can practically hear their rebuke: "Lord, we have a crowd back at the house. More people for You to heal. You don't have time for this. Come on!"

But Jesus walked away from needs—genuine needs, pressing needs—in order to stay with the Father's agenda. "That is what I came out for," He said.

Do you know what you "came out for"? What is your purpose, your calling, pastor?

Start with your calling, your purpose.

What if you clarified in your mind the calling of God on your life and the direction of the ministry to which He summoned you? What if you began to try to refine your ministry and lay aside the lesser things?

To do this would require a lot of things: time to think and reflect, prayer and prayer and more prayer, discussion with the wife and with a few significant church leaders. Some of the questions you would face include-

—What can you turn over to other people?

—Are there others in the congregation who can take some of the jobs from you? And just as importantly, can you turn loose of them?

—Can you make such changes a little at a time so it's not so abrupt and would not be noticed by most of the congregation?

—Can you then focus on your strengths, on your true calling, and do those better?

—Then, once you begin to divest yourself of some of the distractions of ministry and free up some time, you will have to decide what will fill the void: time with your family; time to sit in a room quietly and think and pray and study; time to take a daily walk for your exercise.

Creativity is the first casualty.

When you are constantly tired and meeting yourself coming and going, you will not have the time or energy to work on fresh sermons and new directions for your church.

Creativity, it is said, requires a circumference of silence to do its best work.

Gordon MacDonald pointed out that the three great banes of the pastor's existence are hurry, crowds, and noise. Ask any mother, any schoolteacher, any pastor.

The opposite of hurry, crowds, and noise would be stillness, solitude, and silence. They can be such great blessings in the life of a minister, but they do not come easily or automatically.

You have to choose. You have to make some hard decisions.

A pastor will have to be pro-active. No one is going to do this for him.

Even if some sensitive soul approaches you with, "Pastor, you're working too hard and need to make some changes if you're going to survive," they cannot take it beyond that. The martyr complex in many a pastor thrives on being needed, feeds on ego affirmation from church members, and depends on the carnal satisfaction of feeling worthy because "I'm so busy." All of that is unworthy of a child of God. You will walk by faith and live in the Spirit, or you will work in the flesh and be constantly trying to earn God's love and everyone's approval.

You have to decide.

It's up to you. No one will make you rest.

Chapter Thirty

Pastor, leave sports partisanship out of the pulpit. Here's why.

"Not everyone in the pews cares who won that game. They could care less who Mickey Mantle or Hank Aaron, Joe Namath or Drew Brees was. Tell them a Yogi Berra story and while you stand there waiting on the laugh, they will say, 'Who is that?' An evening at a college football game with you is not a delight for everyone, but punishment." –The voice of sanity

Keep that in mind as you enter the pulpit area.

Dr. Cecil Randall pastored Tuscaloosa's First Baptist Church during the era of Coach Paul "Bear" Bryant when winning national championships became a matter of annual routine and alumni expectation. Later, as a professor in New Orleans Baptist Theological Seminary, he told his students not even once did he mention football from the pulpit.

"Not everyone in your congregation is local," Dr. Randall said. "Some are from those other states, and they cheer for those other teams. Besides, you have bigger things to do today than talk about a football game."

Any pastor who questions that should go back and examine his calling.

There is an exception.

When the entire team comes to your church for a special service, you may talk football. All fifty-five athletes are sitting before you in the audience, along with six coaches and their families. Everyone in the building is fully expecting you to talk about them, what they're doing, the season before them, something. Try to inspire them, pastor, with what they are trying to achieve but without dumping on their opponents, some supporters of which are also sitting nearby and eavesdropping.

Pastors who have difficulty doing this–honoring a team and challenging them but without trivializing the gospel message–should seek advice and suggestions from their mentors.

Leave football out of the pulpit.

Or basketball if you're in Kentucky, Kansas or North Carolina. Soccer if you live in Europe, South America, or Asia.

You are on a mission for the Lord Jesus Christ. You are not a lackey for the local chamber of commerce nor an agent of the community public relations campaign. You want this city to do well—see Jeremiah 29:7. But when you open your mouth to deliver Heaven's message, you have greater goals in mind.

Ask the Holy Spirit to guide you.

There is nothing wrong and everything is right with supporting all that is good in your community. As a pastor, I once headed up the chamber of commerce's beautification committee for our town and often did 10-second television spots promoting a clean and lovely community. And, as a member of the local symphony board, at the end of the worship service I might mention the concert on Tuesday night with the hope more would support it. But our town was not large, and no one was offended.

I was not slamming another team. God told the Israelites in Babylon to "work for the welfare of the city where I have sent you into exile and pray on its behalf; for as it prospers, you will prosper." (Jeremiah 29:7). Literally, He said, "In its shalom, you will have shalom."

A few quick observations on this subject...

One. You're not going to stop people from discussing last night's game before Sunday School. So, don't even try, pastor. Actually, there's nothing wrong with it. They're fellowshipping, and anything is on the table for that.

Two. Personally, even if his preferences are well known, the pastor should wear his partisanship lightly. One church asked everyone to wear a t-shirt for their favorite team the following Sunday. The pastor wore one from his alma mater. My opinion—and that's all this is—he should have worn a plain white dress shirt that day. Or, he could have gotten really creative and had his wife make up a shirt with the logos of a dozen good teams. But if I'm an Alabama fan and the pastor is preaching in an Auburn t-shirt—or vice versa—this is probably not going to be well-received.

Three. This is not to say you cannot use sports analogies or stories in sermons. They're in Scripture. (I Corinthians 9:24-27; Hebrews 12:1; 2 Timothy 4:7)

Four. Never forget the words of the baseball catcher as the batter approached the plate and made the sign of the cross. "Hey Buddy," he said, "Why don't we just let the Almighty enjoy the game?" It's a good reminder.

Five. If you know for a fact that some members of your congregation support "that other team," ask them to let you know if they ever feel you have crossed the line. Assure them of your love for them and respect for their loyalties. If your partisanship is extreme and deep, enlist their help in seeing that you toe the line.

Six. Pastor, leave the pennants and wall hangings from your team out of your office. For all the obvious reasons.

Seven. I'll make a prediction. One of these days you will have in your congregation a professional athlete, someone well known to the sports world, someone who pulls down a zillion bucks a year, someone whose image has graced *Sports Illustrated* numerous times. And he/she will be impressed that you do not swoon, that you stay on course in preaching the gospel message. In my experience, the professional athlete knows better than anyone how ephemeral and shallow are the accolades of his/her profession.

I have known some of those veteran athletes. To my surprise, their lives do not revolve around sports. They actually have normal lives.

Long ago, someone told Coach Bob Devaney of the Nebraska Cornhuskers of a die-hard fan who was overboard in all things Nebraska. The man had even ordered his casket in fire- engine red with "Nebraska" all over it. He had even had the name of the team cut into his teeth.

They asked Coach Devaney, "What do you think about that?" He answered, "I think he should get a life."

Indeed. And that's where you and I come in, pastor. We know the One who is the Giver of Life and that more abundantly.

Tell them about Jesus.

Chapter Thirty-One

The arrogant pastor: peacock in a mudhen parade

Let this mind be in you which was also in Christ Jesus.... (who) made Himself of no reputation, taking the form of a servant, and coming in the likeness of men. Being found in appearance as a man, He humbled Himself and became obedient to the point of death, even the death of the cross. Wherefore, God has highly exalted Him.... (Philippians 2:5-9)

Browsing through the bookstore, I picked up a book written by a pastor somewhere. The cover photo was a full picture of the man himself. In the lower right-hand corner were these words: "Not your typical preacher."

I was offended.

At breakfast the next morning, I asked my wife, "Why did that offend me?"

She didn't hesitate. "Because it was so arrogant of him." My thought exactly.

Either that preacher wrote that line about himself and ordered that his photo be plastered across the front of the book, or he surely approved it. Either way, his ego is all over the place. The man is exalting himself.

I can imagine his office filled with stacks of these books. A hundred photos of his face stare back at him. Each one announces he is better than the average preacher.

He loves it.

I am offended that the man does not want to be identified with "typical" preachers. He is clearly "a cut above," in his thinking at least.

In my opinion, most pastors are humble, hard-working, and dedicated to doing the work of Christ. They are not prideful or self-exalting.

"Not your typical preacher?"

"I'm not like other preachers." Ever heard that?

The last two preachers I heard say something similar about themselves turned out to be hypocrites. One was revealed to be a serial adulterer and the other a gambler and alcoholic. Clearly, they sought to divert attention away from their failings by criticizing other preachers.

No doubt some preachers are attracted to the pulpit because of the attention they will receive. They love the idea of hundreds—thousands, even! —sitting before them, eagerly taking in their every word. They preen and prance and practice their movements in order to impress and enchant.

I'm happy to say I do not know any such preachers. But no doubt they exist.

Egotists love the idea of their sermons being telecast, their thoughts being published in magazines and books, their facial image being recognized across America.

It's not a new thing. We find these peacocks in Scripture.

During our Lord's earthly ministry, the Pharisees were the peacocks. Jesus said of them, "They love the best seats at feasts, the choice seats in the synagogues, greetings in the marketplaces, and to be called by men 'Rabbi, Rabbi.'" (Matthew 23:6-7). He cautioned, "Whoever exalts himself will be humbled, and he who humbles himself will be exalted" (23:12).

Those Corinthians peacocks were billing themselves as "super-apostles." They were not content to lump themselves with the original twelve. They were (ahem) "not your typical apostles."

Paul refers to them in 2 Corinthians chapters 11 and 12. They bragged that they were superior in knowledge and better in the pulpit. Clearly, the most gullible in the pews were swallowing those lies. This reminds us of the Lord's admonition about causing "one of these little ones who believe in Me to stumble," and the fate that awaits them (Matthew 18:1-6). Instead of being the real deal, Paul pointed out, these men were "false apostles, deceitful workers, transforming themselves into apostles of Christ" (2 Corinthians 11:13).

Interestingly—and the Lord's servants will love this—Paul decides to play the game being perpetrated by the super apostles. "Seeing that many boast according to the flesh, I also will boast" (2 Corinthians 11:18). And he does this in the most remarkable way, completely different from what was expected, but totally consistent with the true child of God.

He showed them his scars.

"In labors more abundant, in stripes above measure, in prisons more frequently, in deaths often. From the Jews five times I received forty stripes minus one. Three times I was beaten with rods; once I was stoned;

three times I was shipwrecked; a night and a day I have been in the deep...." (2 Corinthians 11:23ff)

So, Paul implied, you might ask these self-promoting peacocks what scars they bear as a result of their faithful service.

Humility is not just a suggestion of Scripture. It is unfailing evidence of Christlikeness, a requirement for usefulness to the Lord, a rebuke to the carnal nature which feeds on pre-eminence and recognition.

Scripture says we are to humble ourselves. We should never ask God to humble us. He can do it of course, but He does it with a heavy hand. See what He did to Nebuchadnezzar (Daniel 4).

And we must humble ourselves daily. The ego will not go away quietly but will recover from today's humiliation and show up tomorrow insisting to be given the best place at the head table.

"I die daily," said the great apostle (I Corinthians 15:31).

That's the only way to keep the ego in check.

Dan Crawford, retired professor at Southwestern Baptist Theological Seminary in Fort Worth, remembers the time when he was fresh from seminary and a new campus minister at the University of Texas. In the upcoming graduation, he was informed, it was "the Baptist's turn" to handle the invocation and benediction. So, that day, young Dan donned his plain black robe–unadorned since at that time he had not earned a doctorate–and took his place toward the head of the processional in between the president of the institution and the speaker of the day, who was the head of an esteemed university in the state. The long processional of professors was a colorful thing, each robed in reds and blacks and blues, with their colorful hoods indicating their field of accomplishment.

Later, noting how out of place he had looked in that colorful procession, a friend commented, "Dan, you looked like a mud hen in a peacocks' parade."

That wonderful line became the title of a book of reminiscences from Dan Crawford's career.

In my opinion, pastors were intended to be mudhens. "He must increase, I must decrease," said John the Baptist, thus providing a mantra for God's servants ever since (John 3:30).

Frank Pollard, for a quarter century the highly esteemed pastor of the First Baptist Church of Jackson, MS and preacher for the world-wide broadcast of "The Baptist Hour" was being interviewed by a seminary student. Asked how he wanted to be remembered after he was gone, Frank answered, "I don't want to be remembered; I'm just the messenger."

When that seminary student reported his interview to the class, the professor told me you could have heard a pin drop. "Big preachers don't talk that way," he said.

True, some preachers are not content to be humble non-entities. Messengers. Delivery boys.

They want to be known, to be acclaimed, to be recognized, followed, and adored. These are the peacocks in the parade of mudhens.

God help us.

At the risk of over-repetition, I repeat that the minister has to decide anew every day of his life to stay out of the way and to exalt Christ.

Chapter Thirty-Two

You're a pastor; you're not like us.

I was a young pastor, flying home from somewhere. It was a dark and stormy night.

The planes assigned to our Golden Triangle Airport by Southern Airways—I said it was a long time ago!—were the ancient Martin 404s. Prop jets, I think they are called.

We bounced all over the sky that night. Lightning flashed around us, rain pelted our little plane, and thunder crashed. The plane rolled and dropped, lifted and skidded.

You've heard of white knucklers; this was the mother of them all.

The next day in the supermarket, a woman whom I did not know introduced herself. "My husband was on that awful flight from Memphis last night."

Oh yes. That was unforgettable, I said.

"But he told me every time he began to panic, he looked up and saw the pastor a few rows ahead of him, and you seemed to be fine. And that gave him confidence."

I laughed, "That's good, because I was frightened out of my wits."

Why, we wonder, do people think if a preacher or a nun or priest is on board, God is somehow going to take extra care of an endangered flight? As though He loved them more than the others. "God is no respect of persons," Scripture says somewhere.

No one gets by with anything with the Heavenly Father just because they are His favorite children.

They're all His favorites.

September of 1965 we were in seminary in New Orleans. Hurricane Betsy was bearing down on Louisiana and Mississippi. Less than five months earlier, Margaret and I had moved with our two-year-old son into an apartment in back of the church situated on Alligator Bayou, 25 miles west of New Orleans in the tiny Cajun community of Paradis. The eye of Betsy passed over our village that night. During the lull, I walked outside to find peace and calm, and could see the stars in the sky. Ten minutes later, the storm was back, this time all its fury blowing in the opposite direction.

It was a frightening night. And since we were from north Alabama, this was our first experience with hurricanes.

Our friends Ron and Jane Adema from Birmingham were visiting with us. Ron was an up- and-coming preacher like me, and we were trying to encourage one another. So, when we scheduled a revival that September, we invited Ron to preach.

Our church structure was made of two buildings taken from some army camp in and around New Orleans. Paradis Baptist Church was birthed in May of 1945, just as some bases were winding down and the buildings became available.

That night, just after dark and before we lost power, our phone rang. Someone from across the street was calling. "This is scary," she said. "But it's so comforting to look across the street and see lights on in the pastorium."

I said, "Well, we're not doing anything religious. We're playing rook."

I wish I could be counted on to say something more righteous and uplifting in such moments. But that was how I was (and remain to a certain extent to this day, a half century later). "Lord, help me to grow up into a mature man," I still pray to this day.

Or not. I'm not real sure I want to be overly religious. Martin Luther's favorite verse, Ecclesiastes 7:16, fits here. Do not be overly righteous; Why should you destroy yourself?

Our community suffered a lot of damage that night. Because of the huge live oak tree in the front yard, our buildings were spared. Since the greatest damage inflicted by hurricanes is always on the eastern side of their path, New Orleans East and St. Bernard Parish paid the heaviest price with wind damage and flooding.

This preacher was frightened. This preacher prayed. And God did what He wanted to do, in line with Psalms 115:3. Our God is in the heavens; He does whatever He pleases.

Preachers are not a separate class of humans. They are often too human. I smile at the memory of what some friends told me after they moved to Memphis. The house they purchased was across the street from mega-church pastor Dr. Adrian Rogers. One evening, my friend Bob called to his wife, "Wanda! Come here. Dr. Rogers is taking his garbage to the curb." From the kitchen, Wanda said, "And just how did you figure it got to the curb?" He said, "I don't know. I just never thought he would carry his own garbage to the curb."

Preachers are different, right? Give me a break.

Israel sometimes thought they had a get-out-of-jail-free card from God and could do as they pleased since "the ark is in Jerusalem" and "His name is on us." They learned the hard way God had higher standards for His people and held them to stricter requirements, and they would pay dearly for missing that. I Peter 4:17 says, "The time has come for judgement to begin at the house of God."

No one gets a pass.

We are all sinners. We are all in need of a daily outpouring of His grace. And we should all be showing grace and mercy to one another.

What we should not do is expect because someone is holy that the Father is duty-bound to show them special treatment.

Every pastor I know constantly reminds the congregation to "Pray for me." Indeed. If anything, they need more prayer than anyone else.

Chapter Thirty-Three

The burden and fear of handling the Word of God

"...rightly dividing the Word of truth" (2 Timothy 2:15).

One day I posted this on Facebook...

Ever wonder how pastors deal with Sunday morning anxiety? They're about to enter the pulpit and lead a congregation to worship the living God, then open His book and declare its life-changing message. What a responsibility! How do they cope with so great a burden? I'll tell you how. They breathe deeply, commit it all to the Lord, and keep telling themselves, 'Relax, hotshot. This is not about you. '

Most have to say it about 150 times before the message gets through. For some, 600 repetitions are required. And yes, some never get the message and approach this most solemn of responsibilities thinking it's all about them.

That generated quite a response on Facebook. One comment in particular resonated with me.

Longtime friend Frank Hansen, whom I joined to his wife Sheryl half a lifetime ago, expressed concern for those who cope with "the burden and fear of handling the word of God."

Frank gets it. It is precisely that: handling the Word of God is both a burden and a fear.

Standing before groups large and small or even individuals and opening God's Word is a privilege, an opportunity, a responsibility, and a lot of other things. But it's also a burden and a fear.

We must never take this lightly. Lives hang in the balance. The burden of the Lord.

Old Testament prophets sometimes began their proclamation by announcing "The burden of the Lord" (e.g., Nahum 1:1). Any pastor who claims not to feel the burden from time to time has been playing at the business of preaching. Well, that, or delivering someone else's sermons.

Lives hang in the balance. People who hear the Word and believe may live forever. Those who reject Christ will have eternity to regret their decision.

And the determining factor sometimes can be the way the preacher declared the "whole counsel of God."

That's the scary part.

With so much at risk, no wonder some preachers think this is about them. If I do it well, God uses my message to change lives forever. And if I do it poorly or get in the way, those who reject my ineffective message will likely reject my Savior too.

The burden is enormous.

Hebrews 13:17 reminds the church that ministers will someday stand before the Lord and give account for their souls. "Let them do this with joy and not with grief," the inspired writer says, "for that would not be profitable to you."

Yikes. I'm going to account to the Lord for the people hearing me today! How awesome and frightening that is!

The fear of the Lord.

"It is a fearful thing to fall into the hands of the living God" (Hebrews 10:31). While I expect this warning applies to the sinful and rebellious, anyone with an inkling of an awareness of the greatness of our God knows the feeling. The sense of dread is almost palpable sometimes.

I'm going to stand before the Lord and give an account. Oh my.

What if I get this wrong? What if people stumble over my poor delivery and fail to see it's all about Jesus Christ? What if someone misses Heaven because I did a poor job?

It's easy to see why preachers sometimes feel it is indeed about themselves. Their preparation and prayer, their delivery and their connection with the congregation, these and a hundred other considerations occupy so much of their mind and fuel their concerns.

No wonder God has to draft people into His service. No one who knows the weightiness of responsibility and accountability would volunteer for such an assignment.

I keep thinking of that line from the Chronicles of Narnia. Here's the way Mark Buchanan tells the story in his book *Your God is Too Safe*.

In C. S. Lewis' most famous Narnia chronicle, 'The Lion, The Witch, and the Wardrobe,' the children—Peter, Susan, Lucy, and Edmund—enter Narnia through a wardrobe in their uncle's home. Edmund has already given allegiance to the witch and sneaks off to join ranks with her. The other three children go to the home of the Beavers, a wary but hospitable pair. Mr. and Mrs. Beaver tell the children that they will take them to see the King, Aslan.

'Is–is he a man?' asked Lucy.

'Aslan a man!' said Mr. Beaver sternly. 'Certainly not. I tell you he is the King of the wood and the son of the great Emperor-Beyond-the-Sea. Don't you know who is the King of Beasts? Aslan is a lion–the Lion, the great Lion.'

'Ooh,' said Susan. 'I thought he was a man. Is he–quite safe? I shall feel rather nervous about meeting a lion.'

'That you will, dearie, and make no mistake, 'said Mrs. Beaver. 'If there's anyone who can appear before Aslan without their knees knocking, they're either braver than most or else just silly.'

'Then he isn't safe?' said Lucy.

'Safe?' said Mr. Beaver, 'don't you hear what Mrs. Beaver tells you? Who said anything about safety? 'Course he isn't safe. But he's good. He's the king, I tell you.'

Let us approach this most sacred of duties with a full recognition that lives hang in the balance, that God is at work here, that we are dealing with what has been called "the fine china of human lives," and that we shall give account for every idle word (as well as all the other ones!).

Humanly speaking, this is not doable.

Only in the power and strength of the Lord can any of us hope to preach the Word with integrity and authority.

Chapter Thirty-Four

10 lessons on leading God's church, all learned the hard way.

Anyone who begins to pastor a church should recognize two big things: There are lessons to be learned if you are ever to do this well, and most of them are learned the hard way.

The scars will attest to your education.

Most of this is counter-intuitive; that is, not what one might expect.

One. Size is immaterial.

It doesn't matter to the Lord whether He saves by the few or the many (I Samuel 14:6).

Most pastors, it would appear, want to lead big churches, want to grow their church to be huge, or wish to move to a large church. Their motives may be pure; judging motives is outside my skill set. But pastoring a big church can be the hardest thing you will ever try, and far less satisfying than one would ever think.

Small bodies can be healthy too; behold the hummingbird or the honeybee.

A friend says, "At judgement, a lot of pastors are going to wish they'd led smaller congregations."

Two. The pastor's lack of formal education is no excuse.

The pastor of the small church will often have less formal training and education than he would like. Not surprisingly, he sometimes feels inferior to his colleagues with their seminary degrees. I have two thoughts on that...

—It's a mistake. He can be as learned as they are and more if he applies himself. Let the Lord's preachers not be overly impressed by certificates on the wall or titles before their name. Or depressed by their absence.

Better the preacher who's got it on the ball than one who's got it on the wall!

—He can get more formal education if he decides it's God's will and if he is willing. All seminaries and Bible colleges have online programs that make advanced education practical and affordable.

My dad, the oldest of a dozen children, had to leave school after the 7th grade and enter the coal mines at age 14. He worked inside the mines for 35 years before being disabled. But Dad never quit learning. He took correspondence courses and read constantly. When God took him to Heaven at almost 96 years of age, Mom had to cancel four or five magazine subscriptions he was still taking and reading.

Some of the finest preachers of God's word had little formal theological education.

Three. There are no lone rangers or solo acts on the Lord's team.

He sent them out two by two. (Mark 6:7; Luke 10:1)

The preacher who says pastors are not allowed to have friends and thus shuts himself off from colleagues in ministry has bought into a lie from hell that causes him to deceive himself, starve his spirit and limit his ministry. While a pastor may choose not to have close friends among his own members, there is every reason for him to make friends with other ministers who serve the Lord well. Failing to do so limits himself and hurts the kingdom work.

Furthermore, he must have co-workers alongside him. Paul needed Barnabas, Silas, Timothy, and others. Read the last chapters of Romans and First Corinthians and ask God to forgive you for trying to do this work alone.

Four. Doing a job yourself is easier than enlisting and training someone else, but it's a violation of your calling.

"Make disciples," said our Lord. That mandate calls for us to help people come into the kingdom, then nurture and grow them to the point they will know the Word, can share the Word, and can make disciples of others.

Barnabas did not find it convenient to leave Antioch and travel to Tarsus "to seek Saul." (Acts 11:25). But in doing so, he connected the man called as an evangelist to the Gentiles with the opportunity tailor-made for him. We are forever grateful to the best disciple-maker in Scripture, Barnabas!

Five. I cannot lead people to do what I'm not doing.

God did not send me to be a talker only, but first and foremost a doer. Not as a coach only, but as a player-coach. It is enough for the disciple to become like the teacher, said our Lord.

So, as a pastor and church leader, my job is to show them how. Not just tell them. (James 1:22. First Peter 5:2-3. First John 3:18).

Six. Not only is it hard to start tithing our income, sharing our faith, and dealing with

146

trials, God planned that it would be that way.

Watch the butterfly emerge from its chrysalis. The struggle, we are told, is an essential part of its development. Without the struggle, the creature dies.

Only people of faith and determination will set out to learn to tithe and witness and understand the Bible, then stay with it until they are able to do it well. Everyone else drops by the wayside, intending to wait until it's easy. In doing so, they're wanting what never was and never shall be. "Without faith, it is impossible to please God" (Hebrews 11:6).

Members of our churches need reminding that God does not need our money. He is not suffering from a cash flow problem. God is trying to grow disciples. That accounts for the hundreds of teachings on money found in the Word. You wonder when we are ever going to understand this. And when are preachers going to quit fearing criticism and teach stewardship until people do it!

Seven. God makes His leaders servants, not bosses or lords or bigshots.

I have met husbands who want to lord it over their wives because "God made me the head of the home and told her to submit!" Such men may call themselves believers, but they are pagan to the heart and may never have been saved. They certainly don't know the first thing about God's word or Jesus' heart. If they did, they would know that they are sent as servants. "Christ loved the church and gave Himself for it" (Ephesians 5:25).

Bullies on the playground or dictators in the pulpit are cancers of the body and should not be tolerated. The parable of all parables on this subject is Luke 17:7-10. We must keep saying to ourselves—even when we have done everything Jesus required— "I am only an unworthy servant; just doing my duty."

Eight. The more righteous we are, the less we will be aware of it. "Moses knew not that his face did shine" (Exodus 34:29).

I said to the 75-year-old saint in our church, "Marguerite, you are the most Christ-like person I know." She didn't flinch. "Oh honey," she said to her young minister, "if you only knew." I did know, in a way, but have learned a hundred times since: Those closest to the Lord are the last to know it. The nearer to the light we get, the more imperfections and blemishes we will see.

Beware of ever thinking you have arrived. "Let him who thinks he stands take heed lest he fall" (First Corinthians 10:12).

Nine. The Lord's servants who serve well are going to run into the buzz saw of opposition from the nay-sayers, do-nothings, status-quo lovers, and carnal. That's no fun, but it's not all bad.

Reading the mandate of the disciples in Matthew 10:16ff, we cannot say we were not warned. But it has ever been this way. We are swimming upstream in a downstream world.

Jesus prepared us for this by saying that whoever receives us is receiving Him, whoever listens to us is listening to Him, and whoever rejects us is rejecting Him. (See Matthew 10:40 and Luke 10:16.). If being treated like Jesus is not enough for us, we're in the wrong calling.

Ten. Not only does the Lord allow His choice servants to suffer sometimes, but He also even plans for that to happen. Again, see Matthew 10:16ff.

Caesar ain't coming to your revival, preacher. So, the Lord will be needing someone to get arrested for preaching. Then, when the exalted ruler has to rule on this case, he will order the saint in chains to "tell us what you've been preaching." That's how it worked with Paul (see 2 Timothy 4:16-17), and how it has been with His choice servants ever since.

When Paul and Silas were falsely charged, then beaten and jailed, even though their backs were open wounds left untreated and they were hungry, tired, and hurting, "about midnight, they began praying and singing hymns of praise to God. And the other prisoners were listening to them (Acts 16:25). Don't miss that.

They're always listening and watching when God's people suffer unjustly. This is a truism which God uses to reach many for Himself. Outsiders watch to see how we handle the pain, whether we practice what we preach, and if God's people love each other as Jesus commanded.

No one wants to suffer. No one volunteers to hurt. But sometimes it's the only way for some people to get the message.

What God's faithful must never do is groan and bellyache and say, "Why me, Lord?" Your suffering may turn out to be the highest compliment the Father ever gave you. Early believers rejoiced they were counted worthy to suffer. (See Acts 5:41).

Chapter Thirty-Five

Scripture has some strange heroes; we can learn from them all.

Anyone could have told Bartimaeus not to make a fool of himself that day when Jesus came to town. As soon as someone said the Man of Galilee was on His way into the city, the blind beggar commenced to yell and carry on, trying to attract the Lord's attention. When the city fathers tried to shush him "Hey, we're trying to make a good impression here, friend. "Hold it down!" Bartimaeus hollered that much louder.

Anyone could have told him he would have other opportunities to meet Jesus, that the Lord was still a young man some said in His early 30sand He would be back this way again.

No need to lose one's dignity. All things come to him who waits, someone must have said.

They were wrong of course. This was Jesus' final trip through Jericho and the last chance Bartimaeus would ever have to meet Him. He had no way of knowing that. All he knew was that Jesus Christ was the focus of his hopes and dreams, and that given the opportunity to meet him, nothing and no one would stand in his way.

I like to call Bartimaeus the smartest man in Jericho.

Anyone could have told Zaccheus he was wasting his time trying to get near Jesus that same day in Jericho. This little shrimp of a man, tax collector, unscrupulous businessman, traitor to his nation, and thus despised by one and all lost what dignity he had that morning, running around trying to find a good spot to see the Savior. He ended up climbing a tree and hanging from its branches, just for a glimpse of the Man of Galilee.

Anyone could have told him he was not likely to be even noticed by Jesus, certainly not to be personally greeted by Him, and not in a million years to have the Lord and the disciples come by his home for the noon meal that day. Anyone could have told him his record of disdain for the poor and dishonesty in his dealings had surely built an impenetrable wall between him and the Savior.

But they would have been wrong. What they did not reckon on was Jesus' compassion for the lost and the seeking. And since anyone could have told Zaccheus how unworthy he was and not to bother the Lord, Jesus took the initiative: he stopped at that tree, called Zaccheus down, and invited himself to lunch at his home. That day, Zaccheus met the Saviour. Jesus changed his heart and Zaccheus changed his behavior.

Here's to Zaccheus, the richest man in town.

Anyone could have told Joshua that the walls of Jericho would not be falling down just because his people circled it 13 times and blew trumpets. Anyone could have told him the harlot Rahab could not be depended on to keep her word, and they would surely have advised her that with her sordid past she would not be accepted into the Israeli family after Jericho fell.

But they would have been wrong. The walls fell as God said, Jericho was defeated, Rahab's family was rescued, and she went on to become a great-great-great-great-great-great- great-great grandmother of King David and thus occupied a spot in the genealogy of the Lord Jesus Himself, according to Matthew chapter 1.

One would think we would have learned by now not to attach so much weight to the opinions of others. Even our religious publications pad their issues with the latest polls on what people are thinking on this issue or that one. As though it mattered.

The only thing that matters is obedience. And the only obedience that counts is submission to the Will of God.

The prayer Saul of Tarsus prayed that day outside Damascus is still as good as it gets and as much as the Lord requires: "What wilt Thou have me to do?" (Acts 22:10)

Anyone could tell you you're wasting your time and throwing away your life by stepping out of the crowd to follow Jesus. They would say you only go around once in this life and you have to grab for all the gusto you can get, or other foolishness like that. They might cite you examples of people who went overboard for religion and became idiots; there certainly is no lack of case studies.

Jesus had something to say on this subject. "He who loses his life for my sake finds it" (Matthew 10:39).

Or this: What does it profit a man to gain the whole world and lose his own soul? And then, (assuming a fellow makes such a devil's bargain) what will he give in exchange for his soul? (Matthew 16:26)

Pray we will be as smart as the blind beggar of Jericho and grab the first opportunity to meet the Savior. One never knows which will be his final opportunity.

Pray we will be as wise as Zaccheus who although at the opposite end of the economic ladder as Bartimaeus, knew the hollowness of wealth and the foolishness of self- indulgence and did what he had to in order to get to Jesus.

Pray we will start believing in the Lord's word and desire His will above all else.

There will come a day when every eye will see just how true Christ is, every tongue will admit how accurate His claims are, and every knee will drop into the dust in acknowledgment that He alone is Lord and no one else. When that moment comes, anyone could tell you how smart you were to have followed Jesus Christ in your lifetime.

Anyone could tell you that.

Chapter Thirty-Six

Ten of the scariest times in a pastor's life

I sit there listening while my pastor friend tells what he's going through in his church. And sometimes all the alarms go off. I realize he is in a dangerous place in his ministry.

Not always, but sometimes, I can tell him this. If I sense a leading from the Holy Spirit or if he and I already have a close enough relationship, I'll interrupt him.

"Brother Bob, can we pause the narrative here a moment? I need to point something out to you."

"My friend, you are exposed. You are a sitting duck. Life has drawn a target on your back. Satan has his gunsights on you."

"You'd better do something big in a hurry or you're going to get in bad trouble." He sits there stunned, without a clue.

"What do you mean? I'm doing everything I know to work my way through this."

I say, "I'm not talking about what you are going through. I'm talking about where you are personally at this moment. You are in a vulnerable spot, and you need to move before something bad happens."

Older, veteran pastors have learned the hard way to tread softly through this dark valley they have entered. They have seen the carcasses of their peers strewn about, brought down by ego or depression or temptation.

It's the young minister who is more likely to try to brave it out alone. It's the young pastor who is more prone to end up a victim instead of a victor.

Here are 10 danger zones for the pastor to watch out for.

On the highway, signs alert motorists to the scary places up ahead. They are instructed to drive carefully, to slow down, to watch for obstructions.

Would that we had some way to tell God's servants they are entering such zones in their ministry.

1. You are tired.

The sign on the highway might say: Warning, ministers of the Gospel: For the next ten miles, you are tired. Your reactions will be slow, your mind is not sharp, you may find yourself in trouble before you know it.

We think of Elijah. After that great victory over the Canaanites at Mount Carmel, the exuberant man of God ran nearly 25 miles to Jezreel. Arriving there, he learned that Jezebel wanted him dead. Instead of reacting in faith—as he had done on the mountaintop—his fatigue betrayed him.

Jezebel's threats, her dogged worship of Baal, and her control over Israel burst his balloon and destroyed his confidence. Fearing for his life now, he fled, ending up at Beersheba, a hundred miles south.

When we are tired, we don't feel like reading our Bible or praying or doing the Lord's work. As Elijah was to find, what he needed was nourishment and sleep (I Kings 19:5-7).

The minister who thinks of himself as above the need for proper food and rest is setting himself up for a failure in a dramatic way.

2. You are bored.

The sign on the highway reads: Warning: Boredom. Ennui for the next dozen miles. Be careful of distractions. Keep your hand on the wheel and your eye on the road.

We think of David. At the time when most kings were away defending their country, he stayed home. "But David remained at Jerusalem" (II Samuel 11:1). One night when he could not sleep, he rose from his bed and walked on his rooftop and spotted Bathsheba taking her bath. Nothing good followed that.

David had cleared off his schedule and had no important goals remaining before him. There was a void in his life at this point, making him a sitting duck for temptation.

Every minister gets bored occasionally, no matter how exciting his ministry is and how rewarding his relationships are. It's human. What he does with the boredom may well determine whether the rest of his life is spent working for God or picking up the pieces of his shattered dreams.

Your infernal enemy is smart. As Martin Luther said in his hymn, "On earth is not his equal." Satan can see that you are bored. He hears your sermons and knows when the joy has gone from them. He watches your family and spots when the excitement has left your marriage.

This is the time to kick your prayer life and personal devotional life into high gear, child of God.

3. You find yourself at a critical crossroads.

The sign on the highway reads: Intersection ahead. Decision time. Choose carefully your route because you will be on it the next 25 miles.

A change of career, a re-direction in your ministry, a new understanding of God's will for your life—all are critical intersections. These are dangerous times.

In my late 30s, I was bored in my ministry and in our marriage. The president of one of our seminaries invited me to campus to discuss the possibility of taking a staff position.

Margaret and I drove down and spent a couple of days in interviews, discussion and prayer. I recall her tears as she looked at the sad choices of homes available to us on campus. As we left, I was 95 percent sure I would accept the president's invitation.

On the long drive home, God changed my heart. I realized I was already doing the ministry He had called me to, and that I loved my wife and adored my children. I did not want to serve anywhere else or be married to anyone else. I phoned the president and thanked him kindly, then rededicated myself to pastoring that church and leading my family.

A pastor I know resigned a large church in Texas and moved to a smaller one in Mississippi. Later, he admitted to a friend that he had made that decision at a bad time. "I was just exhausted," he said. "And when I got rested up, I was pastor of the wrong church."

I heard one old preacher advise, "Never make critical decisions on Monday or when you are tired." Good counsel.

4. You are angry.

The highway sign reads: Caution: Anger. Blurs your vision, hardens your heart, exaggerates your reactions. Pull over to the side of the road and get control of yourself.

We don't require a biblical example to teach us about the dangers of uncontrolled anger or the benefits of taming this lion. Paul advises, "Let not the sun go down upon your wrath" (Ephesians 4:26). The point of that is to say a) we all get angry from time to time, but b) it needs to be handled promptly. Undealt-with anger is a poison which contaminates everything it touches and destroys every relationship.

In my experience when we are backslidden—that is, out of fellowship with the Lord—we become critical of God's people and angry at the least offense. Likewise, when we are close to Him, we love those same people and are understanding and forgiving toward those who do us wrong.

The anger, therefore, seems to be a "road closed" sign that would interfere with our loving people and building strong and lasting relationships.

Deal with your anger, pastor. Do it before you leave the house today. Leave it at the foot of the cross.

5. You are lonely.

The highway sign reads: Loneliness makes you a target for temptation, lowers your resistance to impurities, and weakens your resolve. Get over it quickly.

Criminologists say that no one ever commits a crime without first justifying it. I suspect those in the Lord's work who step across the lines of fidelity in marriage excuse what they are doing with protestations of loneliness.

You may be lonely. No one is saying otherwise. There is a great deal of unhappiness and even loneliness in many a marriage. And yet, that does not justify breaking the marriage vow.

In his book *The Myth of the Greener Grass*, Allan Peterson reminds us that Satan will use good intentions with good people to entice them to do wrong.

This is not the place to go into all the cures for loneliness in marriage, but our point is that this condition makes the man or woman of God vulnerable to temptation and enticement.

Someone told me of a minister who lost his pastorate, his family, and all the esteem he had built up over the years by an affair with a woman he was counseling. "What was stunning about this," my friend said, "was that the woman was a notorious adulterer. The pastor knew full well what she was and still gave up everything for her."

Loneliness makes one so vulnerable. Be aware. Stay alert. Stay on your knees.

6. You are stressed.

The sign beside the road reads: Stress is a killer. Marital stress, financial stress, internal church stress—all are signals that the bridge could be out on your highway. Slow down and pay close attention.

In the cartoon, the older woman tells the young one, "Stress is not par for the course, dear. It is the course."

Stress is just another word for the pressures that close in upon us. We all have them. The only person without some kind of stress is resting comfortably in the cemetery.

Every marriage encounters stress. Every human has to deal with financial stress at one time or the other. And in churchwork, stress comes in truckloads—people conflicts, schedule conflicts, money problems, doctrinal clashes, personal disagreements, denominational strife, the list is endless.

By itself, stress is not bad. It's a given. It's always going to be there. As the TV character said, "It's always something." Yes, it is.

We build muscle by putting stress on it. When God wants to build His children, He allows us to go through stressful times.

It is good for me that I have been afflicted, that I may learn your statutes (Ps. 119:71).

7. You are smug.

The sign reads: Self-satisfied in your achievements? Smug in your contentment? Do not be surprised if you are blind-sided by some highway obstacle. You will be in the ditch gasping for air and never know what hit you.

The Apostle Paul said, "let him who thinks he stands take heed lest he fall" (I Corinthians 10:12). There is such a thing as too much confidence.

The trick for the servant of the Lord is to find the balance between courage and confidence on the one hand and humility and a sense of dependence on the other. The cocky young preacher—they are not an endangered species, unfortunately, but seem to arise anew with each generation—would do well to study II Corinthians 12 where Paul admits to a thorn in the flesh that would not go away. Eventually, he learned that God's grace is sufficient and "when I am weak, then am I strong."

8. You are depressed.

The sign on the roadside reads: Feeling blue? Don't take it out on the rest of the world! Look up!

Everyone gets depressed at one time or the other. Mondays seem to bring depression for many in the ministry. Their fatigue is surely a factor in that.

It helps to remember that some of the Lord's best workers have battled depression.

Charles Haddon Spurgeon and Elizabeth Elliott come to mind. Mrs. Elliott wrote in one of her books that when she was depressed, she would be unable to make work plans for that day. "So, I learned just to do the next thing," she wrote.

She would make the beds, then ask, "What is the next thing?" If that was to wash the dishes, she did that. And so on. At the end of the day, she had been productive.

What she did not do was let depression rule her life.

9. You are discouraged, maybe even defeated.

The sign on the highway of the ministry reads: Beware of low places! Watch out for unexpected blowouts, failures, setbacks. They can wreck you permanently.

I've known this to happen. Someone has a blowout on the highway and while working to repair the damage, gets hit by a passing motorist.

In the small town in Louisiana's bayou country where I was pastoring, US Highway 90 went through the center of everything. Traffic moved through at 70 mph, as I recall. One day there was a fender-bender. Nothing major. The parties were standing around, inspecting the damage. Suddenly, a car blew through at the speed limit or above and killed a woman standing beside her car.

Breakdowns are bad enough, but often they bring other, more complicated problems. So, when you have a setback in life, be careful. Things could go south in a hurry unless you are careful.

Never forget that discouragement is one of the devil's great fields of play. You must not linger there long. Find out the source of your real encouragement and go there as quickly as possible.

10. You are on a high. Have just had a great, great success. Watch out.

The sign reads: High place ahead! Alert. You may be distracted by the view or the thin air. Pay attention.

Remember the line in a couple of places in the Old Testament about "walking on my high places"? (Habakkuk 3:19 is my favorite.) Think of it as an "Everest" experience. You are on top of the world. The view is magnificent, the feeling is exuberant, but the air is thin, and the footing is slippery.

So, after your great success—the building campaign, the publication of your book, the doctorate, whatever—be careful. This is a vulnerable time for you, minister of God.

Be on the alert, man and woman of God. Be sober. Be vigilant.

Your enemy, your adversary, your opponent, the original slanderer, the one who hates you with a passion, that one would love nothing better than to sabotage your ministry,

He walks about like a roaring lion. Hungry, prowling, relentless, powerful, deadly. Seeking whom he may devour. He comes to steal, to kill, and to destroy.

"Resist him, steadfast in faith" (I Peter 5:8-9).

"But the God of all grace, after you have suffered a while, perfect you, establish you, strengthen you, and settle you. To Him be the glory and the dominion forever and ever. Amen" (I Peter 5:10-11).

Chapter Thirty-Seven

True Humility in the Pulpit. What a Rarity!

"Except you are converted and become like children, you shall not enter the kingdom of heaven" (Matthew 18:3).

What's lacking in the great majority of religious experts—of all tribes, all beliefs, all everything!--is a childlike humility.

I've sat across from the salespeople hawking Jehovah's Witness and Mormon doctrine door to door and been amazed at the sheer gall and arrogance of these know-it-alls.

I've sat in the auditoriums and classrooms when prophecy teachers were spreading out their charts and telling far more than they could ever know, pronouncing their anathema upon anyone daring to believe otherwise and taking no prisoners in the process.

I've sat in massive conferences among thousands of my peers and heard ignorance spouted as truth but camouflaged with alliteration and pious phrases and encouraged and affirmed by thundering echoes of "amens" and "hallelujahs".

--In every case, I longed to hear someone say, "We see through a glass darkly...." (I Corinthians 13:12).

--To hear someone say, "I have not arrived. I press toward the mark...." (Philippians 3:12-13).

--To hear someone say, "We do not know how to pray as we should...." (Romans 8:26)

--To hear someone say, "That which I am doing, I do not understand. I am not practicing what I would like to do, but I am doing the very thing I hate" (Romans 7:15).

Where is the childlike spirit we hear so much of in the Word?

1) I can hear someone say, "Well, we enter the kingdom by that spirit, but thereafter, as we learn and grow, we become teachers and instructors and gain confidence and are allowed to become more bombastic."

Rubbish.

We are expected to be of a childlike spirit all our lives. We are to remain teachable all the way to the end. We are instructed to grow in the fruit of the Spirit, and that includes such traits as gentleness, humility, self-control, and faithfulness (Galatians 5:22-23).

There is no point of maturity when believers may cast aside all humility and childlikeness and run roughshod over the flock or call down curses upon those who dare to disagree.

2) We have seen arrogant unbelievers transform almost seamlessly into arrogant believers.

At one point they knew nothing and railed against anyone claiming to have answers. Then, suddenly, once they were converted, they knew everything and castigated anyone claiming to believe something different.

Meanwhile, the quiet believers who work hard to learn and grow and serve, but who still struggle with questions of Scripture and some matters of faith, are shunted off to the side as irrelevant in the Kingdom.

"Let him who stands take heed lest he fall" (I Corinthians 10:12). Children fall a lot, so they must be careful.

3) The greatest stumbling block to the prominent atheists and humanistic philosophers coming to faith in Jesus Christ is often the requirement that they become as little children. If they could be grandfathered in or brought into the Kingdom under a (ahem) special arrangement for the gifted and wise, some would join Jesus in a heartbeat. But to admit that they know nothing and need to be taught—sometimes by the unlearned who happen to know Jesus from a lifetime of serving Him—is asking more than they can give.

"Truly I say to you, whoever does not receive the kingdom of God like a child shall not enter it at all" (Mark 10:15).

In his masterful work "The Great Divorce," C. S. Lewis imagines a busload of hell's residents visiting Heaven to see if they might want to transfer. In Lewis' story, told to make some wonderful points, anyone on the bus who wishes to remain in Heaven will be allowed to do so.

To no one's surprise, none of the hellish ones "fit" there. The things they lived for on earth just did not work in Heaven. Lewis tells of a learned Anglican bishop among the group from hell—I imagine that must have smarted!—who was considering remaining in Heaven just so long as he was given certain assurances.

"I should want a guarantee that you are taking me to a place where I shall find a wider sphere of usefulness—and scope for the talents that God has given me—and an atmosphere of free inquiry—in short, all that one means by civilization and—er—the spiritual life."

His celestial guide responds, "No. I can promise you none of these things. No sphere of usefulness: you are not needed there at all. No scope for your talents: only forgiveness for having perverted them. No atmosphere of inquiry, for I will bring you to the land not of questions but of answers, and you shall see the face of God."

As the bishop protests and keeps insisting on the free exercise of his intellectual pursuits, the Heavenly One says, "Listen! Once you were a child. Once you knew what inquiry was for. There was a time when you asked questions because you wanted answers and were glad when you had found them. Become that child again, even now."

The Heavenly Guide added, "We know nothing of religion here (in Heaven). We think only of Christ. We know nothing of speculation. Come and see...."

Suddenly the bishop remembers why he will not be able to remain in Heaven. "I'd nearly forgotten. Of course, I can't come (to Heaven) with you. I have to be back (in hell) next Friday to read a paper. We have a little theological society down there. Oh yes!"

In your church each Sunday, after your minister preaches the Gospel of Jesus Christ, it's likely he issues a call for people who wish to respond to stand to their feet and walk forward, down that lengthy aisle, all the way to the front, and there to pray with a counselor "who will assist you in giving your life to the Savior and inviting Him into your life." That is a humbling experience. Ask anyone around you, for most of them have done it.

And that's just the point. If you can humble yourself enough to confess Jesus publicly and to join with these imperfect believers in trying to serve Him, in learning His word and growing in faith, if you can become as a little child, you can enter that door.

That door was built for child-size people.

All others exclude themselves.

Chapter Thirty-Eight

Pastor, ask something great from us.

The reason many of us pastors keep returning to the same few quotes is that they are definitive for us. They so embed themselves in our consciousness that they end up defining who we are.

Somewhere I read of a friend who accompanied Abraham Lincoln to church. Afterwards, the friend asked how Abe had liked the sermon. The future president's answer was something like: "He may be a good man, but he's not a good preacher. A good preacher would have asked us to do something great, and he didn't."

Sometimes a preacher needs a comeuppance like that from a layperson—calling us back to reality, insisting we remember our calling, that we not get so caught up in the minutiae of our work that we forget to issue the clarion call to God and righteousness.

But this is not about Lincoln. It's about his comment, and his excellent statement that a good preacher calls on people to do great things. I completely agree and am betting most pastors would also.

Now, my opinion is that the typical pastor does not call on people to do little things in place of "great" ones. That's not what Lincoln heard, I'm guessing. The pastor did not issue an invitation for people to sign up for janitorial work, volunteer to teach the 3rd grade boys, or bring casseroles on Wednesday nights.

Instead of being that specific, that detailed, and that minor, the preacher did something else.

He issued a broad invitation to do general things without ever making himself clear on what they ought to be doing.

One of the cardinal sins of sermons is to issue fuzzy calls for people to do nebulous things.

Somewhere I heard of a visiting preacher who delivered several sermons in a row on patriotism and the threat of Communism (back when the USSR was in full flower) to America. Toward the end of the week, he lamented to the pastor that he could not understand why the altar call was not getting more response.

The pastor said, "What do you want them to do—join the FBI?"

Growing up, I cannot count all the sermons I heard in which pastors told us that we were to share our faith with others, to win souls, to evangelize the world, to reach the lost. If a single one ever gave us instructions on how to do that, I'd be surprised. In my mind, they didn't.

Only when I was in seminary preparing for a pastoral ministry did I come across a booklet by the delightful title, Here's How to Win Souls. Texas Pastor Gene Edwards was sharing through photos and text precisely how a believer could knock on someone's door and lead them through the steps of understanding the gospel of Jesus and through the prayer of commitment. It was like a feast to a starving man. I read it, devoured it even, and went forth to practice it. I found it on target in every way and am indebted to Pastor Edwards to this day.

Generality is the curse of modern sermons.

I speak as one who has been there, done that.

As a young pastor, I dutifully bought several file cabinets and folders and began amassing clippings for illustrations that would adorn future sermons. In time, the files bulged with items under every conceivable topic. But the thickest folder, the one filled with more illustrations and stories than any ten of the others, was labeled: "Dedication."

When I couldn't think of a subject a particular story fit, I'd drop it into that file.

Whether that was the cause or the effect, my early sermons all seemed to issue in one broad invitation for people to "dedicate yourself to Jesus Christ."

Anything wrong with that? Not as far as it goes. The problem is it doesn't go far enough.

Jim, the fellow in the pew sitting beside his wife Darlene and daughter Brandi, takes in my sermon, hears the invitation, and thinks, "Okay, fine. I want to dedicate myself to Jesus.

Now, tell me how I do that, why I should, and what it means in the daily operation of my life."

The pastor knows Jim. He knows Jim manages a retail furniture store, that he loves classical music, and has a deeply inquisitive mind. Jim loves a great challenge and enjoys doing new things. But Jim and Darlene are sitting close to Bryan and Rebecca, in front of Bo and Oleta, across the aisle from Rudy and Elizabeth, and not far from James and Ann. Every person is different. Every situation is unique. Some have been believers for ages, some are new to the faith. Some are deacons and teachers; others are spiritually in grade school.

No one prescription fits all. And that's why the preacher tends to shy away from specifics. Bryan is the youth minister, Bo runs a competing furniture store, Rudy operates a plant nursery, and James is a professor at the local university.

Darlene is a college student, Rebecca a stay-at-home mom, Oleta is in New York City one day and San Francisco the next, and Ann is a counselor.

Try to make one sermon fit all of those people, Mr. Lincoln! That's the preacher's challenge. And it can be done.

What a preacher does is to tell a story.

He brings the sermon to its climax in which he calls on God's people to "present your bodies a living sacrifice." Yep, he asks them to "dedicate themselves" to the Lord.

But he doesn't stop there, which is what I did for the longest.

When you are nearing the sermon's exit ramp is no place to stop. It's okay to give a turn signal and begin slowing down, but don't stop here. If you do, the audience is stranded.

Get them off the highway and onto the lane where they live. Bring it home.

What an effective preacher does here is to tell what happened when one person made such a commitment.

He tells a story. One they can relate to, can understand, appreciate, and learn from.

I had brought a sermon on tithing from Malachi 3:10. In it, I emphasized that this may be the only place in Scripture where God calls on people to "prove me" or "put me to the test."

I did not just challenge people to tithe their incomes to the Lord through His church. I did, but not in the usual way.

What I did was issue a call for people to try tithing for the three months of the summer, June-July-August. "And see what a difference the Lord makes in your life."

At the end of the summer, I told them, if you do not believe that tithing your income has made a great difference in your life, that you have not been blessed in a hundred ways as a result, if you will tell me and ask for it, we will refund every dime you contributed.

You may believe I had cleared that with our church's lay leadership before making such an announcement. They were all willing to give it a try.

I emphasized to the congregation that I'm not predicting or promising material blessings from your tithing this summer. They may or may not come. But there are hundreds of other kinds of blessings promised to those who are faithful stewards and generous givers worth far more than the money in your pocket.

We came up with a name for this prove-the-Lord three-month-period: "Summer Blessed." In the church bulletin or from the pulpit, we would urge our people to "make this a summer blessed by the Lord."

Jokesters teased that, "Well, summer blessed, and some aren't!"

When that summer ended, one person asked for his contributions to be returned. I told a couple of the appropriate church leaders, then the financial secretary checked the man's records and wrote him a check.

Many, many others in the church wrote notes glowing with appreciation for what God had done in their lives as a result of their getting priorities straight and investing in spiritual matters.

One couple wrote a letter which I still keep and read from time to time, telling how they had gotten married just a year before, burdened with debts and owning two old cars. By tithing their income and being responsible, now, one year later, they had paid off all the debts, had upgraded their vehicles, and were about to relocate to another city where they had been offered better jobs.

Okay, now. See what we did here?

We were at the exit ramp of this article, ready to shut it down. However, it needed an example to get us home, a story that illustrates one way to do the very thing we've been talking about here.

What I did not do was to try to encompass every situation pastor will encounter. Every church is different, every pastor is unique, and the makeup of your congregation is unlike anyone else's.

So, I picked one example out of my own past and told that.

I had asked something great of the people—that they prove God's faithfulness to His promises by doing something hard for themselves.

The challenge is to stay general enough and to get specific enough. To find the balance.

Never forget that you are engaging in big things, matters involving

Almighty God and the beloved, fallen Creation from His own hand, people for whom Jesus Christ died.

"Now unto Him who is able to do exceedingly abundantly beyond all that we ask or think, according to the power that works in us, to Him be the glory in the church and in the Lord Jesus to all generations forever and ever. Amen." (Ephesians 3:20-21)

Thou art coming to a King, Large petitions with thee bring,

For His grace and power are such None can ever ask too much.

from John Newton

Ask ye what great thing I know That delights and stirs me so? What is the high reward I win?

Who's the name I glory in? Jesus Christ, the crucified.

from Johann C. Schwedler

Chapter Thirty-Nine

Let the pastor decide he's going to preach the Bible.

My journal tells of the time our family attended the Billy Joel concert at the New Orleans Arena along with 10 or 15 thousand of our closest friends. If you like Joel's music "Piano Man," "The Longest Time," "She's Always a Woman to Me", you'll understand why a couple of oldsters like Margaret and me were there. Not many our age made the trek, though. Too much trouble. Too expensive (tickets were over 80 bucks). Easier to buy the CD and stay home.

Now, Billy Joel was great. He gave a terrific show; he is an incredible musician. But it was loud. Man, was it loud. Some of the numbers, I sat there thinking, "I'm sure there is a kernel of music somewhere on the inside of all that noise." But I think I know why they made it so loud, added blinding lights, and rocked that building: for the young people. He was appealing to the youth. And apparently, he did, because they were there in surprising strength. They knew the words better than I did.

A couple of times I thought my cell phone was going off. It was my body vibrating.

At the end, I decided that even though Billy Joel is of my generation or close to it, I am most definitely not his target audience. And I'm okay with that.

Earlier that evening before we left the house, our back door neighbor Bill called as I was setting out the garbage cans. "Joe, you got a minute?" I said, "Just about that."

He said, "I preached a sermon recently, and now my home church wants me to preach it there. I need your help."

Bill was a Methodist. He owned a farm in the country but lived and worked here in the city. We were neighbors for some sixteen years. He's a good guy. Quiet. A family man.

"What did you preach about?" I asked.

He said, "That we need to return Methodism to the old ways." I said, "What old ways?"

He answered, "To the ways of John Wesley."

I said, "Okay, so what are the bad things you see in your denomination these days?" He answered, "Hillary Clinton is a Methodist." That is exactly what he said.

I said, "What? Are you talking about liberal politics?"

He said, "Yes. And women in the pulpit. Women bishops. Gender-neutral scriptures. That sort of thing."

I said, "What Bible text did you have?" He said, "I didn't really have a text."

Bill is right. That sermon needs a lot of help, maybe more than I can give. He promised to write out his sermon and let me look it over.

I know a good text for Bill's sermon. Jeremiah 6:16 reads: "Stand by the ways and see and ask for the ancient paths, where the good way is, and walk in it, and you will find rest for your souls."

The problem, of course, is identifying exactly what that old path, the good way, really is and then finding it.

I could have told Bill about the Windsor Town Hall which Sir Christopher Wren designed over 300 years ago. After it was completed, the city manager refused to pay the bill, insisting there were too few columns to hold up the building. When Wren protested that the columns seemed to be doing a good job of it, the manager was adamant. More columns or no money.

The great architect had four more columns installed in the Town Hall, each identical to the others in every respect but one: they lacked a half inch reaching the ceiling. They were not supporting anything.

That municipal building still stands in Windsor as a "Guild Hall."

Now, let's turn this into a metaphor. Let that town hall building represent various structures in our society. Each has columns that are cosmetic for appearance only—as well as columns that are load- bearing. Remove the load-bearing columns and the whole building collapses. So, here's what happens...

When each new generation arrives on the scene, they begin pushing at columns, trying to clear away room to erect their own structures.

We hope the youngsters learn what cosmetic structures are and what is load bearing before they begin shoving too hard.

Some of us can recall how the youth of the 1960s were trying to tear down the schools and the family and the government, all load-bearing institutions which must be maintained for a stable society. They did a lot of damage, some of which has not been repaired to this day.

They're doing this in Bill's church and in a lot of other denominations: throwing out centuries-old traditions and replacing them with modern practices more to their liking.

True, some traditions should be discarded. We recall the Lord telling the Pharisees of His day that their traditions were strangling the Word of God (Matthew 15:3).

Some traditions, however, are essential to the well-being of society. The home. The church. The school. Integrity in government. A free press.

Lord, help us to know which is which.

It's fine for a concert artist to adapt his music to the younger generation. It's not a big loss. But what about when your church replaces the pipe organ with an electronic keyboard and a set of digital drums? Is that all right? What about when the church leaders pack the hymnals away and project choruses on a screen?

Or when they change the wording in the Bible so that God is no longer a "He" or "Father," but "Thou" and "Creator." How does that suit you?

Is it all right for your church to decide that twenty centuries of traditional interpretation of Scripture is in error and that homosexuals should be accepted as full-fledged members of the church and even ordained as leaders? That's being done in more and more churches.

This generation of churches is the first in history to approve abortion on demand. Does that make it right?

Sometime in the dark of deep night, the old clock malfunctioned and struck 13 times. Grandpa rose out of his sleep and shook Grandma. "Honey, wake up!" he said. "It's later than it has ever been before!"

It is indeed.

I could tell Bill about the time I was in a Methodist church in a small Mississippi town and noticed a poster promoting evangelism and revival in that denomination. I thought of that as rather remarkable in that denomination (see my admission below) and moved in closer to read the poster. Underneath the bold headlines, the text was calling on people to return to the teachings and ways of John Wesley. That was the revival they were pushing.

I was disappointed.

No one asked me, but I would have said to them, "Friend, it's not about John Wesley. It's about Jesus Christ. Today's generation doesn't care a whit about Mr. Wesley. Or John Calvin for that matter. Or George Whitefield or Jacob Arminius or even Martin Luther."

Granted, maybe they should. I write as a church history major who benefited from the study of all these church warriors.

Today, people are trying to find their way in life, trying to get through the day and raise their kids and survive in this stressful world. It's pointless to try to filter Scripture's teachings through a citizen of the 18th century when they could open the Word of God and read Jesus' message for themselves. That, I submit, is what John Wesley wanted in the first place.

My admission: I have a lot of Methodism in my DNA. For four years as a child, we attended the Methodist church in a small West Virginia mining town. As a teenager, I attended Methodist Youth Fellowship with my girlfriend. I graduated from a Methodist college. My college roommate became a UMC preacher. My sister served her Methodist church as treasurer for decades. I became Southern Baptist as a sophomore in college when some family members insisted we visit the large Baptist church on a Wednesday night. One visit and I knew. God wanted me here. I was baptized there, met my wife there, was called into the ministry, ordained, and married there. Definitely, a God thing.

I'm on the side of anyone wishing to have a God-sent revival. I want them to emulate the best practices of previous generations. But I grieve when they or any of God's people trash the traditions that have stood them in good stead for centuries in order to accommodate their practices to the tastes of outsiders who never have and will not ever share their values.

It's not about Billy Joel or John Wesley, but about Jesus Christ who alone is the Way, the Truth, and the Life.

Chapter Forty

How to take criticism and make the most of it

Let me say up front that I do not have a formula for enabling anyone to enjoy criticism. No one finds pleasure in being told he is wrong, that she needs to change the way she does something, that an apology is in order. Even the most accurate and helpful criticism can be painful when it arrives. How much more an unfair accusation flung our way.

Simply put, there are two kinds of criticisms: the fair and the unfair. The truthful and the slanderous. The well-intentioned and the mean-spirited.

If you live long enough, you will encounter both kinds. How you deal with them will determine a thousand things about your character and your happiness.

Chuck Swindoll has something to say that fits here:

Anybody can accept a reward graciously, and many people can even take their punishment patiently when they have done something wrong. But how many people are equipped to handle mistreatment after they've done right? Only Christians are equipped to do that. This is what makes believers stand out. That's our uniqueness. (from "Bedside Blessings," a daily devotional)

I'm recalling an early news talk program (a few years back) that was dealing with this very thing. The talkers were wondering something about the conservative politician Sarah Palin.

A shooting had occurred at a political rally in Tucson, Arizona. The shooter, clearly unbalanced, left blogs and notes to express his fear about the way politicians were leading this country. No sooner had this become known than liberal spokespeople began attacking and blaming right-wing conservatives for excessive rhetoric which inflamed the passions of deranged and unstable citizens.

Sarah Palin was in their crosshairs.

What Mrs. Palin did was to strike back. She did what she made a career of doing: finding a microphone to unload on the problem-causers in this country. She took no prisoners, but rather eloquently defended herself and attacked her attackers.

Some of the program talkers pointed out that if she ever attained high office, she was going to have to learn to take the criticism, whether just or unjust, and not strike back at everyone who criticizes her. (My observation is that Donald Trump reached the White House without ever managing to do that, but that's a story for another time.)

If those in the public eye respond to every criticism, there will be time for nothing else. No one enjoys being criticized.

I once found myself on the elevator with Jim Mora, then the coach of the New Orleans Saints football team. After introducing myself, I told him that pastors can identify with coaches, since we also do our work on Sundays and then have to sit idly by while our constituents tear it apart during the week. He laughed and said, "Yes, but they don't do it on television and talk radio." I thought about saying we would be willing to endure that for the kind of money he makes but decided against it.

Anyone in the public eye is going to be criticized. Sometimes it's well-earned and you had it coming. Sometimes it's so unfair you shake your head and wonder what planet the accuser is living on.

Sometimes you respond. Mostly you don't.

The more visible you are, the more your opinion and leadership count, the more critical it is for you to have close advisers who can help you decide what to respond to and in what way.

Sometimes in Scripture, the Lord's servant responded to the criticism.

In Galatians, Paul defends his apostleship. In II Corinthians, he defends his apostleship and his ministry. In Romans, he defends his gospel and his preaching.

Did he not respond to other criticism? Possibly, but since his writings are all we have of these exchanges, the evidence seems to be lacking.

No one exemplifies this better than Moses.

Moses was wearing himself out handling the endless stream of disputes between the Israelites. His father-in-law Jethro watched this debilitating parade and approached him. "What are you doing?" he asked. "Why are you the only one sitting as judge? You don't have time for anything else!" (Exodus 18:14)

"What you are doing is not good," Jethro told Moses. "You cannot do this alone."

One wonders how Moses took it when his father-in-law followed that up with, "Now listen to me. I will give you some advice."

To his credit, Moses listened well and heeded the wise counsel to set up layers of judicial courts to deal with problems, leaving only the heaviest issues for himself.

The quality of character which is necessary for one to take criticism and use it wisely is not a secret: meekness. It is for good reason Scripture tells us Moses was the meekest man on the earth. (Numbers 12:3).

Meekness is strength under control. It is definitely not weakness, not timidity, and not even remotely cowardice. Moses was blustery in a lot of ways and the very definition of strong. Yet, he took the slanderous criticism thrown at him as his daily diet and made his complaints known to the Lord in prayer.

Uncontrolled strength retaliates with force. Controlled strength takes it in and considers whether the criticism might have merit.

David teaches us how to handle criticism, even the unfair kind.

One of the minor characters who appears in David's story is Shimei, a descendant of King Saul. The story is found in segments, in II Samuel 16 and 19 and I Kings 2.

David's son Absalom was leading an insurrection. As David and his entourage fled Jerusalem, they headed down toward the Jordan valley. The hills and roadsides are barren there, enabling one to see vast distances. From a hilltop, this fellow Shimei hurled rocks and curses at David.

"Man of bloodshed!" he called out. "Get out! And don't come back. The Lord is repaying you for all the misery you brought on the household of Saul. He's giving the land to your son Absalom! Murderer!" (II Samuel 16:7-8)

David's nephew Abishai, one of his generals, said, "Sir, if you'll let me, I'll go up and take off this fellow's head."

David answered, "You and your brothers! Can't we agree on anything? Maybe this fellow is cursing me because the Lord told him to do it."

"Look," he continued, "my own son is trying to kill me. How much more this Benjamite. Let's leave him alone. Maybe if I'm merciful to him, the Lord will be merciful to me." (16:10-12)

That response is worth considering. In fact, it contains three great principles for the servant of the Lord who is being unfairly attacked:

1) Maybe this is a word from the Lord. So, listen to it.

2) Put it in context. Understand it.

3) If I am kind to the attacker, perhaps the Lord will bless me as a result. Use it.

As they went along, Shimei continued to harass them, but David's people ignored him.

Now, fast forward. Absalom is dead, the insurrection has been put down, and David is returning to Jerusalem. Shimei is shivering in his sandals knowing he's in big trouble with the king.

According to Second Samuel 19:16ff, Shimei was one of the first to meet David at the Jordan to welcome him home. There's a big crowd there, everyone assuring the king that "we were on your side from the beginning."

Shimei wades the Jordan to meet David on the east bank. He drops to the ground and calls out, "Please don't hold me guilty, king. I don't know what I was thinking that day! I know I have sinned. In fact, I'm one of the first of my tribe down here to meet you."

With that, Abishai turned to David. "Now, will you let me put him to death? Please? Is it okay now?"

David said to Abishai, "You're talking like my enemy. Should any man be executed in Israel today? Do I not know that I'm the king in this country?" He turned to Shimei and said, "You will not die."

Consider the three principles in David's response as great insights for dealing with penitent wrong doers:

1) Anyone counseling vengeance is your enemy.

2) Today is a day of good news. It's a time to celebrate, not to kill or be killed.

3) We have nothing to prove, and we prove nothing by revenge.

As for the rest of Shimei's story, check out the first few chapters of First Kings. We will just say it doesn't end well for him.

Now, let's all go forth and work on developing thicker skin. Smiley face goes here.

Chapter Forty-One

Preaching the Word in a climate of fear

God has not given us the spirit of fear, but of power and love and a sound mind. —2 Timothy 1:7

You, therefore, my son, be strong in the grace that is in Christ Jesus. —2 Timothy 2:1

I solemnly charge you in the presence of God and of Christ Jesus...preach the word! Be ready in season and out of season; reprove, rebuke, exhort, with great patience and instruction. —2 Timothy 4:1-2

The pastor friend called almost in desperation.

"They're almost to the point of giving me my walking papers. The animosity from some of our leaders is so thick you could cut it with a butter knife. What do I do now? How do I stand in the pulpit and preach? And what should I preach?"

If you've never preached the gospel of Jesus Christ while sitting in front of you throughout the congregation were people who hated you, arms folded and brows furrowed, you've missed out on one of the great experiences of the Christian life.

If you've never feared for your job for nothing more than preaching the whole counsel of God, you're in a minority, pastor.

Sometimes the ill-will is for nothing you have done or failed to do. The plotters and schemers have their own reasons and their own private agenda. Sometimes, the problem is you have stepped across an invisible line and intruded into forbidden territory.

You preached against guns when every man and half the women in the congregation were bonafide members of the NRA. They were aghast. "How dare you!"

You preached God's love for all races when the KKK (or their modern successors) were looking around for their next victim. "You are crazy, boy?"

You preached tithing to people who had made idols of their money, preached sexual purity to a gang of partyers, preached God's definition of marriage to a liberal crowd. "Do you know where you are?"

You preached once saved, always saved to a congregation of Pentecostals (who as a rule believe otherwise). You preached the full inspiration of God's word to a liberal crowd. You preached Psalm 139 (the preciousness of life!) to a church with Planned Parenthood in the budget.

They accused you of unnecessarily stirring up opposition. "There's so much else you could be preaching. Why did you choose to preach the very thing you knew would rile them?"

Preach the word.

Pastors preach what they believe God tells them. Otherwise, they should find another profession. Our Lord said, "They hated me without a cause" (John 15:25, quoting Psalm 35:19 and 69:4).

This is not to say the minister should look for a subject likely to light everyone's fuse. Every congregation needs the whole word preached, and not just the texts likely to draw fire.

You don't need to lay your life on the line every time you rise to preach. Do not volunteer to martyr yourself. But if the Lord calls you to do so, go forward. The ministry is no place for the timid.

I've known pastors in Kentucky-Virginia who dared not speak from the pulpit on the dangers of tobacco since some in their congregations made their livelihood from growing the stuff. "Do you know what pays your salary, pastor?"

In coal country, some pastors have hesitated to speak out against—take your pick— environmental pollution, the excesses of labor unions, or the abuses of mine owners— because of the makeup of their memberships. "Look around you, son. You're in West Virginia!"

In the Deep South the pastor who takes a stand for gun control may be in danger of losing his job and/or a sizeable portion of his membership. Or both. The pickups in the parking lot carry bumper stickers saying, "Guns and God." "I fought for this country and was trained to use this gun. You're safe as a result."

Powder kegs have always been around. I remember the early 1960s when the racial tension in this country was so thick you could cut it with a knife. Living in Birmingham, I saw the burned-out bus that had once carried the Freedom Riders. Sit-in demonstrators were active in our city. Martin Luther King was jailed there and wrote his legendary "Letter from a Birmingham Jail" in those days. Meanwhile, I was trying to pastor a small church a few miles north of the city and struggling to discern how much of this to address from the pulpit.

In the late 1960s, following seminary, I pastored in the Mississippi Delta. A few miles east of us, the White Citizens Council had been formed. (They soon dropped the White.) It was a lot of things, but if you think it was a respectable, updated version of the KKK you wouldn't be far off. In most of the Delta towns where the Blacks outnumbered the Whites, they had decided to rise up and demand to be treated as full citizens of this country.

The tension was like electricity in the air.

Pastors who tried to lead their churches to be open to all races usually found themselves out of a job. Many churches in the Deep South were torn apart over this issue.

So, most pastors I knew preached all around the issue. Among our Southern Baptist preachers, rare was the one who took a public stand against racism and kept the support of his congregation.

In Greenville, Mississippi, when our interdenominational ministerial alliance voted to ask the local YMCA to reverse their policy excluding blacks, the rabbi took the floor (we were meeting in my church!) and preached to all us Baptists a sermon on hypocrisy, since our churches were segregated. This was 1968-1969. I recall the pastor of our largest Baptist church saying to the rabbi, "You don't know what it's like trying to lead our people."

At this point, readers are curious about what I did or the stands I took. This article is not about me. However, I did on numerous occasions take a public stand. In the summer of 1969, my wife and I spear-headed an interdenominational and interracial evangelistic crusade at the high school stadium in Greenville. That crusade had the support of sixty churches and drew in five thousand each Sunday afternoon and thirty-five hundred each weeknight. The evangelist, former professional footballer Bill Glass, said it was the most heavily integrated meeting he had held to that point.

Could I have done more? Of course. You will never hear me bragging about "what I did during that war." I was probably as cowardly as anyone.

I remember the climate of fear. Some people who fed on strife between the races and drew their energies from conflict were always watching and listening for anything they could use. They were not friends of the gospel nor supporters of the pastors.

Even church people can be vicious. Proponents of a position of any kind can be self- righteous and dangerous.

What to do...

Pastors who have to address their congregation in a climate of fear and suspicion need to be careful. The enemy loves to entrap God's servants...

—Activate your prayer team. I suggest pastors always have a half-dozen prayer warriors in other cities who touch God in their prayers and who can keep confidences. Rally them from time to time to intercede before the throne as you deal with issues and face foes of the gospel.

—Get the counsel of your mentors. Every pastor should have on standby a couple of battle- scarred, retired pastors who will advise him on matters of critical importance.

—I said to one friend who thinks he may be terminated any day now, "Do not unload on the congregation. Preach the Word. If the Lord will let you, preach something uplifting and comforting from the Lord Jesus. Hit it out of the park." He should be finding out what the Lord had in mind in counseling us to "rejoice in adversity."

—Show each person the love of God in you and the joy of the Lord in your spirit. If Paul and Silas could "pray and sing hymns" in the Philippian jail while their backs were open wounds, their feet were locked into stocks, and the mob outside clamored for their necks (Acts 16:25), you and I should have no trouble rejoicing in the midst of our "momentary light affliction."

—Keep your focus on the Lord, not on men. He is your Source, not some committee or board.

—Once in a while read Matthew 10, beginning at verse 16 and going through the chapter. Become intimately familiar with what our Lord said about what you are now going through. Know that you are now living this very experience. So, be faithful.

—In your sermons, don't be brutal. Be loving and Christlike. Preach to win the opposition, not to clobber them. Preach so that those on the fence will tilt to your side. Demonstrate how we are more than conquerors through Him who loved us (Romans 8:37).

—You may choose to go ahead, however, and pack your bags. I'm not saying God is not going to carry the day in your situation, only that many a faithful warrior for Him has had to suffer, and this may be your turn.

Be faithful, friend.

Chapter Forty-Two

The church's dirty little secret

"Then we will no longer be infants, tossed back and forth by the waves, and blown here and there..." (Ephesians 4:14).

"Church is the only place on earth where people can throw hissy fits and get away with it." —a friend serving his first church after seminary.

My minister friend seemed to think he had made a discovery about the kingdom, something few people knew.

I told him I was sorry he had to learn this dirty little secret about church life. I asked for the story that had led to this discovery. He had two.

A church member attending his class complained because she could not find her workbook. The pastor told her he had borrowed it for another class, and she was welcome to use his. She said, "Okay. I'll go home then."

She walked out.

The minister asked me, "Would she have done that at work? At the doctor's office? I think not."

But at church she had no problem with putting her immaturity on full display.

On another day, a man stormed out of a church leadership meeting because his idea for a fundraiser had been rejected.

My friend said, "Would he have done that in a college class? At work? At home? At the store even?"

He would not have. And this guy was a church leader!

The church—which is the institution which we Christians should respect most— ends up being the least respected by many. And the pastor the least respected professional.

My friend said, "Situations like these used to keep me up at night. By God's grace, they don't anymore."

I'm sorry anyone has to learn this reality about church life; I'm glad my friend is sleeping at night.

A couple of observations come to mind, neither of them original.

–The only way Noah could stand the stink inside the ark was the storm outside.

–That the church still exists, with all its human flaws, is proof aplenty of the grace and mercy of God.

Immature believers abound, and that's all right. Babies must go through each stage of development before they reach maturity. But we should never put an infant in a place of leadership. Leaders must be adults in the faith if the church is to do its work effectively and if they are to be role models for those coming after.

The leader who storms out of a meeting because they did not get their way has just done the church a huge favor. They have identified themselves as unqualified to lead, as surely as if they had hung a sign around their neck. You hope other leaders recognize this and take steps to see that this person is required to grow up before being given more responsibilities around the church.

We are better off without such people representing God's church and making critical decisions. (On the other hand, if that one returns and apologizes before the entire group, which is a sign of growing maturity, and they should be given every encouragement.)

Here are seven "wrong ideas" the spiritually immature–those given to "hissy fits," as my friend put it–have about the Lord's work...

1) They see the church as a human institution belonging to them.

"We can do anything we want to. It's our church. My daddy helped start this church." Or paid for that pew. Or built that shed.

They do not see the church as holy and belonging to Christ. (Matthew 16:18).

Such infants are in for a rude awakening when they appear before the Lord Jesus.

2) They see the pastors as their employees, there to do their bidding, and accountable to them.

"We hired him; we can fire him." "If we are unhappy with him, then he has lost his effectiveness and needs to be replaced."

They do not believe that God sends pastors to churches and places them as the overseers of His flock. (Acts 20:28 and I Peter 5:2)

They are in for a rude awakening when they stand before the Lord Jesus.

3) They see God's work as something the professionals do and their roles as volunteers only when it's convenient and easy.

"We hired him to increase the attendance." "It's his job to visit the sick and reach the lost; that's why we pay him."

They do not see that the commands to be light and salt, to take the gospel to the ends of the earth, were given to the entire church, not just the apostles.

They are in for a rude awakening when they stand before the Lord Jesus.

4) They see their contributions (money, service, teaching, prayer, etc.) as voluntary and not required.

"If I give my money, I expect it to be done the way I want it to do." "I'm not giving my money there anymore; I don't like what the pastor is doing."

They do not see themselves as under Heaven's mandate and fully accountable to the living God.

They are in for a rude awakening when they stand before the Lord Jesus.

5) They see their church's reputation in the community as irrelevant and unity as beside the point.

"We're Baptists. Where you find two of us, you'll have three opinions." "I've been here the longest; I deserve to be heard." "If the community sees our church as divisive, that's their problem and they don't have to come."

They do not get John 17:21 where our Lord prayed for unity among His people "that the world may believe that Thou hast sent me." When the church is divided, the community wants none of what it has to offer, and the Kingdom of God suffers.

Such people are in for a rude awakening...well, you know...

6) They see their childish behavior as no one's business but their own.

"I'm not responsible for what others think of me." "If people make decisions about Jesus based on how I act, well that's just their problem." "God knows my heart."

They do not get Matthew 5:16 where Jesus commanded us to let our light so shine before men that they might see our good works and glorify our Father who is in Heaven. A great deal depends on my faithfulness.

Rude awakening coming.

7) They see themselves as the center of their own universe and think everything revolves around them.

"God wants me happy. I heard a television preacher say that and I believe it." "If I'm not getting anything out of the sermon, it's the preacher's fault."

They do not see that Jesus Christ is the center of everything, and that worship is a matter of "giving to Him the glory due His name." By worshiping Him rightly, they will get a lot from a service; however, if they go into the service to "get something," they will receive nothing from it. It's a matter of focus.

Rude awakening up ahead.

Count this as a call for maturity in leadership and discipleship of the membership.

Pastors should preach constantly that the commands of the New Testament were given to the full church and not just the disciples, and that we shall all stand before the Lord and give account of our faithfulness someday.

They asked a well-known preacher of a past generation, "What is the most important thing we need to get across to the people of God today?" He answered: "Our accountability to God."

"Why do you look down on your brother? For we shall all stand before God's judgement seat. It is written 'As surely as I live,' says the Lord, 'every knee will bow before me; every tongue will confess to God.' So then, each of us will give an account of himself to God" (Romans 14:10-12).

From time to time, if we stay in the Lord's church long enough, each one of us will receive a disappointment from not getting something we had our heart set on. We will be denied some program or event or facility that was dear to us. Nothing tells the story about our maturity like the way we handle our disappointment.

Let us grow up into maturity. Let us be strong in the Lord and thus be able to help others coming behind us.

Chapter Forty-Three

The pastor and his wife cannot agree on moving. What to do.

You're a pastor. And a pastor search committee is all over you, believing that you are the man for their church, God's own choice. They've called, wanting you to travel to their city and preach in their pulpit and give their people a chance to "call" you as their new shepherd.

The church is much larger, the salary provides a hefty boost in your income, and the prestige is twice where you presently serve. This has to be of God, right?

Oh, one thing more. Your wife is unhappy about it.

She is convinced there are good reasons to stay where you are. What does a pastor do in this case?

Most ministers have been there at one time or another.

In my case, it was the opposite. My wife thought the committee was correct, that relocating was of the Lord. I was the holdout, the one who could not decide.

It wasn't that I was opposed to moving. I just wanted a word from God that it was the right thing.

I called one of my mentors for counsel. I did as he suggested, and a half-hour later rose to my feet and picked up the phone and called the chairman of the pastor search committee, asking them to remove my name from consideration. I called my wife and told her, then buckled down to becoming the best pastor for my people I knew how to be. It worked out. Or did it? For the rest of her life, Margaret was not so sure we had done the right thing.

One year later, we accepted the call to another church—yes, a larger and more prestigious church—and it did not go well. After a difficult three years, we left that pastorate and ended up serving a broken church in the New Orleans area at a diminished salary.

This is something every husband and wife have in their relationship attic somewhere: an issue on which they simply agree to disagree. You realize you will never agree to it but love each other anyway.

A pastor's wife e-mailed me about something she and her husband were facing. Kerry gave me permission to use their story.

Dear Brother Joe: Have you ever written anything on your blog that has to do with candidating at a church and you and your wife needing to have unity on the decision? Keith and I are in a bit of an impasse right now and we are praying for unity. The red flags are more serious for me than for him. I don't want to keep him from being at a great church; I just don't think this one is it. Anything you have to say about this type of situation is welcome.

I called my wife and read that letter to her. She said, "What are the red flags she's concerned about?" Good question. So, I asked Kerry that in an email.

Her answer was four pages long. The problems they had with moving to the other church involved:

—medical issues. They would be far removed from the kind of medical specialists the family requires.

—church issues. The congregation had made life miserable for the previous pastor over home schooling. Some powerful church leaders were involved in the public schools and felt strongly the pastor's family needed to support them. Kerry was homeschooling their children for some good reasons.

—personality issues. The committee wanted a pastor's wife to be more submissive than they felt Kerry was.

On the other hand, Keith wanted to be back in the pastorate so strongly, after having had a bad experience in the previous church. Even though this was not a perfect situation, he would be fulfilling his calling and satisfying that inner longing serve God's people as shepherd.

Kerry wanted that for her husband, too. However, she knew that another bad experience in a church would be the worst thing imaginable.

Kerry and Keith talked and prayed and waited. The answer they got came through the pastor search committee. They called Keith to say they would be looking elsewhere for their next pastor.

Was he disappointed? No doubt.

Kerry was relieved. However, she was hurt for Keith. She wanted so badly for him to be back doing what God called him to do. She just wanted it to be in the right church.

My wife and I discussed this at length and came up with these suggestions for those in similar situations.

Talk about these things now, long before a pastor search committee comes calling.

The worst time to try to formulate a plan for handling such differences is in the midst of them. The best time is when no such options are in the picture, and no one can win or lose.

Decide to honor each other. To listen to each other's concerns. To respect the other.

My wife has generally left these decisions to me. However, if she had concerns, she wanted to be heard and to know she had been heard. That put a responsibility on me to pay full attention to her thoughts and concerns.

Decide what you will do if you are at an impasse. In most cases, which will mean that the ultimate decision will belong to the pastor husband.

In one case, I told the president of an institution who was inviting me to join his staff I was "95 percent sure" the answer would be "yes." Then his assistant showed us around the campus, and we walked through the three houses that were available. We could live in any one of the three. My wife cried when she saw them. On the way home, we talked and talked. We prayed some and we probably cried some. That's when I knew in my heart that we were not supposed to make this move.

Her "red flags" had stopped me from making a mistake.

If the wife knows her husband is really hearing her and that he values her input and takes it seriously, even if they cannot agree, she will tend to be supportive.

If, however, this is not the case—that is, if he really listens to her and then overrules her and she becomes resentful and non-supportive—the marriage has serious problems. This decision more likely revealed the problems than caused them. I recommend several doses of marital counseling. (And yes, my wife and I went through a couple of series of those too!)

If necessary–if she feels he is not listening to her or valuing her input sufficiently–it might be necessary to dig her heels in for a while. Not permanently, but long enough to be heard.

I don't deny that sometimes it might be necessary for a wife to do this. But let her husband be such that her hesitation really matters to him enough for him to stop and listen.

Let the wife keep reminding herself that his whole ministry is based on his ability to hear God's will and to follow it.

My heart goes out to pastors' wives. Theirs is an unpaid position with a hundred demands and expectations, and not all from the church congregation. Sometimes it's the preacher- husband who expects her to function as a servant with no mind of her own and no desire except to make him look good.

God, bless all pastors' wives, please.

Once in a while we hear of a pastor who relocated or stayed, based not on his preference for his own ministry but for his consideration for his wife's work. One minister told me his wife had moved several times for his work and now that she had a great job offer in another state, he felt it was only fair that he submit to her needs this time.

It would be unfair of us to judge him wrong.

Each husband/wife team will make their own calls in such situations.

The city where they moved needed preachers too, and soon he was shepherding a good congregation there.

It is to his own master that a servant stands or falls (Romans 14:4). That little verse keeps reappearing in a lot of my conversations with the servants of the Lord. It safeguards us from judging one another in decisions about the Lord's work.

Make sure you are both listening to the Lord. One thing we know: God is not going to send the two of your contradictory messages.

Be a team. Support one another. Together, you will be a mighty force for God. Divided, you will wreak havoc in the church, destroy your home, and end the effectiveness of a good minister of God.

Chapter Forty-Four

Three Big Things to Believe — and One Greater

Sooner or later, one ought to be able to narrow down his major theological (i.e., true life) beliefs to just a few.

The only way to do this is to have lived long enough on this sod as to know oneself thoroughly, to have studied enough to know the Scriptures intimately, and to have interacted with others enough to know the alternatives sufficiently.

Here then are the big three, three non-negotiables which should form the basis of all we hold dear. For me personally, the discussion is closed on these. That ship has sailed. My conviction is solid.

1. WITHOUT GOD, THERE IS NO MEANING.

As a young adult, I struggled with the concept of deity and tried to satisfy my youthful-but-inquiring mind that God is no figment of my imagination, but exists as a genuine Person in back of the universe and the One whom we read about in the Scriptures. The more I learned about atheism, the clearer I saw that all it had to offer was despair and meaninglessness.

Back from that brink — and glad to be — I had to admit that everything inside me resonated with the message of God in Scripture, both Old and New Testaments. It was more than comforting, because a lot of it is disturbing. But it was rock solid, like I was dealing with reality. The teachings of Scripture fit the real world I was living in.

Ravi Zacharias* wrote, "If life is random, then the inescapable consequence, first and foremost, is that there can be no ultimate meaning and purpose to existence." That fact, he says in *The End of Reason*, is the "Achilles' heel of atheistic belief." Even though writers like Richard Dawkins, Christopher Hitchens, and Sam Harris like to promote moral values outside of a belief in God, it does not work. If there is no God, there is no ultimate meaning, and the child molester, the serial killer, Dr. Albert Schweitzer and Dr. Billy Graham or Mother Teresa, all come to a common end of nothingness.

Everyone seeks meaning and purpose. Movie script-writer Leonard Mlodinow (Newsweek, May 4, 2009) tells how he found himself at a

Hollywood party chatting with a successful model when an attorney came up and usurped her attention. It turned out they were both Trekkies, devotees of the Star Trek saga, and knowledgeable about the most minute of details. He writes, "I stood there with a blank look, obviously over my head. Too much detail for my taste.... I was in awe that he remembered all that arcane stuff. Then, somewhere in the middle of his Vulcan dissertation, I realized something."

The philosophy the Trekkies were quoting as Bible, the material they were memorizing and spouting as their gospel, Mlodinow had written.

It was his stuff.

Mlodinow says, "The situation felt surreal. Not just because I'd forgotten my own dialogue—you'd be surprised how easy it is to blank on entire scenes — but that they had remembered it, and in such detail."

It's truly amazing what some people will grab hold of in order to give meaning to their lives.

I sat at lunch with a friend who was pastoring a little church in New Orleans' French Quarter. As he told of people they had led to Christ and some of the amazing things seen in their ministry, I thought, "This, more than any theological argument, is proof to me of the existence of God." Many a person has testified that only in coming to Jesus Christ and meeting the God of the Bible has their lives found the purpose for which they were created and taken on the meaning that gives them the fullest satisfaction.

2. WITHOUT HELL, THERE IS NO JUSTICE.

It will seem strange to some that given a choice of three statements of belief, "I believe in hell" would be one. This was not random, however, and not impulsive.

Without the existence of hell, there is no justice in the universe.

I sat in front of the television, watching a program on the personalities of the Second World War (primarily FDR, Churchill, Hitler, and Stalin). In the days and hours leading up to his suicide in the Berlin bunker, Adolf Hitler was still ordering the execution of his own people whom he suspected of plots against him or favoring surrendering to the Allies.

The man who is about to meet God goes out of this world murdering people right and left.

There has to be a hell, otherwise Hitler got off scot-free. We could add a lengthy list of despots who, if this life is all there is and if they did not repent, beat the system by paying for millions of deaths with their one life. We think of Stalin, Mussolini, Saddam Hussein, Idi Amin, and so many others.

The 73rd Psalm speaks of the fear of wicked people beating the system, of their ignoring God and living their own way and dying in a peaceful sleep at an advanced age. Just when the psalmist was about to give up, he went down to the House of God to worship and suddenly saw something that had eluded him. "Until I went into the sanctuary of God; then I understood their end" (73:17).

The Lord, he continues, "sets them in slippery places. You cast them down to destruction...They are utterly consumed with terrors" (73:18-19).

There has to be a hell, otherwise there is no justice.

In her book, *Help My Unbelief,* Fleming Rutledge tells of a professor who had a major impact in her life. J. Christian Beker was a premier theologian of his day, his book *Paul the Apostle* a classic for decades to come. Rutledge says Beker was a teenager in Holland when the Nazis arrived in 1940. He was sent to a work camp near Berlin where he contracted typhus. In 1945, during the Allied bombardment of Berlin, while lying on his sickbed, Beker felt he was experiencing the apocalypse and committed his life to God. Rutledge notes, "Thus was born a theologian in the midst of evil and death."

However, the news about Beker was not consistently good. "Never were weeds and wheat more entangled in one human life." While, on the one hand Rutledge calls him "one of the most gifted and inspiring Biblical interpreters I have ever known," on the other hand, he was manic-depressive, given to wildly impulsive behavior, and uncontrolled urges. "He cut himself off from most people near the end, and the circumstances leading to his illness and death suggested failure."

I relate that story to make two points: A) judgement is necessary if the universe is to have order and justice, but B) only God can be that Judge. Only He is qualified.

Judgement will result in Heaven for some — I wish it were for all — and hell for others.

Heaven, we are happy to say, "was prepared for (the righteous) from the foundation of the world," while hell "was prepared for the devil and his angels" (Matthew 25).

3. WITHOUT THE CROSS, THERE IS NO SALVATION.

The cross of Jesus Christ is the centerpiece of the universe, the focal point of creation. It points skyward to Heaven, extends downward to hell, and reaches outward to all people and all creation.

The salvation provided in the death of Jesus on the cross is unlike anything offered by any other religious or philosophical system ever known. While no one doubts that occasional teachings of Jesus are paralleled by insights from other religions, no doctrine found anywhere compares to the message of salvation through grace provided by the death of Jesus on the cross for our sins.

"God demonstrated His own love for us in that while we were yet sinners, Christ died for us" (Romans 5:8).

This is about the ultimate everything. The love that spans the universe and conquers all, the vision that sees all people of every age and atones for the rebellions and failures of every last one, the hope of eternal life: this is the gospel.

This supersedes all other religious offerings. To my knowledge, the competition—i.e., all those other religions—speaks of earning, growing, learning, achieving oneness with God through human effort. The cross speaks of receiving what God has given and Christ has provided.

All others speak of work, this alone speaks of grace.

All others offer conditional acceptance and partial improvement; the cross assures us by one offering He has perfected forever those who are sanctified (Hebrews 10:14).

All others depend on the power of oneself and the knowledge of one's mind. The cross is the power of God and the wisdom of God (I Corinthians 1:24).

Where does Jesus Christ fit in this threefold statement of belief? Answer: Throughout it.

Jesus Christ is the best proof of the existence of God. "He who has seen me has seen the Father." (John 14:9)

Jesus Christ taught more about hell than He did about Heaven. He called it "everlasting fire" (Matthew 25:41), "unquenchable fire" (Matthew 3:12), a place where "their worm does not die and the fire is not quenched" (Mark 9:44-49), a place of "torments" and "flame." (Luke 16:23,24), and other horrific images.

Jesus Christ is the sacrificial Lamb on the cross as well as the Great High

190

Priest making the perfect sin offering. When we speak of the power of the cross, we refer to the efficacy of the death of Jesus on that instrument to atone for our sins.

Jesus is Lord of all. That says it all.

Chapter Forty-Five

Ten reasons for the pastor not to resign abruptly.

This word is directed toward the embattled pastor, a servant of the Lord who is struggling against relentless opposition and daily grows weary. One question you face is whether to end the misery by resigning and walking away. As attractive as that seems sometimes, it is rarely the right choice. Consider this…"Therefore, we do not lose heart." (II Corinthians 4:1,16).

From time to time I receive notes like this one

"I resigned from my church tonight. Just couldn't take it anymore. The bullying from a few strong men (from one family in particular) finally wore me out. So, I got good and fed up, and tonight I tossed in the towel and told them I was through. It feels good to walk away and leave all this stress behind. But now, I will be needing a place to move to, a way to support my family, and when the Lord is ready, a new church to pastor. Please keep me in mind if you know of a church in need of my services."

Nothing about that feels right. I want to call my pastor friend, "You resigned in a fit of temper or a moment of discouragement? You walked away from the place God sent you? You quit a well-paying job without knowing where you will move your family or how you will support them? Have you lost your ever-loving mind?!"

I can almost guarantee that the pastor's wife is thinking these thoughts, no matter how loyally she supports her man and hurts to see him struggling under such a heavy load.

I would like to say to every minister I know that unless you are sure the Holy Spirit inside you is saying, "This is the time. Walk away now," don't do it. Do not resign abruptly or impulsively.

Here are 10 reasons not to quit and walk away even when to remain there is killing you….

1) God sent you. Stay until He says otherwise or until they fire you.

You may not be able to keep a church from firing you–some of the finest ministers on the planet have been terminated–but if it's up to you, stay until He tells you to leave.

So, pastor, you found the going to be tough, some of the leaders resistant, and a few members to be criminal in their behavior? You grew tired of fighting them and fed up with the way they treated you?

I have something to say to you, my friend. Grow up.

No one said it was going to be easy, least of all the Lord who called you in the first place. Go back to Matthew 10 and read what He said to the early disciples, starting at verse 16.

Compare your situation with what they were facing, then apologize to Him for your bellyaching.

2) The faithful people in the church need you to see them through this crisis.

There are good people in your congregation who need a shepherd. If you walk away, you are abandoning them to the bullies who have been making your life miserable and (presumably) ruling that church with a heavy hand.

If the bullies remain in place, the church will continue to be sick and stunted in its growth and ministries. Read Acts 20:28ff and notice that from the very earliest days of the Lord's church, it has been this way. Your church is not unusual. It may be sick, but if so, it needs a physician and that's why you were sent. Stay with your patient.

3) If you walk away, the bullies win, they are empowered, and they will try to control the next pastor.

The pastor who follows you will wish for all the world that you had cleaned out that nest of vipers before leaving. As it was, he will feel you took the easy way out, turned over the keys to the troublemakers, and made sure the next preacher would have to deal with them all over again.

I know, I know—it doesn't feel that way. You are at your wit's end and feel you cannot take it anymore. But you can. Stay with the assignment the Lord gave you. Love those bullies and minister to them just as faithfully as you do the precious saints. Follow the blueprint of Luke 6:27-35. By doing loving things for your enemies, you will puzzle the troublemakers, frustrate the devil, and honor your Lord. Furthermore, you will strengthen your church and give your people a picture of a blessed servant of the Lord Jesus for all time.

4) You have a family to support.

As the head of your household, you are charged with providing for your own, a serious assignment from the Lord. To walk away from a steady paycheck because you "couldn't take it anymore" reflects poorly on you and puts your loved ones in a difficult situation.

I think of all those years my coal-miner dad rode that man-trip back into the hellhole just to provide for his family. Wonder if he ever dreaded it. Wonder if he was ever afraid.

Fear was not an option. Neither was dread. He did his job.

Now, it's possible for pastors to go too far in the other extreme. I've seen pastors cave in to the bullies and not challenge them on anything. One said, "I go along to get along; it's how I keep my job."

Each extreme—either caving in or walking away—is unwise.

Stay close to the Lord for His guidance, His wisdom and the kind of self-control available only in Him.

5) If you walk away, your ministry will be changed forever–and almost definitely diminished.

What do you suppose a pastor search committee is going to think when they look at your resume? May I answer that for you?

— "If this guy is so good, why is he without a job?"

— "If he could not get along with the strong leaders in his last church, he'd have trouble in our church, too."

— "Let's not take the chance. Let's see who else is available without all this baggage."

And you are history. I have been on the receiving end of this stuff and have the scars to prove it.

You are seriously handicapping your future service to the Lord by abruptly quitting and walking away.

In the Southern Baptist Convention–always my frame of reference–if you walk away from your present church, in most cases getting another church will take from six months to a year. And that one will be a third to one-half the size of the present one. You will regress in your ministry in a hundred ways if you walk away.

6) Those who walk away and find themselves unemployed often lose confidence in themselves and possibly even in the Lord.

Say what you like about pastoring being different from other jobs, the simple fact remains that most people in our culture find their identity in their work. When you have no work to go to in the morning, you begin to wonder "who am I?" and then "am I a failure?"

I receive heart-breaking emails from unemployed pastors who wonder why God doesn't hear their prayers, why search committees do not appreciate their resumes, and why friends do not recommend them to other churches or invite them to fill the pulpit in their absence.

You do not want to be in that position if you can help it, preacher. If it does happen, try to make the most of it. But don't volunteer for that.

7) God can use this testing time in your life, in your family, in your church, and even in the lives of the troublemakers.

In the weight room, you build muscle by putting stress on it. In the kingdom, God builds believers by allowing us to undergo trials and burdens and oppositions. If we walk away from the work before quitting time, we miss the blessings and often add to the problems of the very people we were sent to encourage and bless.

Did you enter the ministry idealistically? Were you expecting the churches to be filled with saints and every day to be sweeter than the day before? If so, it's clear you have never read your Bible. Look at the ministry of God's shepherds in the Old Testament (Abraham, Moses, Joshua, Isaiah, Jeremiah) and in the New Testament (Paul, Peter, James, John). They all had a tough time with it. Did you think you were better than they?

I don't mean to be unkind here, only to provoke you to be tough with yourself and not jump ship when the going gets rough.

8) Think of how you will feel about this a million years from now. Which is to say, take the long view and not the short-term view.

9) The bullies need you to act courageously and faithfully. Whether they know it or not.

It will be good for the Diotrephes in your congregation (they love to have the pre-eminence—see III John) to see someone acting like God truly is in this place, that the Lord really did send him here, and that he actually expects to have to stand before the Lord some day and give account for this flock (see Hebrews 13:17). It will be eye-opening for the bullies to see you are able to take a licking, then get up and love them again in the power of the Holy Spirit.

You are going to bear witness to them by the power of humility, love and service, and not by playing the game the way they want it conducted (by brute force, big numbers, and power). Be faithful.

10) Your family needs to see you acting maturely, speaking firmly, and confidently dealing with this matter in quietness and strength.

I know adult children of ministers who quit going to church years ago "after seeing how the church people treated my daddy." They grew bitter at the church people and marked them all off as unChristian and hypocritical.

In allowing their children to be hurt, the parents did them no favors.

Pastors should do all they can to protect the family. As much as he can, the pastor should shield his wife from the trouble. She'll need to be in on some of the discussions, but not necessarily all. The children are particularly vulnerable. They do not have the spiritual resources with which to deal with hateful members or cruel leaders. So, try to shield them.

The ministry can be the most rewarding life in the world. But it can also be the cruelest. Either way, it is the Lord Christ whom you serve. And let me assure you, He does not take lightly the wonderful service you render in His name nor the treatment you receive from those who would hinder you. (Hebrews 6:10 has your name all over it.)

Find out and then help your family to see what Scripture means in calling the Lord "our Shield and Defender." (It's throughout the Psalms.)

Now, get on your feet again and get back into the ring, embattled preacher. The worst thing they can do is kill you and all that does is send you to Heaven.

Chapter Forty-Six

Our wish for the preacher-killers among us

They asked Andrew Murray about the greatest thought that had ever entered his mind. "My accountability to God," he said.

My pastor friend Albert was facing a crisis in his church. Here was his message to me...

Twice the treasurer has threatened to cut my pay if I announce plans to stay on. He tells everyone that our church cannot afford a pastor. A couple in the church is spreading gossip about me. A recent survey of the congregation assessed me and my ministry—which is fine—but the board chairman plans to discuss it at the upcoming annual meeting without clueing me in on the results ahead of time.

Nothing about this bodes well for Albert. I've seen too many of these disasters-in-the-making to be optimistic. Some people are determined to have their way and run "their" church as they please.

My friend concluded, "Pray for wisdom, shrewdness, strength and peace for my wife and me."

Ask any pastor. The stresses from these forces are preacher-killers.

In their book *Valley Forge*, Bob Drury and Tom Clavin tell how General George Washington turned a bedraggled, dispirited, starving, half-naked army into a fighting force that defeated the best-trained militia on the planet, the British. And that wasn't all. While battling the British and contending with both the frigid weather and the sparse supply of food and clothing, Washington was constantly being undercut by Congress and competing generals who wanted his job.

The internal strife must have been enormous. Ask any pastor.

Your biggest headaches will not come from the world, young pastor. The community at large may welcome you or ignore you, but they are unlikely to organize against you. People inside the congregation will do that.

Not all, thankfully. Many congregations are healthy and positive, focused on serving God and making an impact on their world for Christ. They remind us of the Israelites who were rebuilding Jerusalem's wall with Nehemiah. When antagonists arrived and dare them to fight, they replied, "We are doing a great work and cannot come down" (Nehemiah 6:3).

God, help your preachers.

When the Apostle Paul told of the price he paid for the privilege of serving the Lord's people and extending the gospel, he listed the beatings and shipwrecks and imprisonments. Then he said, and in addition to all this, there is the daily care for all the churches (2 Corinthians 11:28).

What's the answer?

I have a solution for preacher-killers and church-troublers, although it's something only the Lord can handle.

What I do is ask the Lord to get their attention. That's all. But it's enough.

These people could well benefit from some kind of divinely sent, momentary crisis that awakens them to what's really important in this life.

A radio preacher was telling of the time he was addressing the students in a Christian college. Three thousand people—students and faculty—packed the arena. Just as he began speaking, the air raid siren went off. Security people rushed in and ordered everyone to leave the auditorium, get into the hallways and huddle up close to the walls. Outside, a storm was raging and at that moment a tornado was plowing across the campus. The noise was deafening; the power went out.

After a bit, the leadership announced that everyone should remain in the arena while they checked the conditions and assessed the damage. "Go on with your sermon," they told the guest preacher.

The preacher said he brought a different sermon that day from what he had intended. "I had the undivided attention of the audience. There's something about a life-threatening crisis that puts everything into perspective, which makes you realize the petty things you've been living for."

We could wish for some people a life-threatening crisis to adjust their vision, alter their priorities, align their hearts.

Do not misunderstand. We're not wishing anyone to die and not putting a hex on anybody. Only that a little scare would do some people a lot of good.

A preacher was witnessing to a seatmate on an airplane. Nearby a couple of college students—a boy and a girl—were taking it in and belittling the preacher and scoffing at people who simply had too much religion for their own good. These young intellectuals were too modern and too sophisticated for such religious bunk.

All of a sudden, the plane lurched and began to shake. The turbulence was horrendous and frightening. The plane dropped perhaps a hundred feet or so, but it felt like a mile. Then, just as quickly, the air smoothed out and the plane resumed its flight as though nothing had happened.

The preacher continued his explanation of the gospel with the lady, but he could not help noticing that the college kids had grown quiet and attentive. They wanted to know about God. He had their undivided attention.

In my opinion, the church bosses and preacher-killers in some churches could stand a rude awakening now before they get the real one awaiting just over the horizon, the one the Heavenly Father is preparing for them. If they had such an awakening, they would realize several things-

–This is not my church, and it's not yours. It belongs to the Lord Jesus Christ. He died for it, and I didn't.

–Jesus takes personally how I treat His church and how we all treat His preachers, His messengers. Consider how our Lord spoke of God taking personally the treatment of His servants–Matthew 21:33-41; 22:1-7. See also what Jesus told His apostles as He sent them out to preach. That's Matthew 10:40 and Luke 10:16.

–I will give account to God for my stewardship (stewardship of influence, leadership, possessions, everything). "We must all stand before the Judgment Seat of Christ" should be the most sobering thought any of us could possibly have (2 Corinthians 5:10).

–The Lord will not take lightly those who mess with the Church, which is His Bride and His Body, nor with messengers sent to do His will.

Sobering thoughts indeed. We could wish God would give just a little preview of judgement to these who take so lightly their responsibility and their stewardship.

"Lord, is it too much to ask that Albert's detractors might have the fear of the Lord put into them?"

You did it to Jonah's shipmates in Jonah 1 and to Paul's companions in Acts 27. A little storm, maybe? Thank you.

I love what Elijah prayed on Mount Carmel just before the fire fell from Heaven. "Lord," he said, "let these people know that there is a God in heaven. And while you're at it, let them know that I'm your prophet." That's I Kings 18:36ff, and it's about as good as it gets. I confess to having prayed for that a few times in my ministry.

God came through, I'm happy to report. No fire from Heaven, but just the assurance of His nearness and the work of His Spirit.

Chapter Forty-Seven

The preacher said something I disagree with, so I'm leaving!

Even though this is a book for pastors and not the membership at large, I'm including this little essay because it makes a point we preachers should be teaching our people.

Pastors should train their people to expect some teachings outside their comfort zone and not to be disturbed by it. The wise members will do as the Bereans did...

"...they received the Word with great eagerness, examining the Scriptures daily to see whether these things were so" (Acts 17:11).

When I asked where he went to church, the gentleman working on my house said, "I used to go to church across the river. But the preacher said something I disagreed with, so I left." It was all I could do not to laugh.

But he was serious.

After waiting for him to say more, which he did not, I said, "Man, I would hope so." He seemed interested.

I said, "Wouldn't it be terrible to have a preacher who said only what I already know and taught only what I already believe? What would be the point of going to hear him if I already knew what he was going to say? There's so much more to God than what little I already know!"

Lord, make us teachable.

It's a mark of maturity to welcome correction, to recognize and appreciate constructive insights to make our lives better. The godliest person comes to church hoping to hear something that blesses, something that corrects him, something that inspires her, whether they had previously known it or agreed with it or not.

A quick scan of Scripture produces a long line of people who heard God calling their name, who made themselves available to Him, and then were told something they didn't want to hear!

–Abraham: "You want Sarah and me to go where? And never come back? Are you sure, Lord?"

–Moses: "You want me to go to Egypt and do what? and tell who to let your people go?"

—Gideon: "You want me to attack the Midianites with torches and bugles? And with only 300 people? Is this a joke?"

—David: "You want me to face that giant, Lord? to be the ruler over your people? to build that temple?"

—Amos: "Wait just a minute, Lord. I'm a farmer, not a preacher. I wouldn't be comfortable going up to Bethel and preaching to that crowd. A fellow can get in big trouble that way."

—Jeremiah: "You want me to be a prophet, Lord? I'm just a teenager. Are you sure?"

A sure sign of the worldly, the carnal, and the immature is to want things our way, to appreciate nothing that upsets, to resent anything contrary to our convictions and preconceptions.

You may not believe this....

I have heard people say, "I'm looking for a church that teaches what I believe." I find that stunning for its shortsightedness.

Such warped, self-idolizing thinking is what drives some to create their own religion. This is the guy who would write his own Bible. He would then be worshipping himself.

Imagine a fellow lost in the jungle refusing to follow his rescuer because "You're leading me where I've never been before," "You're disagreeing with me" or "You're telling me something I never heard before."

That would not happen. But it happens in religion all the time.

As bizarre as it seems, many people throw out all common sense when it comes to their religious faith. They can make sound decisions all week, build a business and earn a living and contribute to society. Then, they come to church and believe the strangest things.

There are those who base their eternity on the testimony of a charlatan who said angels showed him golden plates which he translated through a miraculous window, which the angel then took away. And how does one know all this is true? Well, we just have to take his word for it.

If the founder of that religion was around today, his rich uncle in Nigeria would have left him a fortune in a bank account and he would be asking our help in getting to it. He'd be on cable television urging people to contribute money for his latest scheme, in return for which he would be happy to send them a small cloth over which he has prayed.

It has been conclusively proven that the founder of that religion took an Egyptian scroll containing burial instructions for a mummy and since at the time no one could translate hieroglyphics told everyone it was in "reformed Egyptian" and was a message from Abraham himself. And as far as I can tell, there was no mass exodus from that religion. You wish people would wake up.

P. T. Barnum, your descendants are still on the job today.

There are those who sit in good sound churches rejecting the message preached from the Holy Scriptures because believing it would require them to change their ways, to believe differently, to make radical adjustments in their lives. And they cannot allow themselves to do that because a) "this is how I was raised," b) "this is what my daddy believed and taught us," or c) "I wouldn't be comfortable doing it some other way."

Why some disbelieve....

For reasons known only to them, the smartest people often drop their brains off before entering their house of worship. They believe weird things and reject God's truth for the flimsiest of reasons.

Listen closely and you will hear things like these...

– "Well, what I've always believed is..."

– "It seems to me that..."

– "I know what I believe is true because it gives me a warm feeling inside."

– "I don't know what the Bible says but I know what I believe."

– "My mama believed this and it's good enough for me."

– "If that were true, I'd have heard about it before now."

– "Nineveh would be outside my comfort zone."

We have not been left to our own devices, thank the Lord. We have the inspired word of God. " All Scripture is inspired by God, and profitable for teaching, for reproof, for correction, for training in righteousness, that the man of God may be adequate, equipped for every good work" (2 Timothy 3:16-17).

So, the solution to the problem is to get to know what God has said in this wonderful revelation to mankind.

First of all, read your Bible. And begin with the New Testament. Sometime later, after you have become familiar with its message, you will want to drop back and read the background material we call the Old Testament. Only by knowing the New Testament thoroughly, however, will you be able to appreciate the riches of the Old.

Begin by turning to the first chapter of Matthew's Gospel and start reading. Don't stop. Read as much as you can at one time.

Always begin your reading asking the Father to speak to you through His word. "Open my eyes, Lord, that I may behold wonderful things in Thy law" (Psalm 119:18).

When you complete Revelation chapter 22, start all over again. You'll get far more the second time through than you did the first. Repeat this as often as you find it helpful.

When you come across concepts new to you, pay attention to them, think about them, ask the Father to help you understand, and then: Keep on reading. To repeat what we've said several times above, you want and expect the Lord to say new things to you, insights you had never thought of teachings and revelations far beyond where your thought-level had been.

Doesn't it make sense that if the living God were to write a book, it would be better and wiser than any other book? That it would challenge us and rebuke us and teach us?

I suggest you not read commentaries (which are explanations about the Bible) until you are thoroughly familiar with the New Testament itself.

Do not make the mistake of limiting yourself to a few verses here and a few verses there, in the manner of many devotional books. After you are familiar with all 27 books of the New Testament, you may enjoy that. But not yet.

You will want to sit under faithful teachers and devoted pastors. But there is no substitute for sitting at your breakfast table with the open Word and reading for yourself. Read it again and again until it sticks to you, stays in your mind, and becomes part of you.

You do not need a seminary degree to appreciate the Bible. Just read it.

A wonderful new world is waiting for you. Get on with it. And don't be surprised if you emerge at the end of your very first reading of the New Testament a different person than when you entered. God's Word has a way of doing that to us.

That's why the writer of the Psalms used hundreds of verses telling us how wonderful the Word of God is. (Look at Psalm 19 for starters. And later Psalm 119.) The fun thing is finding that out for yourself.

Chapter Forty-Eight

An odd skill pastors need if they are to survive in this work.

Pastors must learn to live with loose ends. Unfinished tasks. Dangling threads that need to be tied up.

When they lay their heads on the pillow at night, God's shepherd can think of 38 things left undone and needing attention tomorrow....

Someone needs a call returned, a member needs a visit, a sermon needs more preparation, a program needs planning, a colleague needs encouragement, an employee needs to be held accountable, the pastor's child needs some dad-time, his wife has been wanting to talk about several issues, he had hoped to begin his physical fitness program this week, the nursing home has invited him to hold a service, the seminary wants him to speak, the denominational committee needs to meet and hear his report, and he should have prayed more today. The family that buried their father last month needs a follow-up visit. The postponed dental appointment should be rescheduled, and his CPA has a question about his taxes.

"There's always something," said Rosanne Rosannadanna (the old Saturday Night Live program). There is indeed.

Pastors will not make it in a long-term ministry if they do not learn to turn this stuff off at night.

You need your sleep.

A second type of sleep-robber involves troubling people and events that did not go as expected....

One of the young mothers in my church was in nursing school. She was having a tough time of it, and frequently called to ask for prayer when she had big tests or was facing a difficult assignment. She got through the program and graduated with honors. I was as proud of her as though she were my daughter. And then....

She and the family joined another church.

They moved their membership to a church two miles down the street without one word of explanation.

Why? What happened?

To this day, I have no idea what happened. Did I fail them? Did they interpret something I said as being offensive? Or did this have nothing to do with me as their pastor? I do not know and assume I'll never know.

A family from a church I served many years earlier messaged to say the husband was suffering from a terminal disease and they wondered if I could be available for his funeral. I said 'yes' and offered that on a future trip through their city, perhaps we could meet. They suggested a meal at a restaurant.

The wife and their two adult daughters and their husbands came. The dinner was a nice visit, and we caught each other up on our lives. (The near-comatose husband was living in a nursing home.) I did what I always do, and sketched the family, which I interpret as a small personal gift I can give them. We prayed together and everyone hugged, and I went on my way.

The family was often on my heart and in my prayers and I gave thought to what I might say at the funeral.

When the man died, the family made other arrangements for his funeral, and no one said a word to me.

What happened? I have no clue. Did I fail them in some way? Should I have been more pastoral at our dinner instead of "Joe the old friend"? Or were there other factors at work here unbeknownst to me? I will never know.

Can I live without knowing? I can and must.

A pastor friend recommended to his deacon leadership that I would be the ideal person to lead a retreat. Two deacons, a man and a woman, made a conference call my way and we must have chatted a half hour, covering principles I would teach in the retreat. I felt I had made two new friends.

And then nothing. Not a word from them afterwards.

What happened? Did they read my deacon book and decide I was too conservative? Did the woman feel I was opposed to women deacons? (I'm not; I say it's an individual church decision.) Was something else going on? I will never know.

And that's fine. I can live without knowing these things. (Clearly, I do remember them; otherwise, they would not be included here.)

A healthy approach to dealing with unfinished loose ends involves these four things:

1) Give it to the Lord.

True, you might have to hand it back to Him again and again until He keeps it. But do not hesitate to do so.

2) Do not obsess over it.

A healthy mind can turn it off; a troubled mind (that is, poor mental health) cannot leave it alone but keeps "picking at it."

Should you call that individual and ask if anything is wrong, if perhaps you failed them some way? Short answer: Obey the Spirit. He will tell you in your spirit whether you should humble yourself and make that call or be strong and move on. But in the absence of leadership from the Holy Spirit, I say "No," that you should not give it a second thought.

3) Pray for the people involved.

The Heavenly Father knows precisely what is going on. Ask Him to bless the people and to help you learn needed lessons from this, if there are things to be learned.

4) Go on to the next task.

You have enough on your plate, pastor, without needlessly worrying over something that may not be an issue at all.

After all, suppose you knew the whole stories...

The family that moved their membership abruptly might say: "Oh pastor, did we not call you? I meant to. Our daughter had friends in the youth group at that church and our son played on their ball team."

The family that had invited me to preach the funeral might say, "We saw by your schedule you were in Mexico on a mission trip and did not want to bother you. We meant to call."

The deacon leadership might say, "We discovered the church had no funds for a retreat, so we canceled it. Sorry we didn't contact you. Should we have?"

They might say that.

Or being honest, I know they could just as easily say that I transgressed some invisible line, said something to which they took offense, or a thousand other things. We will never know.

If I cannot live not knowing what happened, then I have a problem. You'll be happy to know I do not have a problem. (Smiley-face here.)

"...forgetting those things which are behind and reaching forward to those things which are ahead, I press toward the goal for the prize of the upward call of God in Christ Jesus" (Philippians 3:13-14).

Chapter Forty-Nine

The best kind of pastor is a broken man.

The best kind of pastor is not necessarily somebody who has always had it all together.

The best shepherd of the Lord's people will know what it is to go astray and be found, to fall and be picked up, to be wounded and to heal, to sin and be forgiven.

If you have ever sat in a congregation where the pastor is without sin (seemingly), where his sermons show no indication that he knows what it is to be tempted, and where no allowance is given for the human condition, then you know that is no place for a sinner like you.

As a sinner—one whose heart is a rebel, whose mind strays from the paths of righteousness more often than you would like to admit, who constantly needs to repent and receive God's mercy—you have no business in a church made up of perfect pastors and sinless members. You stand out like an invalid at a body-building contest.

The best pastor is one who has sinned and been taken to the Lord's woodshed for a time of discipline and chastisement, who has been forgiven and healed and loved and made whole again. Such a pastor will know how to warn the children from straying and to bind them up in love after they have learned life's lessons the hard way.

The best pastor is one who has been in trouble and doubted and came close to slipping, but at the last minute was rescued by the hand of God. He will value the Lord's mercy. (He will treasure Psalm 73 which describes exactly that experience.)

The best pastor is probably not the kind your pastor-search-committee is looking for. But it should be.

In my humble opinion, too many pastors search committees comb through stacks of resumes looking for the man of God who has had it all together from childhood and whose life has been an unbroken succession of victories.

Whatever are they thinking?

Bring in a pastor like that and get ready to duck.

That preacher does not understand failure, will not tolerate human weaknesses, and can be counted on to make life miserable for the struggling and the stragglers. After all, if his life has been one continuous uphill ascent, so can yours be. If he can do it, you can accomplish it. No excuses accepted.

This is a good place to hear from the Apostle Paul.

"Three times I pleaded with the Lord that (the thorn in the flesh) might depart from me. And He said to me, 'My grace is sufficient for you, for my strength is made perfect in weakness.' Therefore, most gladly I will rather boast in my infirmities, that the power of Christ may rest upon me. Therefore, I take pleasure in my infirmities, in reproaches, in needs, in persecutions, in distresses, for Christ's sake. For when I am weak, then I am strong" (II Corinthians 12:8-10).

It is not the man who has not struggled who makes a great champion for Christ. It is the one who has overcome by the power of Christ. And there is no overcoming without the struggle arriving first.

Dale Oldham was a champion pastor and leader in the (Anderson, Indiana) Church of God for two generations. My grandmother used to speak of him and his national radio broadcasts over a half-century ago. In 1969, I met Dr. Oldham and his wife Polly. I will never forget their story.

As a young couple in evangelism, struggling to live on the pitiful offerings that came in, when the Oldhams saw, they were going to have a baby, they took a pastorate. When the baby was born, their lives were fulfilled. Everything was wonderful.

However, the baby lived only a day or two and then died. The young parents were devastated. "Polly turned her face to the wall and refused to be comforted," Dr. Dale would say. "And for a time, my soul felt as though it had died within me, I was so broken-hearted."

"Lord," I said, "we've been serving you out here to the best of our ability for pitifully small rewards. It does look like the least you could have done was to let us keep our baby." No answer came from Heaven.

"Eventually," Dr. Oldham said, "I was able to say, 'Father, I do not understand this. But one thing I do know: You could never do a hurtful thing. Not ever. So, I'm going to give this up to You and go forward.'"

"Only then was I able to comfort my wife."

Finally, he would say, "I cannot say how many times over the years I have ridden to the cemetery with a young family that is burying their child. And because I have been there, I was able to put my arms around them and tell them, 'Give it up to the Lord. Trust Him. One of these days we'll understand it." (The legendary gospel singer Doug Oldham is the son of Dr. and Mrs. Oldham.)

The Bible tells us we have this kind of Savior in the Lord Jesus Christ.

"For we do not have a High Priest who cannot sympathize with our weaknesses, but was in all points tempted as we are, yet without sin. Let us therefore come boldly to the throne of grace, that we may obtain mercy and find grace to help in time of need" (Hebrews 4:15-16).

I think of Roger who used to sit on my living room floor and cry. "Joe, why doesn't God understand what it's like to be me?"

Roger was a misfit, plainly put. I have no idea whether he was slow mentally or whether the problem was some kind of social maladjustment. But he never fit in, not in school or with any group of his peers. He was lonely and wanted female friends. Sometimes, he told me, knowing he should not ask a married woman for a date, he would stand on the street corner and ask women as they walked past, "Are you married?" Of course, they turned away and rushed by without a word.

I said, "Roger, I can assure that Jesus understands. He knows what it is to be you, to be lonely and misunderstood. He knows exactly how you feel when you are tempted to quit trusting God."

I would urge him to keep telling the Lord how he felt, and to believe that God cares and hears.

The Good Shepherd knows how it feels to be you.

Many years ago, I stood in a courthouse square among a couple of hundred people–mostly teenagers–as we held a public demonstration for Christ. The speaker at our rally was a teenager himself, an 18-year-old preacher from a nearby town who had already amassed a small reputation as an effective evangelist.

As he was introduced, the young man approached the microphone, looked out at the crowd, and said, "As I travel around this great world of ours...."

That's the problem with acclaim that comes early in life. One tends to inflate his sense of self and to conclude that there is something special about himself.

In short, he becomes a pain.

Better to hear from one who after straying from the path was brought back by a merciful God. He's the one with a message of warning and redemption, of grace and mercy.

When Jimmy Carter became president, young men like Hamilton Jordan and Jody Powell became his "advisers." A newspaper columnist observed, "No one should be called an adviser until they are at least 40 years old and have had one great failure in life."

We learn far more from our failures and heartaches, our disappointments and infirmities, than from an unending string of successes and awards.

Better the speaker who was laying in the ditch and picked up by a Good Samaritan, who then bound up his wounds and brought him to the inn and made provisions for his needs. That's a speaker with a message of grace and mercy.

Better to sit before a preacher whose life has paid a severe price for his rebellion and who has been made whole by the power of a risen Savior. He will have a good word for others who are astray from the Father's love.

This is not to imply the preacher should constantly harp on his failures and brokenness, his struggle with drugs or divorce or jail time. That he knows what it is to sin against the Lord and to receive His loving mercy is sufficient to guarantee his message will convey hope and power.

Our Lord probably bit His lip when the Pharisees watched the woman anointing Jesus' feet with the costly oil and grew critical. "If this man were a prophet," they reasoned, "He would know the kind of woman this is—a real sinner."

The Lord told the man a story—don't we love this about Him.

Do you see this woman? When I entered your house, you gave me no water for my feet, but she washed my feet with her tears and wiped them with the hair of her head. You gave me no kiss, but this woman has not ceased to kiss my feet since the time I came in. You did not anoint my head with oil, but this woman has anointed my feet with fragrant oil.

"Therefore, I say to you, her sins which are many are forgiven, for she loved much. But to whom little is forgiven, the same loves little" (Luke 7:40-50).

The pastor who has been forgiven is the one who loves. And the pastor forgiven many times loves more deeply than the others.

Who would not want a loving shepherd? One who understands weaknesses and shows compassion and extends mercy?

Are you such a pastor? Then, stop dwelling on the iniquities in your life that Christ died for, and God has forgiven. Sins forgiven by Him are gone forever. Anyone doubting this should read and start believing I John 1:9 and Hebrews 10:17.

Satan loves it when God's people cannot get their minds off the failures in their past. It means they will never seize the blessings of forgiveness and the grace of God's mercy which will make them far better servants of the Lord than otherwise.

There is a reason Scripture says, "Where sin abounded, grace did much more abound" (Romans 5:20).

They who know the Lord's forgiveness are best able to encourage others to come to Him for mercy.

Those who have feasted from the Lord's bounty are best able to encourage the hungry to enter and partake from His table.

Those who have fallen are able to sympathize with others who stumble.

Are you such a pastor? Good. Then, take your eyes off your past failures and fix them on the all-sufficient Savior who will make you strong in all those broken places.

You will never boast of having sinned, but the day will come when you see that you value the Lord's grace and goodness more after having failed him than had you never strayed.

Somewhere I read of Philip Melanchthon, a colleague of Martin Luther, who was one of the most disciplined and godly men of his age. Luther is said to have told him, "I wish to Heaven you would sin a little. The Lord deserves the right to forgive you of something!"

We do not go out and sin so the Lord will have something to forgive us of and therefore to teach us. For most of us, we sin more than enough without working at it. We have failed God sufficiently for Him to demonstrate His goodness amply for all time.

"He Himself knows our frame; He is mindful that we are but dust" (Psalm 103:14).

I'm remembering the time in 1981 when Margaret and I took the Sunday evening worship service in our church and told the congregation of our marital struggles which necessitated a full twelve months of marriage counseling.

The next morning, the church office phone began to ring as couples called to make appointments for counseling. More than one said, "Now that we know what you have been through, we feel you can understand our problems."

That's why a pastor must never leave the impression that he is without sin, without a history, and without a problem in his past or without one today. It is not necessary for him to display his failures before the congregation, but they should learn enough to see that their shepherd is one who understands.

It's about credibility and trust and compassion. Three essential ingredients in good shepherding.

Chapter Fifty

Pastors need other pastors. That's an iron-clad rule.

"As iron sharpens iron, so one man sharpens another" (Proverbs 27:17).

So, one man sharpens another.

So, one woman sharpens another.

So, one Christian young person sharpens another.

As iron sharpens iron, so one campus minister sharpens another. So, one worship leader sharpens another. So, one deacon sharpens another. So, one missionary sharpens another. And in particular, as iron sharpens iron, so one pastor sharpens another.

I tell you on the authority of Heaven that no matter what level of ministry you are serving in, you need two or three great, close personal friends to help you stay sharp and faithful and work at the highest level.

Over a long ministry, I've known only two pastors who did not like preachers. The first one, it turned out, was a fake. When his last church forced him out of the pulpit, it came to light that he had been spending time at the gambling tables in the casinos, was ordering alcoholic drinks with his meals, and was given to telling dirty stories and sprinkling profanity in his conversation. I believe we would all agree here was a man who had no business in the ministry. His dislike and criticism of other preachers, no doubt, was a diversion to draw attention away from his own misbehavior.

The other pastor, however, seems to have been genuine in his dislike for preachers. I knew him well and saw close up the effects of the isolation he imposed on himself as a result of his contempt for preachers. I'm not a psychiatrist, but only a pastor. However, my opinion is that any preacher in isolation has to contend with two great problems: ego and temptations of the flesh. Now, everyone fights these battles, but the isolated minister does so with one arm behind his back. He has no colleague to confide in or pray for him.

Ego problems range from feelings of worthlessness to extreme pride and egotism. The fleshly temptations may involve impure thoughts, unhealthy reading material, and smutty stories, and in time may lead to pornography and adulterous affairs.

Both kinds of temptation ended the ministry of my friend.

Over the years, I've often wondered how things might have been different had that pastor chosen a few close friends to meet with regularly, to confide in, to trust, and pray together.

"There is a friend who sticks closer than a brother" (Proverbs 18:24).

Everyone needs lots of friends. But we're talking about two or three or four special friends, intimate colleagues, the kind who will be straight with you. We're not talking about your fathers in the ministry or your children. This kind of friend is not someone who thinks you hung the moon and can do no wrong.

Jim Nalls was serving a church two miles from mine and we became close friends. When he was in seminary, Jim and three classmates formed a prayer group. They (humbly, I suppose!) named themselves "the holy brethren" from Hebrews 3:1 and made plans to meet annually for a weeklong prayer retreat. I asked him for more information on this.

Jim said, "The last week of September was our 29th prayer retreat in a row." I said, "What do you do? You don't pray for a solid week." He said, "We pray. But we also talk. We talk about the denomination, our churches, our lives, our sermons, everything. But mostly, we are honest with each other."

I said, "But you only see each other once a year?" He laughed. "No. But we call each other all the time, we visit if one of us is in the area, and at the annual meeting of our denomination, we try to get our families together."

When Jim's wife Linda went to Heaven after a lengthy battle with cancer, the three "holy brethren" ministered to the family and conducted Linda's service.

There must be a hundred reasons for the success of Evangelist Billy Graham, but one reason has to do with the four friends he surrounded himself with in the early days of his ministry: Grady Wilson, Cliff Barrows, George Beverly Shea, and T. W. Wilson. I once heard Cliff Barrows speak of the times when they would be driving down a highway and pass a farmer in his field. One of them would say, "Billy, see that fellow out there on his tractor? But for the grace of God, that's you."

It's what friends do. They pop bubbles of pretension, lift you up when you're down, hold you accountable.

Proverbs 27:6 says, "Faithful are the wounds of a friend, but deceitful are the kisses of an enemy."

I like to think of Proverbs 27:17 as a blacksmith shop verse.

As a kid on the farm in Winston County, Alabama, I enjoyed watching my dad work in grandpa's blacksmith shop. He would build a fire in the forge and let me work the bellows. Dad would put a piece of metal on the fire and leave it until it was white hot. Then, with the tongs he would steady it on the anvil and hammer it into the shape he wanted. To any kid, a blacksmith shop is a great place with its fire, the noise, the smells, the feel of the place.

That boy on the farm could tell you that when "iron sharpens iron," you may expect abrasion, friction, noise, and sparks to fly.

When friends get together—the kind of friends we're talking about here, the kind who sharpen you—expect some friction from disagreements and straight talk, maybe a few sparks. But when you leave, you're sharper and stronger, and that's the whole point. This will mean your special colleagues need to be different from you, perhaps a little stronger in some areas. That difference is what sharpens you.

Elijah or Paul?

Most pastors have preached sermon series on Elijah. There is much to emulate about the man, especially his faith and his courage. But if Elijah had a weakness, it was that he was a loner. Whether that was by choice or due to the circumstances, we'll leave to others. But we can see the effect his isolation had on him.

Elijah was feeling lonely, getting depressed, even wanting to die. Then, it appears the ego took over. Twice in I Kings 19, he tells the Lord, "I'm the only one left standing." After he said it the second time, the Lord stopped him. "Not even close," the Lord said. "I still have 7,000 who have not bowed the knee to Baal or kissed his ugly image."

Had Elijah been foolhardy, and he wasn't he might have argued, "Yes, but where are they? Holed up in the security of a cave somewhere. I'm out here laying my life on the line for you."

Elijah knew no one won arguments with the Almighty. Paul was a different story.

From his testimony in Galatians 1, we get the impression that Paul began his ministry as a loner. When he was first called, he did not drop everything and run down to Jerusalem and sit at the feet of the apostles. Instead, he retreated into the desert and for some three years, spent time with the

Lord. Perhaps the Holy Spirit was teaching Paul a new way of looking at all those Old Testament scriptures he knew so well.

When Paul began preaching in Damascus, there was power and logic in his messages. However, instead of making converts, he made enemies. The disciples slipped him out of town just ahead of the lynch mob.

In Jerusalem, the situation repeated itself, but this time, after escaping the city, Paul returned home to Tarsus. We can assume he went back to making tents and perhaps reflecting on the short-lived ministry he had known and wondered what it all meant.

When a revival broke out in Antioch of Syria, the Jerusalem church sent Barnabas, "Mister Encourager," up to check on things. When he found large numbers of Gentiles turning to Christ, he remembered that God had called Saul of Tarsus to be an apostle to the Gentiles. "Why, that man would be ideal for this. Wonder where he is?"

Acts 11:25 is one of the greatest sentences in the history of this planet: "Then Barnabas departed for Tarsus to seek Saul."

In Antioch, Paul found his calling. Thereafter, he is never alone, but always surrounded by devoted colleagues in the ministry. At Antioch, he is one of five leaders of the church. When God calls missionaries, it's Barnabas and Saul. Later, the teams become Barnabas and John Mark, then Paul and Silas. Soon, it's Paul and Silas and Timothy and Titus and Luke and Epaphroditus and Demas and on and on. Read his epistles—especially read between the lines—and you quickly see how much these co-workers meant to Paul, and how lonely he was without them.

The last chapter of the Romans is generally thought of as a lengthy postscript to the greatest of all epistles. It's mainly greetings to this one and that one in Rome. But two things stand out. We are struck by how many people Paul knew in that church, even though he had never been to Rome. And look how intimately he knew them. These "risked their necks for my life," these are my co-workers, my fellow-prisoners, my beloved, on and on.

Paul is a better role model for the servant of the Lord today. Don't try the ministry alone, minister of God. It's a tough life, and the demands are more than you can meet. You need a few strong colleagues as confidantes, as encouragers, as your buddies.

I promise you if you pull together the right friends, your ministry will be sharper, your marriage will lose a lot of stress, and you personally will find more fulfillment in serving the Lord.

Where to find such a friend?

The little acrostic which Matthew 7:7 gives regarding prayer works here: A-S-K. Ask, seek, knock.

First, ask. Pray. Tell the Lord. Often, when I'm coming to a meeting where I know I'll meet other preachers, I ask the Father, "Give me a new friend today."

Seek. Start paying attention. Look for the Lord to answer your prayer. Stick out your hand and introduce yourself. Learn names, ask questions.

Knock. Or pick up the phone and call him and see if you can get together. Recently a young pastor told me he had been turned down twice by older preachers whom he had called.

"They don't have time," he said.

I said, "Let me make a suggestion. Once you decide on someone you'd like to get to know better, call him up. Tell him you'd like to buy him a cup of coffee. Do not tell him 'I want us to become bosom buddies.' Just fellowship with him a little. See what God does."

Chapter Fifty-One

Seven prayers of a lazy pastor

I know a lot about lazy preachers, considering one myself from time to time.

Every lazy-bones prayer below I have probably offered up at some time in the past.

It's tempting to point at do-nothing pastors as being the anomaly and call for them to leave the ministry and stop being a blight on the name of Jesus. But in truth, many of us who work hard and long in serving Him are naturally lazy and have to fight the urge to vegetate. I would not be surprised if many over-achievers in the Lord's work fight the same battles and are always working to compensate for those Beetle Baileyish desires to rest and then rest some more.

Consider these prayers of a lazy preacher....

1) "Lord, give me a great text for tomorrow's sermon, one no one else has ever noticed before and a clever interpretation of it, one no one else would have ever seen. No rush. Just in the next hour since we leave for the ball game at six. Amen."

2) "Lord, I pray for Mrs. Jackson there in the ICU. Please let her live just a little longer so I can enjoy the ball game tonight. I promise to (ahem) try to see her tomorrow sometime so the family won't feel I've failed them. Thank you."

3) "Dear Lord, please don't let anyone die this weekend or have an emergency. With the family coming in for my graduation, my mama would not understand if I have to leave the dinner to make a pastoral visit. Amen."

4) "Here am I, Lord, send Aaron." (The wonderful Jill Briscoe wrote a book with that clever title.) This is a variation of the lazy layperson's prayer: "Lord, I pray you will use the pastor to reach this world for Christ, but not mess with me or spoil my plans in the process."

5) "God bless all the missionaries and all whom it's our duty to pray for." A friend says this is praying "wholesale," instead of "retail."

6) "Forgive me in advance" (for not studying, not forgiving, not visiting the sick, whatever it is I am determined not to do). This is praying

presumptively, something David prayed against in Psalm 19.

7) "Lord, I'll do that just as soon as…." (Complete the sentence however you need to, most often with something like: "I finish this novel," "get the energy," "this program is over," or "I feel led."

Finally, my brethren…

I've racked my brain trying to think of a preacher in Scripture who would qualify as lazy, who might contribute something worthwhile to this discussion. The only one that comes to mind, and not everyone agrees with this, is when the disciples in the Upper Room prayed, "Lord, show us which of these two men you have chosen as the next apostle" (my paraphrase of Acts 1:24-25). Is that a lazy prayer? It could be, or perhaps just a hasty one.

Seems to me the Lord was preparing Saul of Tarsus to fill the slot vacated by Judas, and the disciples were running ahead of the Lord. It feels to me as though they were saying, "While we're sitting here in the Upper Room waiting for the coming of the Holy Spirit, let's do something profitable with our time." Not a good thing.

In a discussion with the great expositor Warren Wiersbe, I mentioned my concern about that prayer in the Upper Room. I said, "You notice that Matthias is never heard of again after he is chosen." Dr. Wiersbe, who believed that prayer to be legit, said, "True, but several of the apostles were never heard from after that." So, we will leave it there, I suppose.

Chapter Fifty-Two

Get all the education you can. Then, never mention it again.

"Get it. Then forget it." Said a seminary professor to his students.

"Beware of Pharisees. They love the place of honor at banquets and the chief seats in the synagogues, and respectful greetings in the marketp l a c e s, and being called by men, Rabbi. But do not be called Rabbi; for One is your teacher, and you are all brothers; and do not call anyone on earth your father; for One is your Father, He who is in heaven. And do not be called leaders, for One is your Leader, that is, Christ. But the greatest among you shall be your servant." Matthew 23

When given a choice—and we always have a choice—pastors should try not to look and act like Pharisees.

For my money, the best way—the very best way for ministers to come across as a big-shot—is to work this little phrase into conversations as often as possible: "When I got my doctorate…"

I'm not sure why that sets me off, but it does. And I haven't the slightest idea whether it's only me or the rest of the universe.

Ninety-nine times out of a hundred, stating that little phrase is completely unnecessary and meant only to call attention to oneself, to make sure the hearers fall to their knees in abject horror. "Oh my, you have a doctorate?! You must be of superior intelligence, far beyond most mortals." "Forgive me for thinking you put your pants on one leg at a time!"

Okay. It's just me. But hear me out.

I'm of the opinion that most doctorates for ministers are overrated. I have known people with earned doctorates who are almost illiterate and never read a book.

And yes, I have one of those degrees. And yep, it's earned.

The chairman of a search committee called me for a reference for a pastor friend. He said, "Should we be concerned that he does not have a doctorate?" I said, "My friend, I know people with doctorates who have a hard time putting two sentences together. Those degrees are easy to come by these days and are vastly over-rated. Pay attention to the pastor's preaching, listen to his conversation, and get to know the man. But ignore the absence of a doctorate."

I assured him his candidate was a godly minister of the gospel, highly intelligent and wise beyond his years, whom he would come to appreciate in the years ahead.

Two years later, that chairman went out of his way to thank me. The pastor, whom they had brought to their church, was doing splendid work far beyond anything they had a right to expect. And they call him by the finest title I've ever known: "Pastor."

If you are the preacher, get all the education you can, by all means. And then, never mention it again. Never. Mention. It. Again.

Here's another good text...

"Two men went up into the temple to pray.... The Pharisee stood and was praying thus to himself: 'God, I thank Thee that I have written yet another book, as I was telling my publisher just today. I thank Thee that I have a doctor's degree, unlike these lesser mortals, and am addressed as doctor, even by my wife. I thank Thee that I have all these framed certificates on my wall which inform even casual visitors that I am someone special, far above the hoi polloi. You are so good to me, Lord. I couldn't have done it without You. Perhaps." (Okay. This is my corrupted—and very contemporary—version of Luke 18:10-12.)

Have you ever heard of a preacher insisting that he be called Doctor? "I worked hard for that degree, and I have a right to be called that."

I have, and this is not someone you wish to know further. His ego is out of control at the very time his inferiority complex occupies the driver's seat. Get out of his way before you get run over.

"Call me Billy."

I'd give a dollar to know how many people Billy Graham said that to over his life of nearly a century. But I'll tell you one thing: Few people did.

Even though Dr. Billy Graham's doctorates were honorary—many colleges and seminaries honored themselves by awarding him such degrees—he deserved that title as much as anyone we know.

But that's not the point.

The point is that the listing of degrees and the parading of titles are often artificial boosts to the fragile ego, and they erect unnecessary barriers between people.

Religious leaders seem to have loved their inflated titles from the beginning. Jesus cautioned His people, "Do not be called rabbi, father, or leader" (Matthew 23:8-10).

No one calls me Rabbi. The word means "teacher" and implies an exalted teacher. (It's great to honor a teacher; the Lord is talking about titles.)

No one calls me Father, although three call me "Dad" or "Pop," and eight call me "Grandpa Joe."

No one calls me Leader. Germany called Hitler that, I understand.

Rabbi, father, and leader were the big three in Jesus' day.

I recognize that the letter of the law here would probably be a wrong interpretation of what our Lord said, and the spirit of the law is the point (see 2 Corinthians 3:6). So, I am not suggesting we get hung up on those specific words. Personally, I have no problem with the Catholic worshiper calling his priest "father." And, for that matter, I have no problem with someone addressing you as "Doctor" if it fits. That is not what I'm saying.

Just don't require or encourage it. That's all I'm saying.

But since there's nothing in Scripture forbidding it, is it all right if I arrange for people to call me Doctor? Professor? Senior Pastor? Or how about Prophet, Apostle, or His Eminence?

The carnal mind—what Scripture calls "the old man"—sure does love its titles, doesn't it?

A few observations about preachers calling themselves "Doctor"—

One. Pastors were called Doctor before physicians were, so it's not exactly usurping the title. The word means teacher. The word is a first cousin to "doctrine."

Two. However, the word has varying connotations in various cultures. In Germany, for instance, the wife of a doctor is called Frau Doctor Whatever. That's carrying it a little far, we think, but each culture has its own thoughts on the matter.

Three. One calling himself by that title and insisting that others do is completely foreign to the humility and Christlikeness expected of a man of God.

Four. My observation is that the cheaper the degree, the more prominently the possessor of it displays it. Some of the best preachers and professors I've ever known have owned multiple doctor's degrees, but you'd never know it by the way they relate to everyone.

Five. How much more impressive it is when we discover later that someone we have come to know, and love, has an earned doctorate. The fact that he did not wear it prominently and has never called attention to it is a pleasant discovery.

Six. Churches would do well to leave off the degrees of their ministers in their publications. Let people find out accidentally that their ministers are sufficiently educated.

Seven. The pastor search committee that insists that the candidate they present to the church possess a doctoral degree is setting themselves up for all the trouble they're apt to get.

Get all the education you can, pastor. Take Greek and Hebrew. Study systematic theology and take intensives on Isaiah, Deuteronomy, and Paul's epistles. Write your dissertation and defend it before the committee of highly educated professors. Thereafter, never mention it again.

I suspect if this were an enforced rule–that you could no longer call attention to the degree– half the people enrolled in doctoral programs would drop out this week.

Humility is a wonderful thing. And extremely rare.

Chapter Fifty-Three

Slow down and savor the Scriptures.

So, you're reading the Bible through in a year? Or, like a few people I've known, you read it through every year for the umpteenth time.

Fine. But in my humble opinion after you have done it two or three times, that's enough. Don't do it anymore.

Just my suggestion.

Reading the Bible through in a year is like seeing Europe in a week: You will notice a lot of things you wouldn't normally see from ground level, but it's no way to get to know a country.

After a few flyovers—two days in Genesis and one day in Romans, for instance—land the plane and get out and make yourself at home in Ephesians or Second Timothy. Move in with the locals and live with them for a few weeks.

That's the only way to learn about a country. It's the only way to really learn a book of the Bible. Acts 16 will help us make the point.

No doubt you know Acts 16 as part of Paul's second missionary journey (which encompasses chapters 16 through 18). He and Silas had trouble bringing the gospel into Asia and were given the vision of a Macedonian man calling for help (16:9). After meeting Lydia on the riverbank in Philippi they started a church in her house. Soon, the two men were thrown in prison for preaching. After an earthquake knocked the cell doors off their hinges, the jailer came in asking the apostles, "What must I do to be saved?" The answer is one of the most best-known lines for witnessing to the unsaved: "Believe on the Lord Jesus Christ and thou shalt be saved, and thy house" (16:31).

We know these things because they stand out in the chapter. Pastors have preached these points repeatedly over the years.

It's a great chapter, to be sure, but it deserves closer inspection and much more attention than a flyover can provide.

I suggest we land the plane, get off, and camp here.

By savoring each scene before moving on, we see much more drama and teaching points in the story.

WHAT PUT PAUL AND SILAS IN THE JAILHOUSE. (Acts 16:16-24)

All these men were doing was good. They were blessing people, helping them come to Christ and straighten out their lives, and healing the hurting. When they cast the demon from a young woman who was being used and abused by her "owners," that was more than the locals could take. The owners complained to the authorities.

The "authorities" dragged them to the magistrates and slandered Paul and Silas as "Jews who are throwing the city into an uproar by pushing illegal customs for us Romans to accept." Apparently, freeing slave girls was a foreign custom. (Funny how our generation speaks of abortions not as killing babies but as "a woman's right to choose." Just so loosely do people play with language when not wanting to take responsibility for their crimes.)

By then a mob had gathered to do what mobs do best: harass the unfortunate and undefended. The magistrates, sensing public opinion would allow this, ordered Paul and Silas stripped and beaten, then thrown into prison. The jailer, sternly warned to guard them carefully, locked the two missionaries into an inner cell and fastened their feet in stocks.

They were as secure as he could possibly make them. That night, under severe caution from the authorities, the jailer remained at his post rather than trusting an assistant. Good thing he did.

Paul and Silas had to have been miserable. Their backs were open wounds, and the stocks kept them in an awkward position all night long.

WHAT PAUL AND SILAS DID THAT STRANGE NIGHT (Acts 16:25-34)

About midnight, Paul and Silas were praying and singing hymns to God. (16:25)

Wait just a minute. Are you serious? They were singing???

Many of us would have been complaining: "God, where are you? We were just trying to do your will. All we've been doing is blessing these people and look at how they've treated us. Where are you, Lord? Why have you abandoned us?"

Not these two. So much for the prosperity gospel. So much for 'name it and claim it.'

These two knew Matthew 10:17ff's promises. They knew that the Lord does not mind putting His disciples in jeopardy to get the word to people with no intention of attending your revival meeting.

226

Question: Do you suppose Paul said, "You know, Silas, I just feel like singing"? Not hardly.

Sometimes we sing because it hurts too bad to laugh. Sometimes we sing because it's either that or cry. The Psalmist said, "I am in pain and distress.... I will praise God's name in song and glorify Him with thanksgiving. This will please the Lord more than an ox, more than a bull with its horns and hoofs" (Psalm 69:29-31).

"And the prisoners were listening to them" (Acts 16:25). They're always listening. They're watching and listening to see how we are handling the pain and misfortunes of this life. That's why the Lord will not hesitate to allow His children to be mistreated. And it's why we must be faithful when He places us in such a situation.

The jailer was listening too. We know that because of what he did later.

Sometime during the night, the ever-present Lord—the One who had not deserted His faithful workers—sent an angel with a jail-sized earthquake. The building shook, the walls were broken, and the chains were busted. The jailer awakened, looked down the corridor and saw all the doors off their hinges and chains laying everywhere. He knew he had an empty jail. The prisoners had surely escaped, right? It's what prisoners do.

So, just before the jailer fell on his sword and saved the magistrates the trouble of executing him, Paul called out, "Hey buddy! Don't hurt yourself. Everyone is here. No one has left."

That was just one more strange thing on this night of amazing happenings. The jailer called for a torch (which tells us he had assistants in the building), then came in and fell before the two prisoners. "Tell me how to get what you have! What must I do to be saved?"

Paul's answer was the same one you and I repeat today when asked the same question: "Believe on the Lord Jesus Christ and you will be saved, both you and your household."

Then, the jailer did something amazing, something so bold that a few hours earlier he would have died before doing it.

He took the men out of prison and brought them down to his house.

He woke up his wife and mother-in-law (okay, just my assumption here). While one bathed the backs of the two preachers and put salve on them, the other scrambled some eggs and heated the biscuits. All the while, the missionaries were telling them about Jesus.

Then, the entire party went down to the same river where Paul had met

Lydia a few days earlier and they were baptized.

And afterwards, something else strange happened. Paul asked the jailer to return them to prison.

THE NEXT MORNING (Acts 16:35-40)

The next morning early, the magistrates sent word to the jailer to let the men go. The jailer, now a brother in Christ, was glad to deliver the news. "Go in peace," he told them.

"Not so fast," Paul said. Turning to the officers who had come from the magistrates, he said, "Go back and give your bosses this message: You beat us publicly without a trial, even though we are Roman citizens. Then you threw us into this prison without bringing charges. And now you want us to go quietly? I don't think so."

Paul added, "Tell the magistrates they'll have to come and apologize to us personally before we will allow them to release us."

On hearing the men were Roman citizens, the magistrates panicked. Rome demanded that citizens be treated according to Roman law. Citizens had rights others did not.

The magistrates could be in big trouble and knew it.

They hurried down to the prison and apologized to the missionaries, then begged them to please leave and not cause any further trouble.

Paul could have insisted on his rights and put the screws on these lackeys. However, he agreed to allow these officials to escort him and Silas out of town. Their presence would also protect them from any mob action left over from the evening before.

But before leaving town, they made a side trip.

They went by Lydia's home. This was where the fledgling church was meeting, and the two missionaries had been staying. Paul apparently had several things in mind: he wanted to say his good-byes and issue the kind of charge he frequently gave to young churches (see Acts 14:21-23). "There, they met with the brethren and encouraged them."

Also, Paul wanted the church to know about the jailer and his household. Someone would need to do follow-up with these new believers.

Then they left.

It's a great chapter, a wonderful story. But only by reading it slowly and considering it closely do we see the various movements and appreciate the scenes.

The Father wants His children to enjoy the Scriptures. There is nothing else in the world like them. And that will require several things: That we read them regularly, consider them closely, compare them with other texts, meditate upon them, and the big one: Obey them.

Our Lord Jesus said, "If you know these things, blessed are you if you do them" (John 13:17). Obedience is always the point.

Chapter Fifty-Five

Beware the need to be accepted by the world; God intends His servants to be outsiders.

"We have an altar, from which those who serve the tabernacle have no right to eat. For the bodies of those animals whose blood is brought into the holy place by the high priest as an offering for sin, are burned outside the camp. Therefore, Jesus also, that He might sanctify the people through His own blood, suffered outside the gate. Hence, let us go out to Him...." (Hebrews 13:10-13)

Have you ever felt like an outsider? Good. You need to.

As a follower of Jesus Christ, you are not only walking in the footsteps of the Ultimate Outsider, but you have been called to a similar way of life.

The Lord Jesus came unto His own and His own received Him not (John 1:12). He was an Outsider even in His own place, among His own people, attending His own party.

He came to His world, and it did not recognize Him.

He walked into His house, found it to be the haven of thieves and con-men, and proceeded to cleanse it, only to be confronted with demands of "by what authority do you do this?"

You've got to love His answer: "It's my house."

He came to His people, and they crucified Him.

No one taking up his cross and coming after Jesus should be surprised when the world turns its back on him and writes him off as a loser and irrelevant. In following Jesus Christ, one should expect the path to be uphill, the company few, and the flow all in the opposite direction.

An Old Testament lesson worth treasuring.

In the former system, the blood of sacrificial animals was brought into the "most holy place" by the high priest as an offering for sin. However, the bodies of the animals were not eaten (in the pattern of most sacrifices) but were burned "outside the camp" (Leviticus 6:30 and 16:27). The Jews thus had an outside altar as well as the primary one inside the Temple.

Followers of the Lord Jesus see this as one more metaphor—the Epistle of the Hebrews lists many such—which prefigured the coming ministry of our Lord. Quoting scholar Edward Fudge, "In keeping with this figure, Jesus also suffered outside the gate of Jerusalem and therefore outside the camp of Israel, so that he might sanctify the people with his own blood. He not only was treated shamefully (Hebrews 12:2), but He was in the literal sense an outcast."

Writer Neil Lightfoot says, "Crucifixion in ancient times took place outside the cities. Jesus died 'outside the gate,' that is, outside the city of Jerusalem (John 19:20). His blood, in contrast to that of animal victims (Hebrews 9:12), was the means of sanctification and the one acceptable sacrifice for sin (Hebrews 10:29)."

"Let us go forth to Him outside the camp, bearing abuse for him" (Hebrews 13:13).

In its immediate context, the writer of Hebrews is calling for followers of Jesus to break all ties with the Judaic system. Everything in The Epistle to the Hebrews was written to establish that we now have the fulfillment of all the old system promised, that Jesus Christ is the substance for which the old was the shadow. That was the ritual; He is the reality.

In our day, there is a wider application. We who have chosen to follow Jesus and have been chosen as disciples of Jesus Christ are called to live for Him outside the mainstream of this worldly system.

If anyone loves the world, the love of the Father is not in him (I John 1:15).

The specifics of what it means for each disciple—will have to be left to the individual under the leadership of the Holy Spirit.

Originally, when some pastors and teachers began criticizing the styles of women's hair and the length of their hemlines, I imagine it stemmed from a sincere desire to buck the trends of the world, to resist the lure of the carnal siren beckoning God's faithful people to indulge in its fleshly standards. I suspect that's what's behind the Mennonites' and Amish's resistance to modern ways.

Those things have a way of getting out of hand, clearly, and quickly becoming legalism of the worst sort.

My personal conclusion is that I am not empowered nor gifted to instruct pastors on what "serving the Lord outside the camp" means personally. Nor are you able to tell me. The Holy Spirit fills this role nicely.

Christians will always have to fight the desire to be both in the world and "of" the world. We have in mind John 17:11,14, where Jesus says His people are "in the world" but not "of the world." That is the permanent standard.

There will be permanent tension there. And, in most cases I doubt if it will go away in our lifetimes. "We who are in the flesh do groan, longing to be clothed with our dwelling from Heaven" (2 Corinthians 5:2).

What that means and how we choose to resist the alluring ways of the world is an urgent matter, but one for each of us to decide. For some, it means guarding the reading material and entertainment allowed into one's home. For others, it might mean avoiding certain people who want to be friends but who are toxic.

People who write of culture speak of something being "campy," meaning trendy. The word "camp" is used in the same way, whether by happenstance or attributable to this passage in Hebrews. In either case, this is a reminder to us that believers are called to live for Christ outside the mainstream, not caught up in the worldly culture around them, and most definitely not bringing it into the church.

Bringing the world's music, speech, and mode of dress into the church because "we want to identify with those we are trying to reach" might be well-intentioned but is a mistake of the first order.

"Therefore, let us go out to Him outside the camp, bearing His reproach"(Hebrews. 13:13). And therein lies the problem.

We don't like to be reproached. (The word means a disgrace.) We don't like to be excluded or ignored.

We want to be noticed, loved and accepted by everyone, respected and admired by insiders and outsiders, popular and acclaimed by one and all.

That can be our Achilles' heel. The hunger to be approved by the outside world has led many a Christian into big trouble.

Our heart's strongest desire should be to please Jesus Christ. "I delight to do thy will, O God. Thy law is within my heart" (Psalm 40:8).

There is no way to over-emphasize this. God's people have to decide to what extent they mean it when they pray "Thy will be done on earth as it is in Heaven." And when we sing "Have thine own way, Lord."

Okay. Back to our original premise that "the need to be approved by the outside world has led many a Christian into trouble."

When my friend Jerry Clower, acclaimed entertainer and member of the Grand Ol' Opry, was named "king (of a certain) krewe)" for Mardi Gras in New Orleans, he rode in the parade on a massive float, tossed beads to thousands of parade-goers, and withstood a barrage of criticism from fellow believers. He explained to Christians that the stage for his witness for Christ had just been enlarged. My conclusion then was and still is today that only he could decide. "Unto his own master a servant stands or falls" (Romans 14:4). And I'm not his master.

Should a Christian drink socially? Go to cocktail parties? Belong to certain clubs?

Should a Christian actor take a role in a play (or movie) that is profane or otherwise unworthy? Can a Christian even work in Hollywood at all?

Should athletes who take their commitment to Christ seriously play football on Sunday? Some might say, should they even play that sport at all?

Here are three questions worth our considering...

1) What has my discipleship of Jesus Christ cost me? What have I given up for Jesus' sake?

2) Do outsiders see me as "one of the gangs" or someone set apart? We should never forget that holy literally means "set apart." I Peter 1:16 fits here.

3) Am I straddling the fence or making a sincere attempt to walk the straight and narrow? That's an allusion to Matthew 7:14. We remember Elijah accused God's people of wanting to have it both ways in I Kings 18:21.

In this fallen world where God's people live and from which we must not withdraw, there will always be a certain amount of tension between what is and what should be. This will require us to live in the Word, to abide in Christ (i.e., to walk in the Spirit), and to stay on our knees.

Only when we "get home" will we find ourselves truly at peace. Jesus spoke of a day when He would say to the faithful, "Come, inherit the kingdom prepared for you from the foundation of the world!" (Matthew 25:34).

Until that moment, like the faithful of old, "Here we have no continuing city. But we seek a city which hath foundations, whose builder and architect is God" (Hebrews 11:10).

Today, we will walk by faith, not by sight (2 Corinthians 5:7) and will live in expectation of the fulfillment of the promises of God. Let us be faithful.

Chapter Fifty-Five

The pastor must not ignore the culture around him.

That year, the big event on my Spring calendar was a pastors-and-wives retreat for English- speakers in Europe. We would be there several days and have time to run out to Pompeii and check on Vesuvius. This is the Amalfi Coast of Italy, below Naples.

The executive director of the International Baptist Convention, my hosts, pointed out in an email a few things I might want to bear in mind.

All the retreat participants speak English, but not all are Americans. Therefore, guest speakers from the States need to take care not to use idioms and references that outsiders will not get.

I knew that but had not thought of it.

So, I took a second look at some of my choice stories. These include tales of growing up in rural Alabama, of small church preachers and narrow-minded Baptists and Southern ways.

Hmmm. We might have a little problem here. I would need to revisit all my messages and stories and illustrations. And even then, once underway in Italy, there might need to be some fine-tuning and tweaking.

What happens when the preacher does not make an attempt to learn the culture of his audience and adjust to it?

He messes up royally.

A pastor I once knew was on a mission trip into a remote part of Africa where church groups met not in church buildings but under a tree in a field. The pastor, I was told, showed slides of his middle-class home in America with his expensive cars. The missionary was unhappy with that preacher.

I have preached in Mississippi's Parchman Penitentiary. To assemblies of other denominations. To a high school following the tragic deaths of several students. To nursing homes where attention spans are brief, and a few patients seem almost comatose. And to more than one church where a sizable group wanted me gone.

It's a challenge.

In his book *Between Two Worlds: The Art of Preaching in the Twentieth Century*, John R. W. Stott addresses this issue. In the section titled "Crossing the Cultural Gulf," he writes that "preaching is not exposition only but (also) communication, not just the exegesis of a text but the conveying of a God-given message to living people who need to hear it."

It's about bridge-building, Stott writes.

A bridge is a means of connecting two peoples who would otherwise be shut off from one another. Bridges make possible traffic between the two. The chasm between the two—that which the bridge spans—represents the "gulf of mutual incomprehension" between the two groups.

For us, the gulf is two thousand years or more, in the case of the Old Testament which Scripture spans to connect us with the message of Christ.

Stott identifies two errors which we preachers make. The first is withdrawing from the world altogether, banishing the culture to hell, and making our entire ministry about the Bible.

This is the mistake we Bible-believers are more likely to make. "We believe the Bible, love the Bible, read the Bible, study the Bible and expound the Bible." And if we're not purposeful, we end up insulating ourselves from the culture.

Stott says you can tell from our preaching that we have withdrawn and are insulating ourselves from the world. How? We quote Spurgeon a lot. (I didn't say that Stott did!) But mainly, we end up misconnecting with the very people to whom we're bringing Christ's message. (I've included four brief stories at the end which make this point.)

The other error is to join the culture, to surrender to it. This is the mistake of liberals, Stott says. "They find it congenial to live on the contemporary side of the great divide." They are always up to date with the times. They know the latest novels and movies and celebrities. What they may not know is the Scripture.

Such preachers who have joined the world, Stott says, have given up the biblical revelation. Where they get their sermons, "heaven alone knows."

To be fair, Stott adds, "Those of us who criticize and condemn liberal theologians for their abandonment of historic Christianity, do not always honor their motivation or give them credit for what they are trying to do. The heart of their concern is not destruction but reconstruction." That is, they look around and see large numbers of people dismissing Christianity as a relic of the past that is irrelevant to their lives. And, in an attempt to make it relevant—to restate the Christian faith in terms which are intelligible, meaningful and credible to their secular colleagues and friends—they give away far too much. So, a minister of the gospel must make a choice.

First, we can retreat into our studies and come out on weekends to preach the revelation of God with no thought as to how the people in the pews are processing this Word.

Second, we can spend all our time with the people and none in the study and so bring messages entirely of their understanding and approval but with little of God in them.

Third, we can try to study the culture in order to speak God's eternal word to it.

That middle ground is our territory. There will often be tension in those trying to occupy this spot of earth. Should I join this club or see this movie? Is there value in learning Greek and Hebrew? Should I attend that Mardi Gras ball if it would enable me to invite my hosts to our church's revival?

Four stories...

Dr. Stott had some interesting tales about preachers who failed miserably to connect with their audience for lack of thought as to who was listening and how to address them.

The first comes from British author George Eliot.

We should not follow the example of the Reverend Maynard Gilfil, the Anglo-Catholic curate of Shepperton, whom George Eliot introduces to us as "an excellent old gentleman, who smoked very long pipes and preached very short sermons." In fact, "he had a large heap of short sermons, rather yellow and worn at the edges, from which he took two every Sunday, securing perfect impartiality in the selection by taking them as they came, without reference to topics."

Second. A chaplain who visited the construction works on the Great Dam being built on the Upper Nile.

His congregation consisted of men who had to endure great heat, extreme isolation and the strong temptations which assault people who have too much time for recreation and too few facilities for it. So, what do you think he preached about? "The duty of observing all the saints' days in the church calendar—as if they had been a group of the devout widows and spinsters in the home congregation."

"He was a first prize idiot," comments W. M. McGregor, who tells the story.

Third illustration from Stott.

Then there was the Cambridge don of whom E. L. Mascall tells in one of his books who "began his sermon to a group of Cambridge bedmakers (college servants): The ontological argument for the existence of God has in recent years, largely under Teutonic influence, been relegated to a position of comparative inferiority in the armoury of Christian apologetics."

One more.

Yet even this crass stupidity was exceeded by Bishop John Wordsworth of Salisbury (1885- 1911) who, in his sermon at a confirmation service at Sherborne School, "vehemently implored the boys, whatever else they might do, on no account to marry their deceased wives' sisters."

A couple of my own stories fit here—

Dottie Hudson wrote a biography of her father, seminary President Roland Q. Leavell. As a young man early in the Twentieth Century, he pastored a Baptist church in Picayune, Mississippi. When the Ku Klux Klan took a young black man from jail and lynched him, Pastor Leavell dealt with it from the pulpit the next Sunday. He had learned that some of the culprits sat in his congregation. In his sermon Dr. Leavell said, "Any man who masks is a coward... if he will do in a crowd what he would not do alone he is a coward... no doubt, lynching is murder.... children in this town have murderers for fathers... lynching cannot be justified under any circumstances."

Some of the most prominent men in the congregation stood to their feet and walked out in the middle of his sermon. Leavell lasted only two years in that church. (The book is *He Still Stands Tall*.)

In 1995, when I was pastoring in metro New Orleans, the federal building in Oklahoma City was bombed. The nation was shocked, and this was on everyone's minds. Since I had to be out of town that Sunday, one of my assistants filled the pulpit. When I returned home, I had a letter from a visitor who had been in our church that Sunday. "Not one word was mentioned from the pulpit about the bombing of the federal building," she said. "This is inexcusable."

She was right. The staff and I had a conversation about this omission that very day.

Chapter Fifty-Six

Learn about Submission, Pastor. Or the Consequences Will Be Dire.

What started this for me was a "Dear Marilyn" column in the Sunday Parade magazine some years back. Columnist Marilyn Vos Savant was answering a fellow who had asked what the big deal was about compromising and giving in for parties to reach an agreement. "I never give in," he wrote, "when I think I'm right." Marilyn wrote back, "So when do you give in, when you think you're wrong?"

When something lodges in my mind, a story or quote or event even something as inconsequential as that little exchange, I know the Holy Spirit is handing me a spiritual lesson on a platter. My task is to pull aside and consider the message.

What the Parade writer called "compromising" or "giving in to others," the Bible calls "submission." And it makes a great deal of that subject.

We're told that the young child Jesus submitted to his parents (Luke 2:51). We're instructed to submit to the laws of man (Romans 13:1). The church is to submit to Christ (Ephesians 5:24). Wives to their husbands (Ephesians 5:22). The younger to the older (I Peter 5:5). And servants to their masters (Titus 2:9 and I Peter 2:18).

The Parade writer is not alone in disliking the concept. The great mass of humanity lines up with him, each person feeling his point of view is right, that his rights take precedence over all other considerations, and that if he does not look out for "number one," no one else will.

Bible historians tell us that meekness and submission were looked upon with scorn by every society until the Christian faith turned values on their heads and made these into virtues. That did not, however, change how people feel. We have an innate resistance to bowing before anyone or anything. "I am the captain of my soul" is article one in the spiritual credo of untold millions.

Many would call this resistance to submission one of our greatest strengths. If so, sometimes our strength can be our weakness.

Two scriptures commanding us to submit to others may be some of the most ignored teachings in all Scripture.

First: "All of you be submissive to one another and be clothed with humility, for God resists the proud, but gives grace to the humble. Therefore, humble yourselves under the mighty hand of God that He may exalt you in due time." That's I Peter 5:5-6 and it's a command for the people in a church to humble themselves before one another.

Think of that. Every member of the Lord's church is to put the rest ahead of himself. No one insists on his rights. No one promoting himself. No one campaigning to get elected as a deacon, no one's ego on the line when the nominating committee passes him by. No one was upset that he was not chosen senior adult of the year, or she was not named to the blue-ribbon committee. Each esteeming the other's opinion above his own.

Now that's something you hear emphasized and see demonstrated in church all the time. Not!

In fact, a lot of our people would be shocked to find these commands in the Bible at all.

Second: "Obey those who have the rule over you and be submissive, for they watch out for your souls, as those who must give account. Let them do so with joy and not with grief, for that would be unprofitable for you." This is Hebrews 13:17 and it's a command for church people to submit to their leaders.

As difficult as it is for us to humble ourselves before one another and for many it is practically an impossibility, I grant you think how hard it is for a certain element in our churches to humble themselves and obey their leaders. But there it is in Holy Scripture. No amount of parsing the Greek will explain it away.

This teaching to obey the leaders of the church is a clear command of Scripture, which makes it a test of faith for believers. Paul said, "For this reason I wrote to you, that I might know the proof of you, whether you are obedient in all things." (II Corinthians 2:9). The proof of a believer is his obedience.

In our day, the idea of "submission" is a magnet for dissension, the very thing it was put in place to prevent. A few years ago, when our denominational leaders suggested that submission ought to be included in the creedal statement, you would have thought from the furor that erupted they wanted the Communist Manifesto inserted. This doctrine is not for the faint of heart, hard of head, or stiff of neck.

Only the strong can submit.

As much as anything, the command to obey leaders was instituted by our

Lord to get His church on the move.

Imagine how cumbersome it would be if the congregation met to discuss and vote on every decision the church had to make. It would be like a football team that met in the huddle before every play for a discussion and a majority vote on which play to run next. They would be penalized for delay-of-game on every play!

Imagine an army that stopped to consider every situation and took a vote on each decision before acting. They would be sitting ducks for the enemy.

I once heard someone say that if a typical Baptist church were a football team, it would be made up entirely of quarterbacks. Everyone wants to call the signals. That's not entirely true, but close enough.

I love the line from the Song of Deborah in Judges 5:2, "That the leaders led in Israel, and that the people volunteered, O bless the Lord." (Note: It reads this way only in modern translations. The difficulty results from some Hebrew metaphors found in that text.)

That's the plan—leaders leading, and followers doing their job. It takes both to win a war. An army with no officers is a mob. An army of nothing but officers is a social club.

Across America, we have hundreds of tiny churches that were birthed decades ago and never flourished. As a rule, it appears the smaller a church is, the more business meetings it is likely to have, and the more detailed decisions the congregation insists on making in those meetings. I heard a pastor say his church spends an hour discussing whether to spend 15 cents a month on a feature for the office phone.

In my opinion, the church that insists on making every decision in a business meeting may take pride in its democratic principles, but what they are really demonstrating is a failure to trust their leaders. Not one word in the Bible commands the church to be democratic, but there is plenty about trusting and obeying the leaders.

It comes down to a matter of obedience to the Word.

A big difference in the growing church and the stagnated church is often whether the congregation frees its leaders to lead and gets behind them in full support.

In one weekend, I learned of three churches in my city whose members were upset because the pastor was exerting His God-given assignment to lead the congregation. New people were coming in, new songs were being added to the worship services, and new ministries were being inaugurated, so a portion of members were resisting the change. Unable to control the church and incapable of commanding the pastor, they were moving out.

One pastor said, "I'm not unhappy they're leaving. Our congregation would be better without them. They've been miserable for so long."

Another said, "Pray for me. This Sunday I'm drawing a line in the sand and telling the disgruntled members to get in and get with the program or get out. One or the other." He added, "It's scary. It's not my nature to be confrontational like this, but I know what the Lord wants me to do."

I gave the pastors a line from John Maxwell: "If you make changes, you will lose the whiners. Make no changes and you will lose the winners. Either way, you're going to lose somebody. Decide who you'd rather keep."

We could wish that these unhappy church-hoppers knew their Bible and that it mattered to them. I suspect they don't, and it doesn't.

God chose to organize His church so that there would be a few leaders and a lot of non-leaders. He gave the non-leaders a name: Followers. The very definition of a disciple is one who follows Jesus. "My sheep hear my voice and follow me," Jesus said (John 10:27). "Take up (your) cross and follow me," He said in Matthew 16:24.

The problem is, of course, people want to be the leader. Few want to follow. It goes against the grain of our old nature.

It appears so simple on paper that is, until one starts telling his inner spirit that his own opinion is not all that important, that he is part of a team, that he should get in line and follow the fellow up front. "Wait a minute," the little demon inside him cries out, "I have my rights." "My opinion matters too." "I'm somebody."

As often as possible, I say to God's people: Christian, you most certainly do not have any rights. In Christ, you have died. And the dead have no rights.

My beloved friend James Richardson, now in Heaven, used to tell of a fellow who stood in the midst of a vigorous church business meeting and bellowed, "All I want is what's coming to me." A little saint sitting nearby pulled on his coattail. "Sit down, Harry," she said. "If you got what was coming to you, you'd be in hell."

Those who have been redeemed from their self-destructive lifestyles, and that's all of us believers should now live in eternal gratitude for the grace of God. You would think our new lives would be defined by mercy and kindness toward everyone, and that the old ego which made life so miserable before Christ would be cast aside and left to decay as the corpse it is.

You would think.

Personally, I have attended church all my life, first a Free Will Baptist Church, then a Methodist church, then the Free Will again, and from the age of 19 onward Southern Baptist churches. I have been a minister of the Gospel since 1961. You'd have a hard time coming up with church situations I have not seen. And I will tell you....

The faithful practice of Christian submission could stop ninety percent of church fights dead in their tracks.

The Apostle Paul once told some people to submit "for the Lord's sake." That's the idea. Or, to put it another way: you submit "for the greater good."

In the military, an enlisted man salutes an officer not because he's smarter or stronger or better. Not because he's older or richer or more experienced or powerful. He salutes the uniform the other is wearing, for what the officer represents. He salutes and submits and obeys for the greater good. A failure to respect his officers would cause a breakdown of such proportions that it would undermine all the training which in turn would result in chaos during battle.

Our local newspaper announced that a lieutenant in the U. S. Army was on trial for refusing an assignment to Iraq. He insisted the war was unjust and illegal. The military prosecuted this vigorously, maintaining that to allow a soldier to pick and choose the commands he will obey would result in chaos throughout the army.

In the early 1990s our church was mired down in inactivity and attempting to "call" a new staff member to lead the educational program. I asked the congregation for their answers to this question: "Will you get behind the new minister and follow his leadership?" Most agreed to do so, but one man, strong of head, stiff of neck wrote, "I will if I agree with what he's doing."

That may appear to sound reasonable to some but look a little deeper. The man was saying, "I'll follow that minister if I'm already going in that direction." In the firm tradition of the Parade writer, he will not give in when he thinks he's right.

And we wonder why so many of our churches are so ineffective.

When the follower of Jesus Christ decides to respect the leaders of his church— all of them, not just the man in the pulpit—he pleases the God who commanded it, honors the Christ whose reputation and honor are at stake, strengthens the unity of the Body, and bears a strong witness to the outside watching world.

As with a thousand other commands of the Lord, this one can be carried out only by daily humbling before the Lord and asking the Holy Spirit to cleanse and fill and empower us to obey.

It all comes down to one's relationship to the Lord Himself.

A pastor said to me, "I can't preach this in my church. It sounds too self-serving, like I'm trying to convince them that I'm the boss around here." He laughed and said, "I may have to ask my associate pastor to preach it."

I said, "Here's a better idea. Humble yourself before your people and serve them. Stay on your knees before the Lord and when you get up, do what He tells you. He will show you what to preach and how to help your people find the order He has instituted for the church. And He will do it on His own schedule."

Wait on the Lord. Go in His strength. Be strong and courageous. Do not be afraid. Always the right thing to do.

Chapter Fifty-Seven

Pastors will be needing someone to take a bullet for them. Ask God to provide such a friend.

Early in the ministry of pastor and seminary educator Gordon MacDonald he had an incident that he talked about for years. Gordon had become friends with the pastor of the only African American church in his southern Illinois community, so when racial trouble broke out between young people, the two ministers decided to get together and talk.

At Gordon's invitation, the other pastor brought several carloads of young men and women into the MacDonald home for a lengthy discussion. Then, they invited other community leaders to join the dialogue. Eventually, a good number of people were meeting.

"I assumed all my church members would be thrilled," said Gordon. The problem was solved, and peace reigned.

Surprisingly, at the next deacons meeting, a man stood to announce his displeasure with Pastor Gordon over this incident. The pastor had betrayed his ministry by engaging in "social gospel" activities, he claimed. The pastor had no business interfering in the African American community. Unless he renounced what he had done and wrote a letter of apology to the newspaper and promised never to do such again, the deacon would resign from the board and leave the church.

MacDonald says, "It was a tense moment." When the man sat down, silence filled the room. Everyone waited to see what would happen next.

At that point, the chairman of the deacons took the podium. He stood there for a moment, looked the man in the eye, and said, "Walter, we're very sorry to lose you from this board. Now, let's turn to tonight's agenda."

An angry ex-deacon stalked from the room.

Every pastor needs courageous lieutenants standing with him-behind him, beside him, sometimes in front of him-people who do not wait to ask what is right, or take a vote on what the majority wants, but who see the right way and take their stand.

A wise pastor will ask the Lord of the Church to provide such men and women.

Ted Traylor pastors the great Olive Baptist Church in Pensacola. He had not been pastoring there long when it became necessary to terminate a worship leader with a quarter-century of service in that church. He says, "It appeared to me he was in the wrong place now, given the times and our needs. He was gifted in other areas, skills we needed, and I approached him about making a move."

The staff member balked and resisted the move for a full year. Soon their strife became public, and members began to choose sides.

At that point, Pastor Traylor asked for the man's resignation.

That very day, the church held its monthly business meeting. People were upset. Some stood to accuse the pastor, to blame him, to express the wish he would leave. Traylor admits that if a search committee from Toadsuck, Arkansas had shown up, he would have gone with them. In the weeks ahead, the tension intensified as anonymous letters arrived and people vilified his wife. Phone calls in the middle of the night interrupted their sleep. It was the lowest point in Traylor's ministry.

One night, when Pastor Traylor arrived home with his son, he saw three men from the church standing under the streetlamp in front of the house. He recognized them as the best friends he had in the church. Were they there to ask him to leave?

Ted sent his son into the house and walked back to where the men were standing. They greeted each other.

One said, "Preacher, we've been on a little trip today."

Another said, "Pastor, have you ever read Second Samuel 23? That's where David was in battle and wished for water from the well in Bethlehem."

Pastor Traylor said he recalled the incident. David was so overcome by their act he poured the water out as a drink offering to the Lord.

The deacon said, "We remember how you used to talk about the well back home in Pisgah, Alabama. You said it was an artesian well that flows right out of the ground, with water so cold and pure that you'd stick your head down and drink till you almost drowned."

"Well, we got up this morning at 5 o'clock and drove to north Alabama. Preacher, we've been to Pisgah."

"We met your mama and daddy. They showed us the well and we brought you this." A quart jar filled with water from the well at home.

Ted Traylor cried. But that was not the end. They were just getting started.

"And Preacher, remember how you said you used to go out on the brow of the mountain and pray? You were a teenager and several from your high school football team were called to preach, and you would walk out on that rock ledge to practice your preaching. Well, your daddy showed us that rock. And we brought you this." Two large chunks of rock.

"Anytime you get discouraged, Pastor, just go out in the yard and stand on these rocks. The God who called you will be the One who takes care of you."

And there was more.

The deacon pulled out a rusted coffee can, full of moss and dirt, with blooms poking out the top.

"Remember those rhododendrons that grow on the side of that mountain? We want you to set this out in your yard, Preacher. And know that the God who is the Lily of the Valley will always bring a fresh flower to your soul if you will trust him."

The pastor didn't have the heart to tell them that taking rhododendrons was illegal.

Toward the end of their visit, one of the men spoke for the others. "Pastor," he said, "We've talked about this all day six hours up and six hours back and we want to make this statement to you: We will die for our pastor. We will die for you. If you stay straight and be moral and ethical and biblical, we will die for you." Then he said, "However, if you are immoral or unethical or unbiblical, we will kill you."

Another said, "Preacher, we're not serving you. We're serving the King who called you. And we are in this together."

Any pastor would give a year of his life to have just one or two such friends to stand with him.

Gordon MacDonald and Ted Traylor's stories were taken from *Leadership Journal,* Fall, 2004.

Chapter Fifty-Eight

How to preach about America in the worst possible way

A preacher once told me, "I want to preach about America in the worst way." I told him it's been done.

What he said was not what he meant, of course.

The worst way to preach about America is negatively.

"The world is going to hell." "America is decaying from within." "The country is becoming socialist." "The president is our worst enemy." "The Supreme Court is ruining America." "The home is breaking down. Marriage is a thing of the past."

When the U. S. Supreme Court ruled that homosexuals could marry in any state in the union, it forever changed the character of this country. Conservatives did not like it but were stuck with that reality.

Did this mean the United States was through? That God would write 'Ichabod' over what used to be a great country? Should preachers deliver their eulogy from our pulpits?

Not so fast.

When a friend sent his sermon outline for the July 4th message he planned to preach, I noticed it was mostly a litany of what's wrong with America. He asked me to read it, then said, "What do you think is the future of America?"

I mulled that over a few hours before replying. Then I said something like the following....

I don't know what the future of America will be. I'm not sure where this country is going. But I can tell you something about that sermon as you have it laid out so far.

He didn't ask for my opinion, but I was giving it. Oh my. Why do I do these things?

Everything you said is true. But your people already know that. So, the sermon is going to tell them what they already know. And it'll be depressing. Frankly, this is cheap preaching. Anyone can preach about all the negative stuff this country—or any nation—is doing. Nations are made up of sinners, and their leaders tend to reflect that.

All governments have sinned and come short of the glory of God.

Give us some remedies (I told my friend). Tell about someone who is doing it right, who is a strength to America and a blessing to mankind. Yes, go ahead and lay out the problem. But don't dwell on it. Move on to the positive, to examples of people who are doing something helpful, something inspiring, something righteous.

Recently I came across an article of mine from forty years ago urging pastors to tell their church members the right way to lead a family and not just harass them for not doing all they should be doing.

Here is an excerpt...

When I was 19, I joined a Southern Baptist church near my college. Before long, I began hearing negative preaching flowing from the pulpits, usually accompanied by flailing arms and raised voice: "...And our homes no longer have family altars...."

I had to ask someone what a family altar was. The term suggested to this untaught mind a place of human sacrifice.

Often in Sunday School, teachers would drop in testimonials such as: 'In my childhood, Dad would gather us all around after supper and we would spend a half hour reading the Word and praying. People don't do that anymore. What's the world coming to?'

To me, a spiritual infant, this all communicated one huge impression: no one has a family prayer time anymore and this is the norm. If you are not praying together as a family, you're like everyone else. So don't beat yourself up about it and feel guilty.

The negative preaching and teaching had communicated the opposite of what had been intended.

What, I wondered, would be the result if we told stories of parents who got this thing right? I thought of Jim and Sondra. Jim jogs from 5 to 6 each morning, and Sondra from 6 to 7.

While she's out, Jim awakens their preschoolers, dresses them, and plays with them. They have a solid hour together every morning. Sometimes in the afternoon, Jim calls home. "Honey, I've got 30 minutes with no appointments. Get the kids ready." He rushes home from his veterinary practice. He walks in the door, sets the oven timer for 30 minutes, goes into the children's room, closes the door, and plays with them. When the timer sounds, he's out the door and back to work.

As Jim's pastor, I delighted in telling what he did. It's a positive declaration about family life and encourages people rather than depressing them under a load of guilt and worry.

I used to have a veteran deacon who would teach the young men about leading their families. "My wife and I love to use the Open Windows (devotional quarterly). They're just long enough and have excellent readings. And the church provides them free."

He was telling the young men that this was the norm, that as a godly father you should lead your family and here is one way to do it.

Is anything right in America? Then, tell it, pastor.

Is anyone doing something inspiring in America? Let's hear it.

Absolutely, call attention to the areas of concern. No one is suggesting you ignore the dark side and tickle the ears of the congregation. But if the goal is to produce righteous saints who function as salt and light in a dark world, tell how it's done.

When Bryan led a teenager to Christ, he stopped a destructive trend in its tracks. The teen's parents were alcoholics, and her family history was terrible. But suddenly, when Jesus Christ entered her life, she was born again to a living hope. She became a great student in school and went on to do wonderfully in life. She married a terrific Christian guy, and their home seems to be healthy, alive, happy, and godly.

The most patriotic thing I can do for America is to lead a child to Christ, to raise a healthy offspring who becomes part of the answer of this nation and not another of its problems.

I cannot undo any ruling of the Supreme Court. But I can do everything in my power to help the redeemed in Christ to have solid Christian marriages.

Let's build sermons around that, pastor. Let's show them how it's done instead of bemoaning the fact that no one is doing it.

You have a difficult assignment, preacher. It's so hard to hit the themes that need to be mentioned and yet stay on focus with the Good News of Jesus. Finding that balance is tough, I know. But keep trying.

One more thing. When you pray for America in your worship service, model for your people how to pray for a country that has jumped the tracks. Don't tell them "This is how it's done." Just do it.

Chapter Fifty-Nine

What the pastor search committee is looking for when they visit your church

My wife and I were being shown around town by two women who were members of their church's pastor search committee. I will never forget something one said from the front seat where she was driving.

"I told our committee, 'I want us to bring in a handsome pastor, someone who will look good behind our pulpit.'"

Had she slapped me, the blow would not have hurt more.

That shallow assessment of what they needed in the next pastor turned out to be rather symbolic of where most of the committee stood.

Most search committees, I want to assert with no evidence at all other than my own convictions, do not take that superficial an approach to their task. Most of them really do want to find the person God has chosen for their church.

Well, that is...

Just as long as that person is a male, between the ages of 35 and 50, with a doctor's degree from somewhere official-sounding, and with a beautiful wife by his side who clearly adores him.

Sorry for the little cynicism there. I'm not actually disparaging what they do. But still, it feels that way sometimes.

Most committees, once they find "the" person, even if it's not what they originally set out for, are willing to change their requirements and go for it. That's why sometimes a committee will bring in a 27-year-old as pastor and sometimes a 70-year-old. Sometimes they decide this preacher is so fine the absence of a seminary degree is not that big a deal.

And, once in a while, all requirements are jettisoned, and they really do go "outside the box."

In my opinion, here is what the pastor search committee is looking for when they visit your church.

1. The committee is looking for evidence God has His hand on you.

That could be indicated in a hundred ways: the power of the sermon, the strength and freshness of your announcements or casual remarks, the way you lead the total worship experience, or even your greeting before or after the service.

In the car on the drive back home, someone in the back seat will volunteer, "I just felt the Lord there today." Or not.

2. The committee is looking for signs of a healthy church.

The only way they have of anticipating the kind of ministry you would have in their church is by looking at the congregation you're presently leading. They consider the finances, the attendance, the appearance of the buildings from the outside (what realtors call "curb appeal"), and the general mood of the congregation as they arrive and depart. At home, they study the worship bulletin closely for indications and trends.

3. The committee is listening for God to speak through your sermon.

Now, some will have a narrow definition of what that means. They may have been conditioned by their previous pastor to believe all sermons must be expository or topical, timely or timeless, that they must be evangelistic or focus on prophecy. Nothing you can do will change their expectations. As the pastor, what you should do is focus on being true to the Lord, preaching the message He laid on your heart, and loving your people.

Others—hopefully most—are more open to God's voice to be heard in any way He pleases. This is something not measurable, not quantifiable, and definitely not predictable.

Committee members will speak of whether they "felt" God or not.

4. The committee is trying to decide on the character of the man in the pulpit.

Do they like you? Do you come across as someone they can trust? If you tell a joke that disparages women or puts your wife in a bad light, that is one search committee you can forget about. They'll not be back.

If you are desperate and change your style to impress your visitors, some will pick up on it. Don't do it.

Be yourself. If they were to call you as pastor and you turn out to be someone other than the person they thought you were, nothing good will come from it.

5. The committee is studying your congregation.

Fair or not, they want to know who makes up your membership. They wonder if the people are supportive of your ministry. Do they value your preaching and follow your leadership? When you open the Word, do they open theirs? Do you claim their whole-hearted attention?

Are the people in your pews discerning? Could they tell heresy if they heard it? Do they appreciate and encourage depth in your preaching?

6. The committee is looking at your church plant.

Is the bathroom clean? Do the walls need a fresh coat of paint? Do the front steps need the leaves cleared off?

No one expects the pastor to clean toilets, paint walls, or sweep steps. But a clean building reflects well on the leadership. Likewise, a poorly maintained campus speaks volumes of the opposite kind.

7. Often the committee has something else in mind too. But only they know what it is.

One committee I dealt with was being guided by the unseen hand of their retired pastor. He was on a fundamentalist kick and saw liberals behind every tree. When the committee asked for my views on the Bible, sensing what they were doing, I refused to play the game. I used every strong word in my vocabulary to testify to my love for, belief in, and commitment to the Bible as God's Word. Every word except the one they wanted: "Inerrant." And true to form, the old man assured his spies on the committee that I was dangerous, and they moved on. In so doing, they saved us both many a headache—and laid the trap for the next pastor they talked with. Even though they called him as pastor, he was immediately sabotaged by the old gentleman. Interestingly, not long afterwards, God took that retired pastor to Heaven.

Dr. David Uth told me this story. When he was pastoring the First Baptist Church of West Monroe, LA, a committee from the First Baptist Church of Orlando came calling. As the visitors drove around the city the night before, they found it unimpressive. One man said, "I don't think there's anything for us here."

Another man said, "Let's give this pastor a chance. In fact, I've laid out a fleece. If he uses the word 'mission' in his sermon tomorrow, that will be a sign to me that we are to go further with him."

What they had no way of knowing was that each year, Dr. Uth prayerfully chose one word as the theme of his ministry for the coming year. And this being the first Sunday of the year, his one-word-theme for that Sunday morning's sermon was "Mission."

The Orlando committee which entered the church hoping to hear "mission" spoken once in the sermon, heard it a hundred times.

Pastor David Uth has enjoyed a long and fruitful ministry in Orlando, by the way.

And so, pastor, you're anticipating a special search committee next Sunday? May I pass along a suggestion or two?

First, stay on your knees and close to the Father. Seek to please Him above all.

Second, go over that sermon repeatedly so you will know it so well, the distraction of distinguished guests in the worship center will be no hindrance to you.

Third, assign a small team to walk over your campus and make sure it's clean, attractive, and welcoming to all visitors.

In truth, you may want to do those things every week. And who knows—you might begin enjoying your ministry so much, you'll want to stay right where you are and tell that search committee to keep on going.

It's a wonderful feeling to be in your rightful place and know it.

Chapter Sixty

What church members have a right to expect of their pastor?

I hesitate to say one group in the church has a "right" to expect anything of another.

Insisting on our rights will almost invariably result in resistance, frustration, anger, and division. And yet in a very real sense believers who support the work of the Lord with their tithes and offerings and time and energy have a right to expect certain things from their shepherd. That's what this is about.

Let's admit up front that we are all unworthy, that if we got what we deserved, we would be in hell.

The Christian life is not about getting our rights or having others meet our demands. Far from it.

We have died with Christ. We are bondservants instructed to submit to one another. That is a far cry from the so-called "catbird seat" from where one may call the shots.

Much better for us to appreciate anything we receive from the people around us, no matter how small or poorly given.

At the same time, the simple fact is that when people go to the trouble coming to church with their families, often at great inconvenience, and do so year after year through the good and the bad, it is not unrealistic for them to expect a few basic things to be present.

One. People want to hear a thought-provoking sermon on Sunday. They have a right to this.

The faithful servant of the Lord must give priority to preparing the sermon and attention to delivering it effectively. The hour of worship is the best opportunity in the week to touch the largest number of members. Therefore, this should receive priority.

However, the people do not have a right to expect the sermons to compete with the celebrity television preacher for entertainment value.

Two. People want to hear a message thoroughly biblical, consistent with the teachings of the Lord Jesus. They should hear that.

Therefore, the pastor should know the Word and work at knowing it better. Even if the minister has not studied Greek or Hebrew, study helps are available and great commentaries easily accessed. With every seminary offering online courses these days, the minister has almost no excuse for not being a Bible scholar.

However, the people do not have a right to expect every sermon to be at a high level of scholarship. The typical congregation is made up of children, youth, parents and seniors, the highly educated and the less educated, singles and married, rich and poor. What touches one often misses another. Therefore, not every sermon will be equally relevant to all.

Three. Even if what they are hearing is the traditional message on a subject, they are familiar with worshipers want it fresh and relevant to their lives. That is not asking too much.

Therefore, pastors do well to stay attuned to incidents, news events, conversations, anything and everything happening around them, that could sharpen the impact of the sermon. A child's off-the-wall comment or a slip-up from a celebrity or an item in today's paper may trigger something in the minister's mind to enhance the message.

However, the people do not have a right to demand this. Some pastors come by this easily and naturally, while others work hard to connect the biblical word with the lives of the pew- sitters.

Four. People want their pastor to be a person of prayer. They will be asking for intercession for their own needs and concerns, but they also need confidence that the preacher is living in the power of the Holy Spirit. They have a right to this.

Therefore, pastors will want to pray without ceasing. They will want to set aside time every day for concentrated prayer, but also to send up "prayer arrows" as they travel, work, and play. The wise pastor will find books that help the pray-er and will always be working to learn to pray more effectively.

However, church members do not have a right to check out a pastor's prayer life. This is a matter between the minister and the Lord.

Five. People want their pastor to be moral in every way Scripture teaches. If the preacher is single, they expect celibacy; if married, faithfulness. No minister can insist that what they do in their private time is their own business. Pastors have no private time which is not the concern of their flock.

Therefore, pastors will want to work to be strong, disciplined, and yielded to the Lord. A wise pastor will have a couple of mentors to counsel him and will enlist a few prayer warriors to intercede for him regularly.

However, as a rule, church members do not have a right to inquire about the goings-on in the pastor's home, or about the relationship of the pastor to his spouse. (The exception would be when realistic questions arise about the minister's behavior.)

Six. People want their pastor to be law-abiding and patriotic. We expect our ministers to pay their taxes and to respect the government.

This is true no matter what country we live in.

When a pastor is constantly running down the government and its leaders, some in the pew will love it—not everyone in the church has good mental health or is interested in obeying the Word—but humble men and women of God will grow uncomfortable with such antics.

Scripture commands us to obey the government, honor the king, and pray for those in authority. While it's true we must "obey God and not man," our focus should always be on serving the Lord and preaching His word. The government is neither our salvation nor our problem.

Therefore, the pastor will work to stay on course, seek professionals to help with taxes and investments, and obey the laws. Even if the membership does not inspect his tax records, they should be so well-done that he would not hesitate to show them if it should become necessary.

However, the members do not have a right to see the pastor's tax records, any more than he has a right to see theirs.

Seven. The members want their pastor to be a strong leader who serves with confidence and authority, but they also want him to be accountable to the church leadership. They have a right to this.

The pastor who is given authority over the entire church but with no accountability to anyone for anything is being set up for trouble. The most loving, responsible, and faithful gift for a new pastor is a small team of believers who will stand by him in good times and bad. If he is doing wrong in some way, they will be the ones to hold him accountable.

However, the members do not have a right to boss the minister, to hold him to a time schedule, or to expect a report on how he spends his time, whom he visits, and such.

The list is probably endless. Church members want their pastors to be paid well, but do not have a right to know what exactly they are receiving.

That's why they have a finance, personnel, and/or administrative committee to represent them in making these decisions.

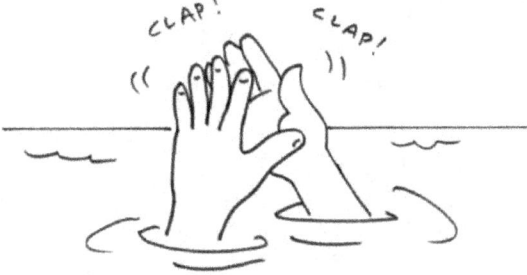

Chapter Sixty-One

Last of all, plan to finish strong.

A pastor put in over 40 years with one church. On the day of his retirement, the congregation celebrated in a big way and gave him a new automobile and many expressions of their thanks. A few days later, he announced he was leaving his wife. He divorced her, moved to another state and married his secretary. His abandoned wife was left in the town where they had served so many years to face the world and deal with broken hearts and disappointed friends.

Anyone who spends Saturday afternoons watching football games has seen this happen. A team starts strong, moving the ball, scoring points, intimidating the opposition and impressing the fans. But later in the game, they begin to fizzle. Either their first string grew tired, or the reserves were unprepared, or the other team figured out how to counter them. They ended up losing the game which they had started so well.

No one gets credit on the scoreboard for having started well. It's how we finish that tells the story.

The fun thing about pulling in an Old Testament story, particularly one from Second Chronicles, is that so few of us are familiar with the players. Many of us are hearing these tales for the first time. The account of King Asa is a perfect illustration for our point. It begins in II Chronicles chapter 14.

Asa reigned over the Southern Kingdom of Judah for a total of 41 years. In introducing him, the writer says rather ominously, "The land was undisturbed for ten years during his days." (14:2)

He started right. So far, so good.

From the first, Asa earned the approval of the Lord by tearing down the pagan altars, fortifying his cities, and building up the military. He spoke words of faith and trust and seemed to have been a good man. He was humble. When he heard a good sermon, he obeyed it. In chapter 15, the prophet Azariah preached to the king and the nation about faithfulness. At the end, Asa responded to the altar call. "When Asa heard these words and the prophecy which Azariah spoke, he took courage and removed the abominable idols...and restored the altar of the Lord. "

Asa led the people to make a great sacrifice to the Lord and led them into a covenant of obedience to God. He put his wicked grandmother out of business, removing her from the exalted position of queen mother due to her idolatry.

For the first 35 years of Asa's reign, things went well. The enemies left the little nation alone and Asa was like a father to his people.

Then things went downhill.

In the 36th year of Asa's reign, the king of the Northern Kingdom of Israel, a rascal named Baasha, brought his army up and besieged Judah. On paper, Asa should have been ready.

He had been building up his army for years. But when an actual threat loomed, he panicked.

Asa brought out gold and silver vessels from the Temple of God and sent them to the king of Syria, Ben-hadad, to purchase his support. We note that he was buying the protection which God was offering for nothing, and he used God's vessels to do it. The Lord was not pleased. Ben-hadad knew a bargain when he saw one and took the job. His army frightened the Israeli forces and Baasha called off his little escapade and returned home. That was not, however, the end of the story.

God had something to say.

The prophet Hanani showed up to tell Asa what the Lord thought of his foolishness in turning to a foreign, pagan king for security. In his brief sermon, Hanani uttered one of the great lines of Scripture: "The eyes of the Lord move to and fro throughout the earth that He may strongly support those whose heart is completely His" (Second Chronicles16:9).

The prophet was saying, "King, you could have had God's favor! It is always available. But you blew it."

Asa had occupied the throne for so long, he thought it was his personal property. How dare this prophet criticize him. He grew angry and arrested Hanani. Then he did even worse. And Asa oppressed some of the people at the same time (16:10). He arrested one and enjoyed it so much he began to persecute others.

Then we read, "In the thirty-ninth year of his reign Asa became diseased in his feet. His disease was severe, yet even in his disease he did not seek the Lord" (16:12).

Bible students can think of a number of scriptural characters who started well and finished poorly. King Saul may be the most obvious one in the Old Testament. And who is better than Judas in the New?

Finishing strong is an ideal goal for any organization and any individual. But for a Christian, it's essential. Just on the other side of the finish line is the grand prize: Heaven itself and an eternity beyond our fondest dreams.

I have read that trapeze artists and tightrope walkers are in their greatest peril just before taking that last step to safety. They've been in the spotlight, done the hard death-defying acts, and now they are finished. The only thing that remains is to get down from the heights and accept the applause. But because they let their guard down and become careless, they are in danger of falling to their deaths.

A pastor must never let his guard down. In one's middle years, the temptations of youth are still there but they take other forms. In retirement, what we call one's golden years, a new set of temptations will present itself. There is no time in this lifetime to drop one's guard.

We must be eternally vigilant, always faithful.

If you have stayed with me this far, I have a reward for you.

I'm going to tell you how to finish this life strong, how to go out with a flourish.

Live well and faithfully today. Read your Bible, pray, love everyone, serve God. Then, if God gives you tomorrow, do the same. If He grants you another day, then live the same way that day. Eventually, one day will be your last and you will go out with a flourish. You will finish strong.

A famous preacher used to tell of the piano lessons his mother taught him in childhood. In the middle of his very first recital, he forgot the piece he was playing. His mind went completely blank. There was nothing to do but walk off the stage in complete humiliation. Afterwards, his mother gave him some great advice. "Darling," she said, "anytime you mess up in the middle, always end with a flourish. End with a flourish and no one will ever remember what you did in the middle."

That pastor would then say to the congregation, "I suspect some of you have messed up in the middle. But I'm here to tell you, you can still end with a flourish. Start today, start right now, where you are, and get it right from here on in."

The good news of the Gospel is that God does not discard us when we do wrong. He allows us to repent and humble ourselves and to begin anew. Even for those of us who have done poorly for many years, it's still possible to finish strong.

But we must get started now.

About the Author

Joe McKeever is a native of Alabama, the son of a coal miner. He is one of six children and the third of four boys. His oldest brother Ron is a preacher in the Birmingham area.

Between the two of them, Joe and Ron have been preaching the gospel of Jesus Christ over 120 years.

Joe was educated at Birmingham-Southern College (bachelor's degree) and New Orleans Baptist Theological Seminary (Masters and Doctorate). He pastored six churches, the last three being the First Baptist Churches of Columbus, MS, Charlotte, NC, and Kenner, LA, followed by five years as leader of the Southern Baptist churches of metro New Orleans.

Joe has written eight books and had perhaps a dozen books of his cartoons published over the years. His books are: "Help! I'm a Deacon!" "Pray Anyway" "A Healthy Church" "Grief Recovery 101" written with his wife Bertha. "Sixty and Better: Making the Most of Your Golden Years" written with his wife Bertha "Hearing from God." "Help! I'm a Pastor!"

Joe has been a cartoonist his entire life. When he was a preschooler, his mother sat him down at the kitchen table with tablet and pencil and ordered, "Now sit there and draw!"

Instead of making him into an artist, Mrs. McKeever was trying to keep him occupied so she could do her housework. That day, Joe found that he loved to draw. When he started to the first grade at Nauvoo (AL) Elementary School, the other children would gather around to watch him draw. His first published cartoon article (other than in local newspapers) was in 1972 in Lifeway's "Outreach Magazine." For the last quarter century Joe has been a featured cartoonist for the Baptist Press website www.bpnews.net with a cartoon each weekday. An easy way to see his drawings is to google "Joe McKeever cartoons." As a sketch artist, Joe draws thousands of people a year. When he guest-preaches in a church, before the service he sits at a table in a high traffic area and sketches people. He draws for weddings, conventions, banquets, and schools.

Joe was married for 52 years to Margaret Henderson of Birmingham. Two years after the Lord took her to Heaven in 2015, Joe married Bertha Fagan, the widow of a pastor friend and seminary classmate of Joe's from the 1960s.

Joe and Bertha live in Ridgeland, MS, a suburb of Jackson. Bertha has two children and six grands, while Joe has three children and eight grands.

Joe's favorite scriptures are Psalm 103 and Romans 8.

His website is www.joemckeever.com.